Prisoner's Dilemma

Prisoner's Dilemma
A Study in Conflict and Cooperation

—

by *Anatol Rapoport*
and *Albert M. Chammah*
with the collaboration of
Carol J. Orwant

Ann Arbor
The University of Michigan Press

Preface

THIS book is addressed specifically to experimental psychologists and generally to all who believe that knowledge about human behavior can be gained by the traditional method of interlacing theoretical deductions with controlled observations. Those who believe so do not by any means comprise all students of behavior. Many psychologists, sociologists, and especially anthropologists and psychiatrists raise serious objections against routine attempts to "extend the methods of the physical sciences" to the study of man. These objections cannot be dismissed simply on the grounds that they are not constructive; for inherent in the objections may well be a conviction that there can never be a "behavioral science" as scientists understand science. Whether there can be such a science or not will be decided neither by citing successful applications of "scientific method" to carefully circumscribed sectors of human behavior nor by pointing out what has not yet been done. Therefore on the question of whether a behavioral science can *in principle* be constructed, we shall take no sides. That *some* kinds of human behavior can be described and even predicted in terms of objectively verifiable and quantifiable data seems to us to have been established. The question is how far this "beach head" can be extended. Perhaps the critics of "hard" behavioral science are entirely right in their conviction that the "hard" methods cannot cover the whole gamut of human behavior. Indeed, perhaps "behavior" is not an adequate foundation on which to build our understanding of man. However, as long as there is more to be found out by the established methods, we see no reason why we should not continue to try.

We are thus of the opinion that the method of experimental psychology should be nurtured, refined, and extended. At the same time, we are not, however, unaware of the limitations of the method as it is currently practiced. Of these limitations there are two kinds. One is the narrowness of the experimental field in which psychological data have been *systematically* accumulated and integrated. Traditionally, this field has been that of physiological psychology and psychophysics, where it has been possible not only to gather data but also to link various sources of data together into comprehensive theories, for example, a theory of sensory perception, a theory of motor integration, etc. But how one uses knowledge of this sort to get a psychology *proper*, pertaining to the complex world of thought and emotion remains obscure. The other limitation is on the range of application of scientific method to "real psychology," the realm of personality, intellect, and moral commitment. To be sure, students of these areas have designed innumerable procedures to translate observables into hitherto elusive traits, which emerge as "factors" and "score profiles." However, the results of investigations in these areas remain, for the most part, isolated from each other. Typical conclusions are arrived at by applying intricate scaling techniques and sophisticated significance tests to masses of data highly specific to the *particular* question under investigation. Such conclusions are frequently no more revealing than that "people who score high on test T_1 are somewhat likely to score high on test T_2." Regardless of whether these results are trivial or dramatic, the fact remains that little has been done to enhance a broad understanding of man from these fragments. The knowledge so gathered remains a catalogue of "findings." The closer the observations get to what supposedly matters in psychology, the more theoretically impoverished and isolated from each other these findings become.

We believe that a source of the difficulty lies in the way the questions are put to begin with. A psychologist is interested in some psychologically important matter. Intuition and impressions gathered from observations or else vaguely formulated psychological theories suggest a hypothesis. The scientifically-oriented psychologist attempts to translate the hypothesis into an experimental procedure. Thus he has already determined the framework of thought in which he will work. The bulk of his effort will go into designing tests, scaling them, interpreting the results, and establishing their statistical significance. After all this work, he will perhaps come up with a simple yes or no answer: his hypothesis will be accepted or rejected, or, to put it in more sophisticated terms, he will have justification for rejecting a null hypothesis (at a given level of significance) or else he will not. With this his investigation is *concluded*. The job of linking his investigation to the remaining body of knowledge (aside from a cursory comparison with related results obtained by others) has not even been started.

Perhaps this impasse can be circumvented if one starts at the other end, as it were. Instead of asking a complicated question (as all psychologically important questions must be) and coming up with a very simple answer (often in the form of yes, no, or maybe), one might try asking a very simple question (such as, "given a choice between two alternatives what will a person do?") and derive a rich and complex avalanche of answers. No "theory" needs to be implied in the original question. Therefore the format of the answers need not be prearranged to shed light on the "theory." The data themselves (protocols of choices) are straightforward and not subject to misinterpretation. People choose on various occasions the one or the other alternative and their choices can be represented as frequencies, including several degrees of contingency, which perhaps depend on certain conditions. Thus one proceeds to construct a theory solely from the statistical regularities one observes in the data. The data are already quantified (as frequencies of chosen alternatives), and so one need not worry about scaling, factorization, or the like.

So far psychology has not entered the theory at all. The aim of the theory is only to organize the voluminous data, in particular to discover dynamic or stochastic laws which govern the *generation* of the data. Such a theory, being mathematical, is already welded into a logical structure by the interlacing mathematical deductions. And mathematical deduction is, after all, the most potent unifier of theories known to man. Only after this purely formal theory is well under way, may psychological interpretations be attempted. Since the formal theory is already considerably integrated (by the mathematical relations deduced from the data), this integration will be reflected in the emerging psychological theory. This has been the dominant method of mathematical psychology, first applied to rote learning situations. The work described in this book follows the same method.

Prisoner's Dilemma is the nickname given to the two-choice situation with which we have been working. The situation was designed not by psychologists but by game theoreticians, as an example of a game which has no satisfactory solution. That is to say, whatever choice is recommended by "rational considerations," has something wrong with it in spite of the fact that nothing remains unknown about the situation. In other words, the chooser cannot do better by finding out more. Hence the dilemma. The simplicity of the situation is misleading. Attempts to analyze it carry one deeper and deeper into a maze of intricate and interrelated questions, which are impossible to keep on the purely "rational," i.e., strategy-calculating level. For this reason, we think that our requirement has been fulfilled. The question asked is a simple one. The answers obtained are involved and rich in psychological overtones. The psychological theory suggests itself naturally, as it were.

The work described here was supported by the National Institutes of Health Grants M-4238-01, M-4238-02, M-4238-03, and M-4238-04.

The authors worked on the project from its incipience. Others were associated with the project for varying lengths of time. We deeply appreciate the help given to us by the following: Howard Berland, John Boyd, John Dwyer, and John Gyr, who assisted in conducting the experiments; Sui Chang, John Fitts, Jane Jackson, and Carolyn Toll, who assisted in data analysis; R. De John, Marcia Feingold, and Richard Cabot, who assisted in programming the computer operations; Dr. J. E. Keith Smith, with whom we consulted on statistical questions. During the last stages of organizing the data, Philip Dale and Abbe Mowshowitz did the bulk of the work in data analysis, programming, and simulation.

We thank all these workers not only for their material help but also for the esprit de corps which they brought to our group and for their enthusiasms for the project, which equaled our own in all respects.

The Mental Health Research Institute was extremely generous in providing us with every available facility and secretarial help. Finally our thanks go to Mrs. Claire Adler and to The University of Michigan Office of Research Administration staff for invaluable assistance in editing and typing several successive drafts.

Contents

Part I

Observed Regularities

Introduction

THE MATURATION OF PSYCHOLOGY as a science is beset
by difficulties similar to those which accompanied
the maturation of physical science—a bifurcation between rigorously demonstrable and intuitively inspired
knowledge. In the case of physical science, these difficulties have been obscured by the nearly total victory
of rigorous standards over the intuitive ones. In a confrontation between mathematical formalism and intuitive understanding the verdict goes to the former
as soon as its predictive power is demonstrated. Thus
Newtonian celestial mechanics eventually had to be
accepted in spite of the fact that the notion of "action
at a distance" seemed to many philosophically unacceptable. Also Maxwell's formal mathematical theory was eventually adopted as "the" explanation of
electromagnetic phenomena while attempts to translate the formalism into intuitively acceptable mechan-
ical models were abandoned. Finally, the formalism
of quantum mechanics has achieved almost universal
acceptance, at least in the West, in spite of its clash
with preconceived notions about the "ultimate" determinism of nature and about the "ultimate" independence of physical events from effects of observation—
both philosophical convictions.

In the physical sciences the choice between formal
mathematical explications and intuitive ones was
forced, because scientists had to choose between them
with regard to the same phenomena. In psychology,
this is not the case. Psychological theories based on

3

objective evidence and rigorous deduction do not usually address themselves to the same phenomena as do the psychological theories based on insightful understanding. Scientific (i.e., experimental) psychology has been possible because the subject matter of study has been carefully selected on the basis of its suitability for the application of experimental methods. Thus the beginnings of experimental psychology coincided with the birth of psychophysics. The intensities of stimuli, the magnitudes of motor responses, the time intervals between stimuli and responses are all physically measurable quantities, indeed measurable largely in traditional physical units—times, forces, energies, velocities, etc. Psychophysics, then, is physics applied to certain strictly circumscribed aspects of behavior. Only the advent of the theory of rote learning (observed largely in animals) made possible the extension of the experimental method to events which are clearly psychological and conceptually detachable from physical measurements.

In a learning experiment, the typical formulation is a specification of a set of clearly recognizable events (recognizable by the experimenter, that is) called "stimuli," another set of such events called "responses," and still another set called "the outcomes of responses." The data are sequences of these events. The data are organized in such a way as to display certain relations among the frequencies of stimuli, responses and outcomes. These relations can often be described mathematically and the descriptions can sometimes be derived from a set of postulates, i.e., mathematical models, which serve as "learning theories."

In this way, the rigorous method of physical science has been extended to the study of phenomena which are clearly not subsumed under those studied in physical science. To be sure, it can be maintained that a "response" is composed of physical events (e.g., muscular contractions), behind which there are other more minute physical events (e.g., sequences of neural impulses), and that all these events are interlocked by physical causality. Nevertheless this philosophical conviction is of no help in constructing a *tractable* theory relevant to the behavioral events observed. Such events are far too complex to be described in a way sufficiently detailed to reveal all the causal connections.

Nor is this all. The correspondence between the behavioral events and the underlying physical ones is by no means one-to-one. Although on the basis of our philosophical convictions we might contend that the same sequence of neural events should "map upon" (result in) the same behavioral events, it is by no means true that a repetition of an "identical" behavioral event implies the same sequences of neural events leading to it. A bar can be pressed or a turn can be made in a maze in innumerably many ways. In fact, an important question raised in the methodology of experimental psychology is whether or under what conditions it is permissible to "lump" vast numbers of events into a single "stimulus" or a single "response," considering that what the experimenter identifies as "the" stimulus may not be identified as such at all by a nonhuman subject.

However, if one is interested in formulating tractable theories, one must accept, at least in part, the pragmatic dictum that conceptualizations are to be evaluated by how much they help to make sense of what we observe. If by labeling certain recognizable events "stimuli" and certain others "responses" and by organizing them into classes, we can make sense of the data, then we must accept such classifications as corresponding to something we can call "reality."

The absence of one-to-one correspondence between be-havioral events and their underlying physical "causes" does not necessarily invalidate the method of experi-mental psychology. On the contrary, the assumption that behavioral events are identifiable entities eman-cipates psychology from physics, because the sort of "causalities" which can be postulated to govern the relations between behavioral acts (the subject's and the experimenter's) need not have any connection to physical laws, no matter how universally physical causality governs all physical events. To the extent that these relations are consequences of psychological postulates and to the extent that the data support the postulates, we have obviated the necessity of relating behavioral events to physical causes, which are, in any event, irrelevant to the goals of a psychological theory.

The question, then, is not to what extent an auton-omous scientific psychology is possible. The question is rather to what extent does scientific psychology have a bearing on psychological questions.

Psychophysics contains, after all, very little psy-chology. What we see as a connection between psy-chology and psychophysics is our conviction (again a purely philosophical one) that since our mental and emotional life is governed to a very large extent by stimuli which impinge on our sensorium, it fol-lows that understanding the sensorium is relevant to the understanding of the psyche. The point is made, but it seems farfetched. It is a very long way from psychophysics to what we feel to be essential psychol-ogy. It is perhaps not quite so far from experimental behavioral psychology (where behavioral rather than physical events are the objects of study) to real psy-chology. Here one can introduce ideas of motivation (relations between learning and reward and punish-ment schedules), primitive intelligence (via learning rates), etc. If, however, we mean by genuinely psychological matters those which are unquestionably central to the idea of the psyche, the distance from "scientific" psychology to "interesting" psychology is still enormous. To give an example of "interesting" psychology consider the following statement.

"The reason Ivan Karamazov hated his half brother Smerdyakov was because Smerdyakov revealed to Ivan the latter's evil inner self, stripped of the veneer which Ivan had acquired by virtue of his superior intellect. Smerdyakov precipitated a psychosis in Ivan by pointing out to him that although Smerdyakov did the killing, Ivan was his father's real murderer."

Now we submit that the above statement is about psychology. It is also clear that at present there seems to be hardly any way to make "scientific sense" of the statement, as it stands. In order to do so, one would have to define *operationally* terms like "hated," "revealed," "evil," "intellect," "real murderer," etc., and also design ways to deduce predictions from the statement in order to pit these predictions against observations. The orthodox behaviorist or positivist of the old school would not be dismayed by these difficulties. He would simply declare the statement to be operationally meaningless and by implication exclude from consideration the questions it raises. Then he would go back to his rats, levers, and mazes, in short to scientific psychology.

However, whether one dismisses the above statement as meaningless or whether instead one declares the method of "scientific psychology" to be less than adequate to deal with the psyche, depends on one's basic orientation about which *non disputandum est*.

To us it seems uncontestable that matters which traditionally were of primary interest to people concerned with the psyche ought not to be excluded from psychology. However, it also seems to us uncontestable that knowledge based on controlled observation and rigorous reasoning is more reliable than intuitive insights, regardless of how much more relevant the latter may be to matters pertaining to the psyche. The problem, then, is how to extend the scope of the rigorous methods further, not only beyond physics (as was already done in experimental psychology) but actually into the area of "interesting" psychology.

The problem, is, of course, being attacked in a variety of ways. Quantitative methods have been extended to personality assessment. Controlled experiments are not unknown in situations definitely related to depth psychology, for example, experimental studies of suppression, aggression, regression, etc. Operational definitions of psychological concepts, experimental or observational controls, quantitative descriptions of data all spell the extension of "hard" methods.

It was inevitable that in this development, statistical methods should have come to play a predominant role. At the level where behavior is observed there simply is no "determinism." Allowances must constantly be made for fluctuations of results. And so quantitative results in psychology are stated almost universally in statistical terms. The statistical techniques are applied, for the most part, to evaluate the significance of the results. As for the results themselves, their quantification is still largely of the primitive sort: simple comparisons of pairs of quantities embodied in conclusions like "People having characteristic A are higher on scale S than people having characteristic B." It appears that the more "psychologically relevant" is an investigation (i.e., the more it deals with matters of genuine psychological interest) the less "mathematical power" is applied to the results themselves. "Mathematical power" goes instead into arguments which purport to indicate how much credence ought to be given to the results.

This diversion of mathematical effort from building a theory into statistical assessment could be avoided if the experiments were endowed with sufficient statistical stability to begin with. At times statistical stability can be achieved by the sheer mass of data. Large amounts of data can be gathered in experiments in which "identical" acts are repeated many times. Experiments on rote learning are of this sort and this is why they admit the application of relatively sophisticated mathematical models.

Is it possible to tap in this manner psychological characteristics more interesting than those related to rote learning? It seems to us that we have found such a situation, namely one where interactions are governed by psychologically interesting motivations. These are the situations in artificially constructed games of strategy.

Games of Strategy and Conflicts

A game of strategy, as currently conceived in game theory, is a situation in which two or more "players" make choices among available alternatives (moves). The totality of choices determines the outcome of the game, and it is assumed that the rank order of preferences for the outcomes is different for different players. Thus the "interests" of the players are generally in conflict. Whether these interests are diametrically opposed or only partially opposed depends on the type of game.

Psychologically, most interesting situations arise when the interests of the players are partly coincident and partly opposed, because then one can postulate not only a conflict among the players but also inner conflicts within the players. Each is torn between a tendency to cooperate, so as to promote the common interests, and a tendency to compete, so as to enhance his own individual interests.

Internal conflicts are always psychologically interesting. What we vaguely call "interesting" psychology is in very great measure the psychology of inner conflict. Inner conflict is also held to be an important component of serious literature as distinguished from less serious genres. The classical tragedy, as well as the serious novel, reveals the inner conflicts of central figures. The superficial adventure story, on the other hand, depicts only external conflict; that is, the threats to the person with whom the reader (or viewer) identifies stem in these stories exclusively from external obstacles and from the adversaries who create them. On the most primitive level this sort of external conflict is psychologically empty. In the fisticuffs between the protagonists of good and evil, no psychological problems are involved or, at any rate, none are depicted juvenile representations of conflict.

The detective story, the "adult" analogue of a juvenile adventure tale, has at times been described as a glorification of intellectualized conflict. However, a great deal of the interest in the plots of these stories is sustained by withholding the unraveling of a solution to a problem. The effort of solving the problem is in itself not a conflict if the adversary (the unknown criminal) remains passive, like Nature, whose secrets the scientist supposedly unravels by deduction. If the adversary *actively* puts obstacles in the detective's path toward the solution, there is genuine conflict. But the conflict is psychologically interesting only to the extent that it contains irrational components such as a tactical error on the criminal's part or the detective's insight into some psychological quirk of the criminal or something of this sort. Conflict conducted in a perfectly rational manner is psychologically no more interesting than a standard Western. For example, Tic-tac-toe, played perfectly by both players, is completely devoid of psychological interest. Chess may be psychologically interesting but only to the extent that it is played not quite rationally. Played completely rationally, chess would not be different from Tic-tac-toe.

In short, a *pure* conflict of interest (what is called a zero-sum game)[1] although it offers a wealth of interesting *conceptual* problems, is not interesting psychologically, except to the extent that its conduct departs from rational norms.

Besides the "irrational" deviations, the psychologically interesting aspects of conflict are those stemming from mixed motives, where the confrontation is not only between the conflicting parties but also between the conflicting motives within each participant. These conflicts are formalized in game theory as nonzero-sum games.[2] One "species" of game belonging to this "phylum" is the subject of this book.

An experimental approach to nonzero-sum games seems to us to be an excellent vehicle for pursuing genuinely psychological questions by objective quantitative methods. The essence of Prisoner's Dilemma represents a mixture of interpersonal and intrapersonal conflict. Experiments with these games yield data in the form of "acts" of sufficiently short duration to permit accumulation by tens of thousands, thus insuring statistical stability.

Our main motivation for conducting these experiments was a conviction that the potentially rich contributions of game theory to psychology will derive from the failures of game theory rather than from its successes. The wide interest in Prisoner's Dilemma among both psychologists and game theoreticians is in its status of a genuine dilemma or paradox. It seems to us that this paradox is of the sort that appeared at times on the intellectual horizon as harbingers of important scientific and philosophical reconstructions. Such has been the paradox of incommeasurables discovered by the Pythagoreans. Such has been the Achilles' paradox discovered by the Eleatics. Both paradoxes were precursors of modern mathematical theories of the continuum. Such have also been the logical paradoxes with self-negating propositions as kernels, the precursors of the modern critiques of the foundations of mathematics.[3] The paradoxes of relativity and of quantum physics also initiated a far-reaching philosophical *reconstruction*.

All these paradoxes have emerged not so much from occurrences of altogether unexpected events as from impasses in thought, contradictions arrived at by seemingly flawless reasoning, and impossible to resolve until the principles of "flawless reasoning" themselves were subjected to careful scrutiny. Thus the Achilles' paradox was not resolved by observing that the athlete of less than Achilles' running prowess can easily outrun a tortoise. Indeed the empirical facts only strengthened the paradox: reasoning led to the conclusion that the athlete could not overtake the tortoise; yet the senses insisted that he did. Nor are the genuine paradoxes, as distinguished from ordinary false conclusions, resolved by finding a flaw in the deduction as such. They are resolved rather by a realization that the framework of thought in which they emerged has only a limited range of application and that the reasoning which led to the paradox transgressed the limits of that range. Thus, if one confines oneself to the arithmetic of rational numbers, it is indeed true that the diagonal of a unit square has no specifiable length; yet there it is—the line segment, connecting opposite corners, which must have *some* length. The paradox disappears when arithmetic is enriched by the limit concept, which redefines the continuum in such a way that irrational numbers become admissible entities.

In the game called Prisoner's Dilemma, the rational choice of strategy by both players leads to an outcome which is worse for both than if they had chosen their strategies "irrationally." The paradox remains unresolved as long as we insist on adhering to the concept of rationality which makes perfect sense in zero-sum games but which makes questionable sense in nonzero-sum games. Thus the paradox forces a reexamination of our concept of rational decision. Herein lies a potential contribution by game theory to psychology and to behavioral science in general. It will be useful, therefore, to give a brief résumé of how the concept of rationality must be redefined as one proceeds from the simplest to more complex conflict situations.

Rationality in Different Contexts

It is especially important to understand the multiordinality of the meaning of "rationality," because there is a widespread notion that game theory provides a rigorous mathematical foundation for a general theory of rational conflict, it being tacitly assumed that a formal definition of rational conflict (e.g., "one where opponents act strictly in accordance with their self-interest with due regard to all the constraints of the situation") is sufficient to make. its meaning unambiguous.

The one type of conflict which admits of a theory and so deserves to be called rational is the type which can be cast into a zero-sum game. Both "game" and "zero-sum" have strictly circumscribed meanings in this context. A situation is a game if each of the participants has at specified times a range of choices of action (the range at each specified time being deter-

mined by certain rules) and if the totality of the choices
made by the participants determines an outcome which,
in turn, determines a set of payoffs, one to each participant. If the sum of the payoffs is zero, no matter
what the outcome, the game is a zero-sum game. In
particular, if there are just two players, the one's
gain is always the other's loss. The interests of the
two are thus diametrically opposed. It is within this
context that game theory can be most justifiably said
to have laid the mathematical foundations of a theory of rational conflict. For in this context there is
no question of what it means to "play rationally"—
it is to choose from among the available courses of
action those which are most conducive to maximizing
one's own payoff (and so minimizing the other's).
The criterion of rationality seems clear enough, but
it is important also to know how it can be applied
in particular situations, and this is just where game
theory sheds a brilliant light on the theory of decision
in conflict situations.

As an example let us examine three games, Tic-
tac-toe, Race-to-Twenty, and Morra. In Tic-tac-toe,
each player in turn places a pebble (the pebbles of
the two players being distinguished) in one of nine
squares of a grid. Only one pebble is allowed to be
in a square. The object is to place three of one's own
pebbles in a straight line before the opponent does.
As is well known, neither can win in Tic-tac-toe unless one makes a mistake. That is to say, for every
move of one player, the other has at his disposal a
counter move which will prevent the first-mentioned
player from getting three in a row. Two conclusions
follow. First, the outcome of every game of Tic-tac-
toe played rationally by both players is determined
in advance; second, there is at least one "best" way
to play Tic-tac-toe, so that if one plays this way, one

need not lose (but neither can one win, because the other need not lose either).

Race-to-Twenty is a simple variant of the ancient game of Nim. It is played as follows. The first player says either "1" or "1,2." The second player continues the count with either one or two consecutive integers; then the first player continues in the same way, etc. The player who says "20" first, wins. A moment's reflection shows that the player to start the count will always win. He should say "1,2." Then regardless of whether the second player says "3" or "3,4," the first player can end his count on "5." Next, whether the second player says "6" or "6,7," the first player can end on "8," similarly on "11," "14," and "17." Now whether the second player says "18" or "18, 19," the first player can end on "20."

Games like Tic-tac-toe and Nim are called *games of perfect information*. In such games each player knows following each move just what has transpired from the beginning of the game. For example, in Tic-tac-toe, the pebbles already placed on the squares are in view. In Nim, one remembers what numbers were said. One of the important theorems in game theory concerns such games of perfect information. The theorem asserts that in all these games there is at least one "best" way to play open to each player, in the sense that if he plays this way he can win all he can possibly win (or will lose no more than he must lose) if the other also chooses the course of play best for him.

The games of perfect information we have just mentioned are extremely simple, so simple, in fact, that one can learn the best way to play them in a few minutes (a few seconds in the case of Race-to-Twenty), and so it becomes pointless to play these games. However, games of perfect information need not be simple. Chess also is a game of perfect information. According to the theorem just mentioned, therefore, there is at least one best way to play Chess for White and at least one for Black. If these best ways were found, every game of Chess would always end the same way, either always in a win for White or always for Black or always in a draw. The outcome, therefore, would be intrinsic in the very structure of the game (if played "rationally") and so Chess too would not be worth playing. The fact that it is played and continues to fascinate brilliant minds is only because the infallible "best" ways of playing Chess have not yet been discovered. Nevertheless, when a chess situation becomes simplified, as in the end game, it very frequently becomes clear that one or the other player *must* win, or else the game *must* end in a draw. If we conceive of such an end game as a complete game, this game too is of the sort which is not worth playing. Indeed mature players usually break the game off whenever analysis makes clear what the outcome must be.

None of the argument just presented applies to Morra. In this ancient game two players simultaneously show either one or two fingers and at the same time each guesses aloud how many fingers the other will show. If only one player guesses correctly how many fingers the other has shown, he wins an amount equal to the sum of the fingers shown. Otherwise, neither player wins anything.

It is instructive to examine a somewhat different version of Morra. Suppose the rules are as before, namely each player shows either one or two fingers, but the payoffs now depend on the outcomes as follows. If both players show one finger, the first player wins one cent. If the first player shows one finger and the second two, the second player wins three cents. If the first player shows two fingers and the second player shows one finger, the second player wins five cents. If both show two fingers, the first player wins four cents. Is there a "best" way for the first player to play? Is there one for the second player? There is. Before we inquire into this matter, however, let us examine a much simpler version of Morra, in which if the sum of the fingers is odd, one player wins; if even, the other wins one unit.

Suppose this simple Morra is played many times in succession. Common sense dictates that the best way to play is to avoid any "pattern" in the choices. For if there is a pattern, there is a chance that the other will "catch on to it" and use this knowledge to his advantage. For example, it would be foolish to commit oneself to play "1" all the time. For if one does, the other will always play "1" or "2" depending on whether he wins on even or odd. Likewise, it is not wise to alternate regularly between "1" and "2," as small children sometimes alternate between hiding the button in one or the other hand when playing Button-Button. For this pattern too can be discovered. It may seem possible to develop a pattern just to snare the other into following with winning responses and then to shift suddenly and so win more than he has won. But this assumes that the other is less clever, and that one can entice him without being oneself enticed. On the other hand, if one avoids any pattern whatsoever, one can guarantee oneself no-win, no-loss in the long run, because against a perfect random sequence no pattern can insure a long-run positive return. Assuming that the other player also is aware of this fact, the conclusion is that the best way to play simple Morra is to randomize one's choices completely, for example, to play "1" or "2" depending on whether a fair coin falls heads or tails. The long-run payoff expectation resulting from this policy (called a "mixed strategy") is zero.[4]

The situation is different in the more complicated version of the game described above. Here the payoffs are not equal, and this must be taken into account in calculating a best "mixed strategy." It can be shown, in fact, that for the first player the best way to randomize his choices is in the ratio 9:4 in favor of "1" and for the second player in the ratio 7:6 in favor of "1." As a result, the first player will lose (in the long run) an average of 11/13 cents per play, while the second player will win this amount. *In no way can either player improve his long-run expectation*.

It appears, then, that there are games for which there exists at least one "best way" to play (one for each player) and there are other games in which, in order to do the best he can, a player must sometimes play one way, sometimes another, mixing his strategies in just the right proportions. These findings form the foundation of the mathematical theory of games of strategy. The bulk of the theory has to do with the clarification of concepts which lead to these results.

For example, the concept of strategy was first precisely defined in its game-theoretic context. We have already used the far-from-precise expression "a way to play." "A way to play" or a "strategy" can be defined precisely only by specifying how "a way to play" is to be described in a given case. It turns out that such descriptions become enormously complex whenever a game consists of more than a couple of moves. Some strategies, however, are simply stated. For example, the winning strategy (which is available to the first player only) in the simplified game of Nim described above (Race-to-Twenty) can be stated so: Begin with "1,2." Thereafter say either one or two numbers, always in such a way as to end on 5, 8, 11, 14, 17, and 20. A simple argument shows that this is indeed an available strategy for the first player. This strategy is not available for the second player, because if the first player begins with "1,2," the second player must end either on 3 or 4, either of which makes 5 available to the first player, and so on. However, there is a "best" strategy for the second player in the sense that he can take advantage of a mistake if the first player makes one. A single mistake by the first player immediately throws the victory to the second. For a mistake in this game can mean only taking one step when he should have taken two, or vice versa. Either way, one of the winning numbers 2, 5, etc., becomes available to the second player, and if one becomes available, they all become available. The second player's best strategy, therefore, can be stated as follows: If an opportunity presents itself to end the count on 2, 5, 8, etc., take it. Thereafter end all successive moves on numbers which, upon division by 3, give a remainder of 2 (for this is the property of all the winning numbers). This strategy will not win against a player who plays his winning strategy, but it will win if the first player makes a single mistake, and in that sense it is the best.

Our example illustrates the idea of strategy in a trivially simple game. In games only a little more complex, the job of describing a best strategy (if there is one) becomes extremely difficult. The reader may verify this by trying to describe the best strategy in Tic-tac-toe in a single set of directions. Game theory teaches that this can be done but not how to do it.

In short, a strategy, whether best or not, must specify what a player will do in every conceivable situation in which he may find himself during the course of the game. This description generally becomes unwieldly because, although one specifies a single choice at each move of the game as far as oneself is concerned, one must allow for every possible *combination* of choices which the opponent may make, and of these there is usually a very large number.

In practice, rational players do not worry about such large numbers of possibilities. In "planning ahead" one does well to consider only the most reasonable responses of the opponent. However, in a mathematical theory one wishes to establish *logically necessary* results (not merely plausible results), and so the problem looms of specifying *all* the strategies (good and bad) available to each player.

Game theory derives its power from having by-passed the problem of listing all the strategies in any specific instance. This was done by conceptualizing a game in so-called normal form. In this conceptualization, the strategies available to each player are simply assumed as *already* listed. The typically super-astronomical number of such strategies does not in-validate the arguments to come, for the number of strategies, although enormous, is finite, and so one can reason about a "set of strategies" in the same way one reasons about any finite set of objects.

And so suppose the strategies have been listed. If there are two players, the totality of strategies and of outcomes can be represented by a rectangular array, that is, a matrix. A game so represented is said to be "in normal form." The (horizontal) rows of the matrix are the strategies available to the first player; the (vertical) columns are the strategies available to the second player. The definition of strategy implies that once both players have chosen a strategy each, the outcome of that particular play of the game is determined. Therefore each box of the matrix, i.e., the intersection of a row and a column, represents an outcome. In this box, we enter the payoffs, one to each player associated with that outcome. If the game is a zero-sum game, only one of the payoffs needs to be entered since the other payoff must be the same number with the opposite sign attached. By convention, the payoffs entered are those to the first player who chooses a row.

Now we can list the principal results of the theory of two-person zero-sum games.

1. If among the entries of the game matrix, there exists one which is both the smallest in its row and the largest in its column,[5] then the corresponding row and column represent a pair of the best strategies for the respective players. Such an entry is called a "saddle point," so named after the corresponding point on a saddle which is lowest with the respect to the horse's longitudinal plane and highest with respect to the vertical plane at right angles to the longitudinal plane.

2. If the game matrix has no saddle point, there exists for each player a best "mixture of strategies," i.e., a way of randomizing strategies on successive plays such that each strategy is chosen with a given relative frequency. If both players choose their best mixed strategies, each will insure for himself an expected payoff which is the largest he can receive under the circumstances. If the game is played repeatedly and if payoffs can be cumulated, the expected payoffs will be realized as long-run average payoffs.

These two principles are illustrated respectively by the abstract games pictured in matrix (normal) form (cf. Matrix 1 and Matrix 2).

	A_2	B_2	C_2
A_1	-3	-6	12
B_1	-1	5	2
C_1	-6	10	-8

Matrix 1.

	A_2	B_2	C_2
A_1	-3	-6	12
B_1	6	5	2
C_1	-6	10	-8

Matrix 2.

In Matrix 1 the saddle point is in row *B*, column *A*. It is the smallest entry in its row and the largest in its column. Player 1 can do no better than choose row *B*; player 2 can do no better than choose column *A*. One way of coming to this conclusion is by an argument based on security. In each row there is an outcome which is worst for player 1. In row *A*, the worst outcome pays −6 (column *B*); in row *B*, the worst payoff is −1; in row *C*, it is −8. Of these three worst payoffs, −1 is clearly the best (least worst). From the point of view of player 2, the worst payoff in column *A* is +1 (for recall that the game is zero-sum); in column *B*, it is −10; in column *C*, it is −12. Therefore for player 2, the most prudent choice is column *A*. His "best of the worst" corresonds to player 1's best of the worst.

The saddle point is also called the minimax. We see that in a game with the saddle point, if both players choose in accordance with the minimax principle, their choices result in the outcome where the saddle point is.

In the game represented by Matrix 2 there is no saddle point, because no entry which is minimal in its row is at the same time maximal in its column. If now each player chooses the strategy which contains the best of the worst for him, the result is entirely different. In Matrix 2, the best of the worst for player 1 is now +2 in row *B*. But for player 2 (who must scan the columns) the best of the worst is −6 in column A. If both players were to choose in this way, player 1 would win 6. But clearly if player 2 thought that player 1 would choose according to the minimax principle (i.e., row *B*), he, player 2, would choose column *C*. But *knowing this*, player 1 would *not* choose row *B*; he would choose row *A*, where he gets 12 in column *C*. But *knowing this*, the column player would choose column *B*, which, if foreseen by the row player would lead him to choose row *C*, etc., *ad infinitum*.

The game-theoretical prescription in this case is for player 1 to choose not a specific row (there is no "best" row as there is in games with saddle points) but to randomize his choices among the first two rows, the relative frequencies being in ratio of 1:6. Player 2 should also randomize his choices among the second and third columns, namely in proportion of 10:11. When both do so, player 1 will win in the long run 3-3/7 units per play, which player 2 must lose. As we see, player 1 can do better than be satisfied with the guaranteed minimum of 2 units per play, which he can get if he plays only row *B*, and player 2 can do better than be satisfied with never losing more than 6, which he can assure by always playing column *A*.

Essentially, then, the idea of the mixed strategy allows an extension of the notion of rational play from the situation where best strategies for both players exist to situations where they do not, as long as the games are zero-sum. This extension is possible if the principle of maximizing expected utility gain is accepted as a principle of rational decision.

The two-person zero-sum game without a saddle point constitutes in our opinion the limit of applicability of game theory as a normative (or prescriptive) theory. That is to say, the minimax mixed strategy can be both rationally defended and intuitively accepted as a "best course of action" in a certain sense. Once the limits of two-person zero-sum games are transcended, game theory, while remaining a powerful tool for analyzing the logical structure of conflicts of interest, loses its prescriptive power. In this realm, strategically rationalizable courses of action are frequently intuitively unacceptable and vice versa.

Prisoner's Dilemma is the best known example of a nonzero-sum game where the "best" decision remains ambivalent. The game is illustrated in Matrix 3.

	C_2	D_2
C_1	1,1	−2,2
D_1	2,−2	−1,−1

Matrix 3.

Matrix 3 represents a nonzero-sum game, because the sums of the payoffs in outcomes C_1C_2 and D_1D_2[6] are not zero. Therefore the payoffs to both players must be entered for each outcome. By convention, the first of the pair of payoffs is that accruing to the first player (the row chooser). Of these outcomes, C_1C_2 obviously is preferred to D_1D_2 by both players. However, strategy D *dominates*[7] strategy C in the sense that D is best both against C and against D, whichever is chosen by the other player. Therefore the choice of D is dictated as the only strategically sound choice. But this strategy is dictated to *both* players, and when both choose it, D_1D_2 obtains, which is worse for both players than C_1C_2. Hence the dilemma.

The nickname Prisoner's Dilemma, attributed to A. W. Tucker, derives from the original anecdote used to illustrate the game. Two prisoners, held incommunicado, are charged with the same crime. They can be convicted only if either confesses. Designate by −1 the payoff associated with conviction on the basis of confessions by both prisoners and by +1 the payoff associated with acquittal. Further, if only one confesses, he is set free for having turned state's evidence and is given a reward to boot. Call his payoff under these circumstances +2. The prisoner who has held out is convicted on the strength of the other's testimony and is given a more severe sentence than if he had also confessed. Call his payoff −2. The game so defined is identical with that represented by Matrix 3 where *D* represents "confess" and *C* "do not confess." It is in the interest of each to confess *whatever* the other does. But it is in their *collective* interest to hold out.

Cooperative and Noncooperative Games

The theory of nonzero-sum games distinguishes between cooperative and noncooperative games. In a cooperative game, players can make agreements to choose strategies jointly. In noncooperative games they cannot do so. Prisoner's Dilemma is, by definition, a noncooperative game. If it were a cooperative game, the dilemma, it is argued, would disappear, because then the prisoners could make a pact not to confess, a pact from which each would derive a benefit. It is clear, however, that if the pact is not enforceable, a new dilemma arises. For now each of the prisoners faces a decision of keeping the pact or breaking it. This choice induces another game exactly like Prisoner's Dilemma, because it is in the interest of each to break the pact regardless of whether the other keeps it.

Therefore if agreements arrived at in cooperative games are to make a difference in the choice of strategies, they must be *enforceable* agreements. However, if the agreements are enforceable, clearly the payoffs are not the same. Enforcement means the application of sanctions for breaking the agreement. It is well known that in the underworld sanctions against squealing are exceedingly severe. And so if a prisoner is considering a choice of strategy, namely whether to abide by the agreement to keep silent or to break it, he must include in his payoffs not only those shown in the game matrix but also the consequences of turning state's evidence. Suppose the sanctions against this choice (by friends of the convicted partner) amount to − 10 units to be added algebraically to the previously mentioned payoff of +2. Then it is not the game in Matrix 3 which is at issue but rather the game shown in Matrix 4.

	C_2	D_2
C_1	1,1	−2,−8
D_1	−8,−2	−1,−1

Matrix 4.

Here strategy D no longer dominates, and we have an entirely different type of game. It follows that if we wish to keep extraneous payoffs out of the picture, we must concentrate on the theory of the noncooperative game.

It is sometimes argued by game theoreticians that the choice of the minimax strategy D (observe that in Matrix 3, D is a minimax for both players) is a rational choice. Although the outcome D_1D_2 looks bad compared with C_1C_2, it is argued that the former is the only outcome which is defensible on rational grounds. In short, it is the only outcome feasible under the constraints of the game. The fact that it is worse than C_1C_2 merely reflects the inability of the two players to communicate.

There is some merit in this argument, but the case seems much weaker if the game is repeated a finite and known number of times. To show this, let us design another game, an extension of Prisoner's Dilemma. This new game will consist of two moves, each move being made simultaneously by the two players, whereby the second move is made after the outcome of the first move has been announced. Each move is a choice by each player of one of the strategies in Prisoner's Dilemma.

We shall now list the strategies available to player 1. There are eight such strategies (in spite of the fact that he can choose his two moves in only four different ways). The eight strategies are as follows.

1. Choose C_1 both times regardless of what player 2 chooses on the first move.

2. Choose C_1 on the first move; on the second choose the same as player 2 chose on the first.

3. Choose C_1 on the first move; on the second choose the opposite of what player 2 chose on the first.

4. Choose C_1 on the first move; on the second choose D_1 regardless of what player 1 chose on the first.

5. Choose D_1 on the first move; on the second choose C_1 regardless of what player 2 chose on the first.

6. Choose D_1 on the first move; on the second choose the same as what player 2 chose on the first.

7. Choose D_1 on the first move; on the second choose the opposite of what player 2 chose on the first.

8. Choose D_1 on both moves regardless of how player 2 chooses.

Clearly player 2's strategies are exactly analogous. This two-move Prisoner's Dilemma, which we shall call PD^2, can be represented in normal (matrix) form, as shown in Matrix 5.

Note that there is no longer a dominating strategy for either player. For example, strategy 8 (the totally uncooperative strategy), which we shall designate by $D^{(2)}$, is best against strategy 8 and also against strategy 4, but not against strategy 2. Strategy 3 or 4 is best against strategy 2 but not against strategy 3. The compelling argument for choosing D in the game played once (namely that D is best against either strategy of the other) does not apply here to $D^{(2)}$. However, a strategic argument can still be made for the

	1	2	3	4	5	6	7	8
1	2,2	2,2	−1,3	−1,3	−1,3	−1,3	−4,4	−4,4
2	2,2	2,2	−1,3	−1,3	0,0	0,0	−3,1	−3,1
3	3,−1	3,−1	0,0	0,0	−1,3	−1,3	−4,4	−4,4
4	3,−1	3,−1	0,0	0,0	0,0	0,0	−3,1	−3,1
5	3,−1	0,0	3,−1	0,0	0,0	−3,1	0,0	−3,1
6	3,−1	0,0	3,−1	0,0	1,−3	−2,−2	1,−3	−2,−2
7	4,−4	1,−3	4,−4	1,−3	0,0	−3,1	0,0	−3,1
8	4,−4	1,−3	4,−4	1,−3	1,−3	−2,−2	1,−3	−2,−2

Matrix 5.

totally uncooperative strategy $D^{(2)}$. We put ourselves into player 1's position.

"Suppose," muses player 1, "player 2 has already chosen strategy 2. My best reply to this strategy is clearly 3 or 4 (cf. Matrix 5). But since player 2 is rational and knows that I am rational, he must have already figured out that I shall play 3 or 4 against his 2. But if I play, say 4, his best reply is not 2 but 8, to which my best reply, in turn, is 8. Now his best reply to 8 is 8, and my best reply to his 8 is 8. Therefore neither of us has any better choice than strategy 8. Both of us know it and each knows that the other knows it. Therefore I must play 8."

In the meantime player 2 has gone through the same reasoning. Consequently both players come to the "rational conclusion" that 8 is the only feasible strategy. With this strategy, they lose 2 units whereas they might have won 2 units if they both had played strategy 1 or 2.[8]

The same argument is extendable to any number of plays. Suppose the game is played 100 times. Then whatever happens during the first 99 plays, it is clear

that on the 100th play D should be chosen. Whatever apprehensions one may have had that one's choices
of D will be "punished" by the other's choosing D
in retaliation, do not apply on the last play, because
there is no opportunity for retaliation after the last
play. But if the outcome of the last play is *certainly*
DD, it no longer figures in the strategic calculations.
Thus the 99th play becomes the last play, and so on,
until the "rational" player is forced to the conclusion
that $D^{(100)}$, i.e., D played all 100 times is the only
feasible strategy.

In consequence, both players lose 100 units, whereas
had they played CC 100 times they would have won
100 units.

Confronted with this paradox, game theoreticians
have no answer. Ordinary mortals, however, when
playing Prisoner's Dilemma many times in succession
hardly ever play DD one hundred percent of the time.
To be sure, long stretches of DD choices occur, but
also long stretches of CC choices. Evidently the run-
of-the-mill players are not strategically sophisticated
enough to have figured out that strategy DD is the
only rationally defensible strategy, and this intellectual shortcoming saves them from losing.

In this book we shall describe how human subjects (University of Michigan students) play Prisoner's Dilemma many times in succession. (There are a
number of ways to play this game; see Appendix I for
one set of instructions given to subjects.) The record
of each sequence of repeated plays (the protocol) is
typically a mixture of C choices and D choices. This
record is a rich source of statistics. From these statistics we shall attempt to construct a theory. We believe
that the theory is pertinent to psychology, at any
rate to the psychology of situations in which mixed
motives play an essential part. The bulk of the theory
will be derived from a description of regularities ob-

served in the data. We shall attempt to unify these regularities by means of mathematical models. It is from the parameters of these models, not from any a priori assumptions about the psychological determinants of the situation that we shall derive our psychological interpretations. As it will turn out, the mathematical parameters are extremely suggestive of psychological characteristics. They will be interpreted as such.

Methodology

A few words are in order about our orientation toward methodology. First, although we hopefully call our theory psychological, single individuals will not be differentiated in it. We shall be concerned with a fictitious "average" individual, whose behavior will be measured by variables derived from averaging protocols of populations of individuals. This approach was dictated not by a lack of interest in the individual, but rather by a desire to understand the gross dynamics of behavior typical in repeated trials at Prisoner's Dilemma. As will become apparent, the dynamics of this behavior are intricate and pose difficult mathematical problems. We used our effort in attempts to solve these problems in preference to trying the immensely more difficult task of assessing individual differences.

Second, we have not resorted to intricate statistical methods of evaluating the significance of the results. Again it was a question of choosing where to direct the effort. The distributions of our variables are not of the well-known types: hardly any of these distributions looks like a Gaussian. For the most part, appropriate statistical methods for evaluating significance are either nonexistent or exceedingly complex. Our purpose was not to establish definitive results but rather to suggest interesting hypotheses. We hope work of this sort will continue for a long time, and that there will be plenty of opportunity to single out some of the more intriguing hypotheses derived from the data and put them to really severe tests. However, we are fortunate in having obtained some results which are both interesting (in our opinion) and whose significance is obvious to the naked eye. Partly the definitiveness of some of our results is due to the large masses of data. Massed data have an intrinsic stability. The individual is lost but the basic system dynamics of the situation tends to emerge. It is this system dynamics which was always at the center of our interest.

Related to the foregoing considerations is also our incomplete utilization of the stochastic models we have proposed. We fully recognized the power of such models in the study of interactions and we have not altogether neglected them. But we have concentrated on the much simpler deterministic models, again in order to bring out the characteristic systemic properties of the situation abstracted of the individuals in it. Thus at one point we have delved into a classical equilibrium analysis of the sort studied by Lewis F. Richardson[9] and have found it gratifyingly instructive in revealing some essential features of our situation. These classical (continuous and deterministic) theories are admittedly inadequate and have been developed here for heuristic purposes only—to bring out salient features rather than to predict the results.

We agree with the proponents of stochastic models that such models are probably more appropriate in the situation with which we are concerned. However, as those will recognize who have worked with stochastic theories of learning, in situations of this sort the difficulty of applying those theories while preserving their fully stochastic character are already formidable when only one subject is involved. With two interacting subjects, the difficulties are multiplied manyfold. To give an idea of what is involved, consider the number of parameters that must be estimated. In the case of a single stochastic learner with two choices, one rewarded, one punished, the estimation of four parameters is involved (if complete fixation or complete extinction of the response is not assumed). The same model applied to two interacting subjects (where there are four outcomes, instead of two) requires the estimation of eight parameters if the response probabilities "learned" are those of C or D; but it requires 256 parameters to construct a stochastic learning model of conditional responses. By making drastically simplified assumptions, this number can be reduced to thirty-six. It would have led us far astray if we went about doggedly estimating parameters with a view of deriving the relevant statistics of the process, as is prescribed by stochastic theories. Our aim at this point is not prediction of specific experimental results but a better understanding of what goes on. We have therefore contented ourselves with conjectures suggested by the data, hoping that these conjectures will provide good points of departure for future work.

Chapter 1
In Search of an Index

OUR FIRST TASK will be to find some convenient way of studying behavior in Prisoner's Dilemma in relation to the payoffs. Clearly it is desirable to have some index derived from the payoffs and to relate observed behavior to this index.

The matrix which represents Prisoner's Dilemma has eight entries in it. The magnitudes of these entries can vary independently within certain constraints. Therefore any behavioral index derived from "performances" on this game can be conceived as a function of eight independent variables. Such a relationship is far too complex to be grasped intuitively. Fortunately there is a natural way to simplify the situation. Four of the entries are the payoffs to one of the players, and four are the payoffs to the other. We can confine our attention only to those forms of the game which are symmetric with regard to the players, that is, look exactly alike from the point of view of each of the players. To realize this symmetry, we let the payoffs corresponding to each outcome depend only on how the players have chosen, not on how the players are labeled. To be sure, this symmetry in the entries does not necessarily represent psychological symmetry, since the payoff units may have different meanings (utilities)[10] for each of the players. But equalizing the entries is the best we can do.

Our game matrix now appears as shown in Matrix 6. The letters representing the payoffs are meant to be suggestive. *R* stands for reward; it refers to the payoff each of the players receives as reward for co-

	C_2	D_2
C_1	R,R	S,T
D_1	T,S	P,P

Matrix 6.

operating. S stands for sucker's payoff. This is the payoff received by the player who cooperated while the other defected. T stands for temptation, the payoff a player may hope to get if he can defect and get away with it. P stands for punishment, meted out to both players when both have defected.

In order to have the situation defined as Prisoner's Dilemma the following inequalities must be satisfied:

$$S < P < R < T. \qquad (\text{I})$$

Specifically, when a player gets the sucker's payoff S, he must be motivated to switch to the defecting strategy so as to get at least P. If he gets the cooperator's payoff R, he must be motivated to defect so as to get still more, T. If he gets the defector's punishment P, he may wish there were a way of getting R, but this is possible only if the other defector will switch to the cooperative strategy together with him.

Besides these inequalities, we shall wish to introduce one additional constraint, namely

$$2R > S + T. \qquad (2)$$

If this inequality did not hold, that is, if $S + T$ were equal to or were greater than $2R$, the players would have at their disposal more than one form of tacit collusion. One form of collusion is the tacit agreement to play CC, which is the expected "cooperative solution" of the Prisoner's Dilemma game. However, if $S + T \geq 2R$, there is also another form of collusion, which may occur in repeated plays of the game, namely alternation between CD and DC. Each such alternation gives each player $S + T$, i.e., at least $2R$, which each player would have obtained from two consecutive CC outcomes. The question of whether the collusion of alternating unilateral defections would occur and, if so, how frequently is doubtless interesting. For the present, however, we wish to avoid the complication of multiple "cooperative solutions." Accordingly the inequality (2) will be assumed to hold throughout.

Having reduced the Prisoner's Dilemma game to a matrix with four parameters, independent within the constraints imposed, we make one additional step toward simplification. Namely, we set $S = -T$. This cuts the number of independent parameters to three. In the three-parameter game, S and T become mirror images of each other, and therefore whatever effect they exert on the performance, they exert together. In all games with which we shall be concerned, we shall have $T > 0$, consequently $S < 0$. Further, since in all our games $T + S = 0$, we must have $R > 0$, since $2R > T + S$ [cf. (2)]. Therefore it should be kept in mind that when we write "S increases," this will imply that the numerical value of S *decreases*, i.e., that the sucker's punishment becomes smaller. Mutatis mutandis "S decreases" will mean that the sucker's punishment becomes larger. Similar remarks apply to P when $P < 0$, as it will be in all our games. We shall sometimes refer to different Prisoner's Dilemma games as "mild" or "severe." Mild games are those where T is not much larger than R or where P is numerically large, i.e., those where it does not pay very much to defect. Severe games are those where temptation to defect is strong or the punishment for double defection is weak, or both.

We are now in a position to ask a straightforward question. Are the motivations inherent in the relations among the payoffs reflected in the performances?

Specifically, R rewards cooperation. Is it true that if the other parameters are held constant, while R increases, more cooperation will be observed?

T represents temptation to defect. Is it true that as the other parameters are held constant, cooperation will decrease as T is increased? Note that the numerical magnitude of S, i.e., the magnitude of the sucker's punishment, increases together with that of T in all the games to be considered here. Hence in the three-parameter model any effect attributed to T can with equal justification be attributed to S.

Finally, P represents punishment for failure to cooperate. Is it true that cooperation increases as the magnitude of this punishment becomes greater, i.e., as P decreases?

We shall offer answers to these questions in terms of the frequencies of cooperative responses observed in many repeated plays of Prisoner's Dilemma averaged over many pairs of subjects. We shall refer to the cooperative response as the C response. When there is no danger of confusion, C will also mean the frequency of the C response and its unconditional probability. Similarly D will mean the defecting response, its frequency, and its probability.

Experimental Procedure

We let seventy pairs of University of Michigan students (all males) play Prisoner's Dilemma games three hundred times in succession. The pairs were matched randomly. Except in a very few cases, the members of a pair were not acquainted with each other. The instructions read to the subjects are given in Appendix I. Following each play, the outcome was announced. Each pair played only one variant of the game. There were seven such variants, so that ten pairs were assigned to each. The seven payoff matrices are shown below. We have kept the number designations of the games to avoid confusion. Games VI through X are not shown here. They were used in other experiments.

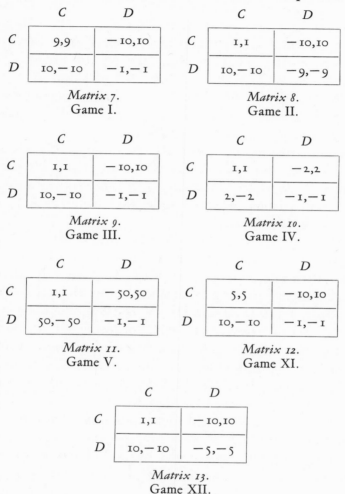

	C	D
C	9,9	− 10,10
D	10,− 10	− 1,− 1

Matrix 7.
Game I.

	C	D
C	1,1	− 10,10
D	10,− 10	− 9,− 9

Matrix 8.
Game II.

	C	D
C	1,1	− 10,10
D	10,− 10	− 1,− 1

Matrix 9.
Game III.

	C	D
C	1,1	− 2,2
D	2,− 2	− 1,− 1

Matrix 10.
Game IV.

	C	D
C	1,1	− 50,50
D	50,− 50	− 1,− 1

Matrix 11.
Game V.

	C	D
C	5,5	− 10,10
D	10,− 10	− 1,− 1

Matrix 12.
Game XI.

	C	D
C	1,1	− 10,10
D	10,− 10	− 5,− 5

Matrix 13.
Game XII.

From the matrices of the seven games, the following can be observed. In Games III, XI, and I, T, S, and P are held constant, while R increases from 1 to 5 to 9. One would expect, therefore, that in these games C would be largest in Game I and smallest in Game III.

Next observe that in Games IV, III, and V, *R* and *P* are held constant while the magnitude of *S* and *T* increases from 2 to 10 to 50. One would therefore expect that in these games *C* would be largest in Game IV and smallest in Game V. Finally in Games III, XII, and II, *R*, *S*, and *T* are kept constant while *P* decreases from −1 to −5 to −9. Therefore we would expect *C* to increase from Game III to Game XII to Game II.

We combine these conjectures into Hypothesis 1. *If other payoffs are kept constant, C increases as R and S increase and decreases as T and P increase.*

Comparisons of Games III, XI, and I, Games IV, III, and V, and Games III, XII, and II are shown in Figure 1. Without inquiring into the significance of the comparisons, we conclude that the results tend to corroborate Hypothesis 1.

Hypothesis 1 implies certain rank orderings with respect to *C* among the games. But the rank order of some of the games is not established by the hypothesis. For example, nothing is implied about the rank order of Games I and II, II and IV, IV and XI, or XI and XII.

To get a theoretical rank ordering of all seven games, we need an index composed of all our parameters, *T*, *R*, *P*, and *S*, i.e., an index which is a function of four independent variables. It would be all but futile to try to get an idea of this function by examining our data, for that would mean plotting values of *C* in five-dimensional space. We can, however, make some a priori arguments about the general character of such a function on the basis of some available theory.

Assuming an Interval Scale of Utilities

The theory in question was developed in a purely formal context. To our knowledge no conclusive evidence has ever been offered favoring the conclusion that the theory is valid in *behavioral* contexts. We are re-

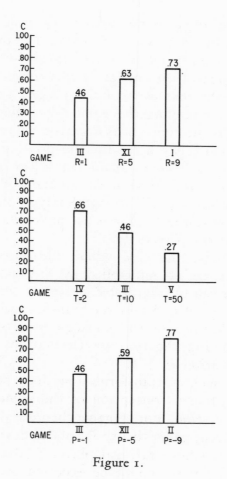

Figure 1.

ferring to the concept of utility, as it has been used
in the theory of games. In game theory, utilities (which
are supposed to be the entries in the payoff matrices)
are almost always assumed to be measured on interval
scales at least in two-person games.[11] This, in turn,
means that, if all the entries u ($u = T$, R, P, or S) in
a game matrix are replaced by $au + b$ (where a and b
are constants, $a > 0$), all the conclusions about the
game resulting from this transformation should be
identical to the corresponding conclusions about the

original game. It seems reasonable to expect this with respect to rational players. Suppose, for example, a given two-person game is transformed by adding a constant to each of the entries. If this constant is positive, this means that each of the players gets a fixed amount just for playing the game (regardless of how he plays it). If the constant is negative, this means that each player must pay a fee for the privilege of playing the game each time, again regardless of how he plays. Either way, these fixed amounts should not make any difference in the *strategic* analysis of the game, precisely because the fixed reward or fee does not depend on what the players do.

Consider next the case where the entries of the payoff matrix are all multiplied by the same positive number. This can be interpreted as simply changing the units of the payoffs. Again the transformation should make no difference in the strategic structure of the game. Combining the two transformations, we have the transformation $au + b$.

Whether such a transformation does not in fact change the players' conception of the game is a psychological question, not a game-theoretical one. But as we have seen, game theory is totally devoid of psychology. It assumes "rational players," that is, "perfect players." These cannot be expected to be human and therefore cannot be expected to have a psychology. We shall, to be sure, be concerned with real subjects and with their observed behavior in the games under discussion. But it will be useful to forget this for the moment, to assume players devoid of psychology and to stay with this assumption as long as we can. Accordingly we shall assume that the behavior of our players remains invariant if the payoff matrices of our Prisoner's Dilemma games are subjected to a linear transformation, i.e., to a transformation of the form $au + b \, (a > 0)$.

An immediate consequence of this assumption is that our behavioral variable C should depend not on the parameters, T, R, P, and S individually but rather on the ratios of their differences.[12] For example, $(R - P)/(T - S)$ is one such ratio; $(T - P)/(P - S)$ is another. Formally speaking, thirty such interval ratios can be formed from the four parameters. Of course fifteen of these will be reciprocals of the other fifteen and so can be immediately dismissed from consideration as independent variables. It can be further shown that only two of these interval ratios can be independent: the remaining ones can all be derived from just two. The two can be chosen in many ways. We choose the following:

$$r_1 = \frac{R - P}{T - S} \quad \text{and} \quad r_2 = \frac{R - S}{T - S}. \tag{3}$$

As an example of the dependence of the other ratios on r_1 and r_2, observe that the interval ratio $(P - S)/(T - S)$ is obtained as $r_2 - r_1$; $(T - R)/(T - S)$ is obtained as $1 - r_2$; $(P - S)/(T - R)$ is obtained as $(r_2 - r_1)/(1 - r_2)$, etc. In short, all the fifteen interval ratios and their fifteen reciprocals can be obtained either as linear functions or as bilinear functions (ratios of two polynomials of the first degree) of r_1 and r_2. Thus if r_1 and r_2 are given, all the thirty interval ratios upon which the rank-ordering index of the game can depend are also determined. It suffices, therefore, to consider such an index as a function of the basic pair r_1 and r_2 alone.

In choosing the basic pair given by (3), we were guided by the convenience of having $T - S$ in the denominator. Since $T - S$ is the largest of the six differences [cf. inequality (1)], this guarantees against infinitely large values of r_1 and r_2, because the denominator cannot vanish without the numerator vanishing simultaneously. In fact, for all permissible values of T, R, P, and S, we must have $0 < r_1 < 1$ and $0 < r_2 < 1$.

Now let us examine the dependence of r_1 and r_2 on the four parameters. We have

$$\frac{\partial r_1}{\partial R} > 0; \quad \frac{\partial r_1}{\partial P} < 0; \quad \frac{\partial r_1}{\partial T} < 0; \quad \frac{\partial r_1}{\partial S} > 0. \tag{4}$$

Since Hypothesis 1 implies

$$\frac{\partial C}{\partial R} > 0; \quad \frac{\partial C}{\partial T} < 0; \quad \frac{\partial C}{\partial P} < 0; \quad \frac{\partial C}{\partial S} > 0, \tag{5}$$

it also implies that C increases with r_1. As we shall see, this determines the rank ordering of Games II and III. This rank ordering is already implied by Hypothesis 1 and so puts no new restriction on the theoretical rank ordering of the games. However, as we shall see, the dependence of C on r_1 also establishes the rank orders of Games IV, XI, and XII, in that order, which Hypothesis 1 does not do. Hence the assumption that C increases with r_1 is a stronger hypothesis than Hypothesis 1. We shall call it Hypothesis 2:

$$\frac{\partial C}{\partial r_1} > 0. \tag{6}$$

We turn to r_2. Taking the partial derivatives, we get

$$\frac{\partial r_2}{\partial R} > 0; \quad \frac{\partial r_2}{\partial T} < 0; \quad \frac{\partial r_2}{\partial S} < 0. \tag{7}$$

We see that while the partials of r_2, with respect to R and T have the same sign as the corresponding partials of r_1, the partial of r_2 with respect to S is negative, while the corresponding partial of r_1 is positive. Hence the dependence of C upon r_2 is not determined by Hypothesis 1. If such dependence is to be assumed, an independent hypothesis must be proposed. There seems to be no a priori justifiable reason for supposing either $\partial C/\partial r_2 > 0$ or $\partial C/\partial r_2 < 0$. We therefore can have either of the following hypotheses:

Hypothesis 3:

$$\frac{\partial C}{\partial r_1} > 0; \quad \frac{\partial C}{\partial r_2} > 0; \tag{8}$$

Hypothesis 4:

$$\frac{\partial C}{\partial r_1} > 0; \quad \frac{\partial C}{\partial r_2} < 0. \tag{9}$$

Both Hypothesis 3 and Hypothesis 4 include Hypothesis 2 and hence a fortiori Hypothesis 1. But Hypotheses 3 and 4 are mutually exclusive. The data can therefore support the one or the other (if any) but not both.

Table 1 shows the values of r_1 and r_2 in each of our seven games.

TABLE I

Game	r_1	r_2
I	1/2	19/20
II	1/2	11/20
III	1/10	11/20
IV	1/2	3/4
V	1/50	51/100
XI	3/10	3/4
XII	3/10	11/20

We see that Games II, XII, and III all have the same value of r_2 but the respective values of r_1 decrease in that order. Therefore the rank order should be II > XII > III according to our Hypothesis 2. But this was already implied by Hypothesis 1. Next, Games IV and XI have the same value of r_2 and therefore are rank ordered IV > XI according to the respective values of r_1. This was not implied by Hypothesis 1 but is consistent with it.

Examining games which have the same value of r_1, we find that they are Games I, II, and IV. On the basis of Hypothesis 3, C increases with r_2; hence these games must be rank ordered I > IV > II. On the basis of Hypothesis 4, on the contrary, these games must have the opposite rank ordering, namely II > IV > I. Finally, XI and XII have the same value of r_1 and consequently must be rank ordered XI > XII if Hypothesis 3 is assumed, or XII > XI if Hypothesis 4 is assumed.

All these implications of the hypotheses can be expressed in the form of lattices shown in Figure 2. A link connecting two games shows that their rank order is implied by the corresponding hypothesis, the game with the higher value of C being on the higher level. The rank order is transitive. Where no link connects two games, no rank order is implied. Observe that only Hypotheses 3 and 4 imply a rank order of all seven games.

Let us now compare all of these conclusions with data. There are several sources of data. In addition to the experiment described on page 36, we have performed several other experiments under somewhat varying conditions. Our present aim will be to check the extent to which the conclusions concerning the rank ordering of the games with respect to C are valid. The variations of the first experiment will serve as quasi-replications. We shall at this point make no use of statistical analysis to test the significance of the results. In certain instances significance will be apparent almost to the naked eye. In other cases rather involved procedures would be required to test for significance, since, as we shall see, the distributions are not of the sort which allow an application of con-

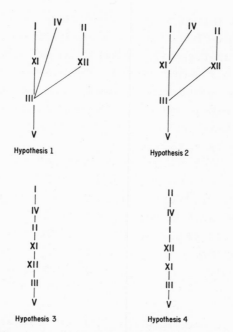

Figure 2. The rank orders of games implied by the various hypotheses. Links connect games whose rank order is implied. Games with greater frequency of cooperative responses are shown on higher levels.

ventional parametric tests. We shall on occasions use nonparametric tests (cf. Appendix II), but for the most part we shall forgo such analysis in order not to detract from the main line of thought. As has already been stated, the generation rather than the establishment of hypotheses has been the main purpose of the work described here.

Variants of the Experiment

We shall now describe the different variants of the experiment with the Prisoner's Dilemma game. The condition under which the experiment has been described will be called the *Pure Matrix Condition*, to indicate that a given pair of subjects plays the same game (not mixed with other games) throughout the session (three hundred plays) and the subjects see the game matrix displayed. That is to say, their performance on that game is not "contaminated" by their performance on different games. As has already been said, ten pairs play each of the seven games in the Pure Matrix Condition, seventy pairs in all or twenty-one thousand responses.

In the *Block Matrix Condition* each pair of subjects plays all seven games. Since learning has an important effect on performance, the order in which the games are played must be varied in order to distinguish the effects of the payoff matrix from the effects of learning. Accordingly our design in this condition was a Latin Square—seven orders of blocks of fifty plays of each game of the seven. There were two such Latin Squares, the orders in the second being the exact reverse of the orders in the first, or a total of fourteen orders. There were five pairs playing the seven playing games in a given order or seventy pairs in all. Since there were fifty plays per game, each pair gave 350 responses.

In a third condition, called the *Mixed Matrix Condition*, each of ten pairs played seven hundred times or one hundred plays per game. Here the games were presented in random order slightly modified to allow each game to be represented exactly one hundred times. The matrices of the seven games were displayed.

The *Pure No Matrix Condition* was introduced by having pairs of subjects play the games without having the game matrix in front of them. However, the payoffs to both players were announced following each play. The *Mixed No Matrix Condition* is defined analogously.

Thus there were five different variants, all independent, in the sense that the corresponding subject populations were nonoverlapping—each pair playing in only one condition. In Table 2 the frequencies of

TABLE 2

Game	Pure Matrix Condition	Block Matrix Condition	Mixed Matrix Condition	Combined Matrix Condition	Pure No Matrix Condition	Mixed No Matrix Condition	Combined No Matrix Condition
I	73.4	70.0	70.0	71.5	32.4	33.4	32.7
II	77.4	68.6	60.9	71.3	44.6	30.2	41.0
III	45.8	49.2	61.0	49.4	22.3	34.7	25.4
IV	66.2	67.5	71.6	67.5	45.8	29.2	41.4
V	26.8	39.5	40.4	34.2	22.6	19.1	21.7
XI	63.5	66.0	67.0	65.1	34.5	32.6	34.0
XII	59.4	59.1	60.3	59.4	33.4	26.0	31.5
Hypothesis 1	13/13	13/13	11/13	13/13	12/13	8/13	12/13
Hypothesis 2	14/14	14/14	12/14	14/14	13/14	8/14	13/14
Hypothesis 3	19/21	20/21	17/21	20/21	16/21	13/21	18/21
Hypothesis 4	19/21	18/21	15/21	17/21	16/21	11/21	18/21

the C responses (in percent) are shown for each of the seven games and five conditions. In addition, the conditions in which the matrix is displayed are combined (Combined Matrix Condition) and also the two conditions in which the matrix is not displayed (last column). In the last four rows of the table the entries show crude measures of agreement between the rank order of the games as observed and as implied by the four hypotheses. Recall that only Hypotheses 3 and 4 rank order all seven games. Hypotheses 1 and 2 imply only partial ordering. Thus Hypothesis 1 implies the ordering of only 13 of the 21 possible pairs, namely I > XI; I > III; I > V; XI > III; XI > V; III > V; IV > III; IV > V; II > XII; II > III; III > V; XII > III; XII > V. Of course, not all of these inequalities are independent. There are only six independent ones among them. In fact each of the four hypotheses implies an ordering of only six independent pairs. But the strength of each hypothesis is reflected in the number of paired comparisons *implied* by the independent six pairs. In the case of Hypothesis 1, there are 13 such pairs; in the case of Hypothesis 2, there are 14; each of the last two hypotheses implies an ordering of all the 21 pairs (among seven games taken two at a time). Our crude measure of agreement is simply a fraction showing how many of the paired comparisons implied by each of the hypotheses in each condition are consistent with the corresponding hypotheses. The weak Hypotheses 1 and 2 are completely corroborated in the Pure and the Block Conditions and also in the combined conditions with matrix displayed. The strong Hypotheses 3 and 4 are nowhere completely corroborated. Of the two, Hypothesis 3 seems to be corroborated somewhat more than Hypothesis 4. No further attempt will be made at this point to estimate a confidence level for these hypotheses, which were proposed here not for the purpose of explaining the data but merely as points of departure for a theory. In Part II, we shall develop a mathematical model in which a rank ordering of the games will be derived as a consequence of certain dynamic considerations. At that time the questions raised here will be discussed more fully.

Summary of Chapter 1

If the payoffs are varied singly, common sense suggests that the frequency of cooperative responses ought to increase with the reward parameter R, ought to decrease with the temptation parameter T, and ought to increase as the magnitude of the (negative) punishment parameter P increases. These conjectures, embodied in Hypothesis 1, have been corroborated in the Block and Pure Matrix Conditions.

If the payoffs are equated to utilities and if the

theory of utility used in game theory is assumed, then the behavior of Prisoner's Dilemma ought to depend not on the payoff parameters themselves but on ratios of differences between them. It was shown that only two such ratios are independent.

Two hypotheses have been proposed in the form of directional dependence of cooperative frequencies in each of the two independent difference ratios. Neither of these hypotheses was corroborated perfectly in any of the conditions. One of them, however, was almost completely corroborated in one of the conditions and both were somewhat less completely corroborated in another condition. On the whole, one of the hypotheses was favored somewhat more than the other.

Chapter 2
Effects of Mixing Games and Concealing the Matrix

So FAR we have been mainly concerned with the effects of the payoff parameters on performance. Now let us examine other effects. Our data come from a number of experiments. In all of them Prisoner's Dilemma is played by a pair of University of Michigan students several hundred times in succession. However, as we have seen, certain conditions vary from experiment to experiment. For example, as we pass from the "Pure" to the "Block" to the "Mixed" conditions, the games become progressively more mixed. In the Pure Matrix Condition, each pair plays only one kind of game. In the Block Matrix Condition, each pair plays all seven games, but there are fifty successive plays of each game. In the Mixed Matrix Condition, all seven games are entirely mixed, following each other in random order. A natural question to ask is whether the games "contaminate" each other in the sense that the games, which in the Pure Matrix Condition are characterized by very low C, show a higher value when mixed with other games, and games with a high value of C in the Pure Matrix Condition show lower values when mixed with other games.

An examination of Table 2 (p. 47) shows that this indeed may be the case. The game with the highest C in the Pure Matrix Condition is Game II. The value of C in this game is considerably reduced in both the Block and the Mixed Matrix Conditions. Next, Game V, which is the lowest in all conditions, shows a considerably higher C in both the Block and in the Mixed Matrix Conditions compared with the

Pure Matrix Condition. In short, the range of C is reduced in the Block and in the Mixed Matrix Conditions. We can also examine a somewhat more refined measure of the spread of C, namely its variance. This turns out to be .02 in the Pure Matrix Condition, .011 in the Block Matrix Condition, and .01 in the Mixed Matrix Condition.

These results we would expect on commonsense grounds, if we assume that the response propensities are determined by the interaction of the players and tend to spread over all the games played by a pair of players.

Now let us examine the effect upon performance of the displayed matrix. The comparison can be made in the Pure and in the Mixed variants, since both variants appear in our design with matrix displayed and with matrix not displayed. The idea behind this variation was originally inspired by discussions about the relative merits of game theory and learning theory in describing performances on repeated games. Actually the idea is older than game theory. It stems from some early findings in experiments on animals in learning situations in which responses are reinforced probabilistically.

As a simple example consider an animal in a T-maze in which right and left turns are differentially reinforced in the sense that food in the same amounts appears at random at the one or the other end with unequal probabilities. It was noted that in many cases the trend is toward a steady state distribution of right and left responses whose probabilities are proportional to the probabilities of finding food at the right or the left end respectively. Observe that this "solution" is not "rational" from our human point of view. Such a situation would be classified in the theory of rational decisions as decision under risk. Ordinarily in such

situations the maximization of expected gain is prescribed by normative decision theory. If the relative
magnitudes of the two probabilities were correctly
estimated by the subject (note that it is not necessary
to estimate their numerical values but only their relative magnitudes), then expected gain is maximized
if the turn which results in the greater probability
of reward is *always* taken. However, the distribution
of right and left turns in accordance with the respective probabilities of reinforcement is a consequence
of a stochastic theory of learning (Bush and Mosteller,
1955, p. 68 ff.) and so has its "rationale" also, although it is not the rationale prescribed by rational
decision theory. Here, then, we have a clear-cut di-
chotomy between two theories of behavior and an
experimental situation in which they can be pitted
one against the other.

In recent years other experimental situations have
have been designed with the specific purpose of pitting
some game-theoretical prescriptions against the predictions derived from stochastic learning theory (Suppes
and Atkinson, 1960). In particular, a two-person zero-
sum game with probabilistic payoffs lends itself to
such a treatment. If such a game has a saddle point,
game theory prescribes to each player the choice of
strategy containing the saddle point. Thus the solution of such a game is for each player to choose a single
strategy and to play it always. Learning theory, on
the other hand, may predict an alternation between
the strategies. If the two-person zero-sum game does
not have a saddle point, game theory prescribes a
unique mixed strategy to each player. Here learning
theory may also predict a mixed strategy, but possibly
a different mixture. In all these cases, therefore, opportunities are offered to compare the prescriptions
of game theory with the predictions of learning theory.

In the case of Prisoner's Dilemma, game theory either fails to prescribe a strategy altogether (a point of view taken by those who consider game theory to be entirely a branch of formal mathematics and so not even a normative theory of behavior) or else prescribes a counter-intuitive strategy, namely the strategy $D^{(n)}$ in a Prisoner's Dilemma game played n times.

We did not expect to see $D^{(n)}$ chosen when $n = 300$, and we did not see it. Hence in our case it was not a matter of comparing game-theoretical predictions with learning-theoretical predictions. We hoped at best to see whether two different learning processes were involved, depending on whether the logical structure of the game was immediately apparent to the subjects or had to be learned from the outcomes. Some of us thought, for example, that the effect of the displayed matrix on C would be inhibitory. We argued that in a trial and error process, the tacit collusion solution CC would be sooner or later hit upon and would persist because of the steady positive payoffs it affords to both players in contrast to the unilateral states CD and DC, which ought to be unstable (because one of the players loses the largest amount in each of them), and in contrast to the DD state, which is punishing. When the matrix is displayed, however, so our argument went, the dominance of the defecting strategy is a constant inhibitor against cooperating. One always is subjected to the temptation of defecting from CC to get the bigger payoff T, and one is afraid to leave DD for fear of getting S. It would be better for cooperation, we thought, if these brutal facts were not explicitly before the subjects' eyes.

The results turned out to be exactly the opposite. The amount of cooperation observed in the Pure No Matrix Condition is just about one half the amount observed in the Pure Matrix Condition. The comparisons are shown in Figure 3.

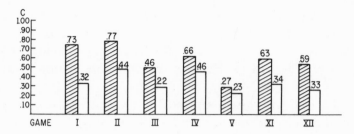

Figure 3. Comparison of frequencies of cooperative choices when game matrix is displayed (left) with when it is not (right).

There is no question of the significance of this result. Even a simple sign test (a very weak test of significance) shows the result to be significant on the $P < .02$ level if only the Pure Matrix Conditions are compared. If both the Pure and the Mixed Matrix Conditions are taken into account, the sign test gives an even greater significance of the difference.

It follows that our original conjectures about the effect of the displayed matrix had to be revised. Instead of serving as a reminder of the prudence of choosing D, the matrix seems to serve as a reminder that a tacit collusion is possible quite regardless of what the formal game theoretical prescription (the equilibrium strategy) might be.

In summary, we find that mixing the games makes them less differentiated. In the extreme case where the seven games are presented in random sequence and the matrix is not displayed, the differentiation of the games practically disappears altogether except that the most severe Game V with its very large temptation payoff still stands out as the game that induces the smallest frequency of cooperative responses. The effect of the displayed matrix is a salutary one from the point of achieving tacit cooperation. It manifests itself in all the seven games both in the pure and in the mixed conditions.

Chapter 3
Effects of Interaction

ONE QUESTION which interests both the psychologist and the layman is what role personality plays as a determinant of performance in a Prisoner's Dilemma game. On the face of it, this question seems eminently sensible. The choice in Prisoner's Dilemma appears to be the choice between competing and cooperating, between conflict and conflict resolution, between trust and suspicion, between loyalty and betrayal. To be sure, everyone recognizes that a contrived laboratory experiment of the sort discussed here is far removed from life and cannot be expected to serve as a reliable test of people's deep attitudes. Still, one might argue, if personality factors are going to emerge in any laboratory experiments, perhaps the ones described here are as good as any, precisely because they do not simulate life in any content-pegged context. One might argue that attempts to simulate life in the laboratory only emphasize the artificiality of the laboratory. The more "realistic" the simulation, the more the participants may be aware of the artificiality and consequently behave in ways unrelated to the ways they would behave in real life. On the other hand, a situation such as the apparently trivial game, Prisoner's Dilemma, because of its very triviality may tap the player's psychological propensities more thoroughly than attempted reproductions of real life.

Another thing in favor of a trivial game repeated hundreds of times is the difficulty of "presenting a front." For example, a subject who knows that others attribute to him a tendency toward hostility in argument or discussion may deliberately act in a friendly manner in a group dynamics experiment. In a Prisoner's Dilemma experiment it is not immediately apparent to the subject what he is being tested for, and even if he gets the idea that the choice between C and D is essentially a choice between cooperation and pursuit of self-interest, the costs and consequences of each choice are not clear-cut. What happens depends not on him alone but also on what the other does. Under these circumstances it is difficult to decide once and for all how "one will act" (what "role" one will play). Finally the quickness with which the decisions must be made (every few seconds) also militates against a thought-out policy. It can be assumed, therefore, that the patterns of responses contain a good deal of spontaneity and so the situation may, after all, tap some basic attitudes and propensities in a significant way.

It would seem, therefore, that a search for personality correlates of performance in a Prisoner's Dilemma game might reveal something. There have been a few attempts to find such correlates (Deutsch, 1960; Lutzker, 1960).*

We can expect the emergence of personality effects if (1) performances of different but homogeneous populations are compared, or (2) the subjects play the game only a very few times. The first condition was fulfilled in Lutzker's experiments, the second in Deutsch's. However, if the game is played many times and if the pairs are randomly matched, the effect of personality on performance may well be masked by the interaction between the paired players. To take an example, suppose the interaction effects are so strong that the two

---

* Lutzker's game was, strictly speaking, not Prisoner's Dilemma, since the payoffs were ordered $T > R > S > P$ instead of $T > R > P > S$, as in Prisoner's Dilemma.

players become exact copies of each other—what one does in many repeated plays, the other is sure to do. If this happens the personalities of the two can no longer be reflected in the performance in the sense that some distinguishing features of the individual performances can serve as indices of underlying personality characteristics. Under these conditions attempts to find correlations between individual performances and personality correlates in experiments with repeated games are doomed to failure.

There is a quick way to find out whether the strength of the interaction effects is such that the search for individual correlates in experiments with repeated games is unwarranted. The members of pairs playing Prisoner's Dilemma are randomly matched. Therefore if each is assigned some quantitative index of some personality trait, the covariance or the product moment correlation of the two indices of paired subjects, taken over a large population of pairs, ought to be zero. Further if the performance were completely determined by the magnitude of this personality index, then the correlation of the performance indices ought to be zero also. In particular the product moment correlation of the frequencies of cooperative choices of two pair members C_1 and C_2 ought to be near zero when taken over a population of pairs playing the game under the same conditions.

In our experiments just ten pairs played under the same conditions (i.e., the same game) in all cases except the Block Matrix Condition. Here seventy pairs played under the same conditions except for the order in which the games were played. We assume for the moment that the effect of order is not large compared to other effects (such as payoffs, personal propensities, and some chance effects to be discussed below). Under this assumption, if individual personality correlates play an important part in determining C, then the individual indices C_1 and C_2 ought not to be significantly correlated in the Block Matrix Condition, and any spurious correlation is likely to be inhibited by the comparatively large number of pairs.

The correlations $\rho_{C_1 C_2}$ are given in Table 3. Although a population of ten pairs is not large enough to establish confidence in a correlation, we have twenty-three replications represented in Table 3, since each ten pairs is an independent sample.

TABLE 3

The product moment correlations $\rho_{C_1 C_2}$ between the frequencies of cooperative responses of paired players. The correlations were not computed for each game separately in the Mixed Conditions.

Game	Pure Matrix Condition	Block Matrix Condition	Pure No Matrix Condition	Mixed Matrix Condition	Mixed No Matrix Condition
I	1.00	.90	.96		
II	.99	.82	.83		
III	.98	.89	.62		
IV	.98	.87	.89		
V	.96	.95	.90		
XI	.92	.86	.98		
XII	.91	.93	.23		
Average	.96	.89	.77	.87	.96

We see from Table 3 that $\rho_{C_1 C_2}$ are all positive and for the most part very large. In the Mixed Matrix Condition this could be attributed to the similar effect of each game, i.e., to the fact that some games elicit more cooperation and some less cooperation in all players. However, as we have seen, the games are only weakly differentiated in the Mixed Matrix Condition and hardly at all in the Mixed No Matrix Condition; so this effect cannot be very important. We surmise, therefore, that the consistently high correlations are results of strong interaction effects between paired players. What one does the other is also likely to do.

Interaction within Individual Sessions

There is another way of detecting interaction effects in Prisoner's Dilemma. A given string of plays yields a "protocol," i.e., a sequence of "states" labeled CC, CD, DC, or DD. Suppose there were a strong positive interaction—one player tended to behave like the other. Then the matched responses, CC and DD, would predominate, while the unilateral ones, CD and DC, would be rare. Suppose, on the contrary, there were a strong negative interaction—each player would tend to do the opposite of what the other did. In this case the "unilateral" states CD and DC would predominate, while the matched states would be rare. From our examination of the correlation of C_1 vs. C_2, we already know that the interaction tends to be strongly positive. This correlation, however, reflects only the gross interaction effect—how dependent is the overall degree of cooperation shown by one player on that shown by the other. We wish to examine the effects of the interaction more closely. We wish to see whether it operates in the sequence of individual plays. To do this, we assign arbitrarily value 1 to C and value 0 to D and examine the product moment correlation coefficients of the random variables C_1 and C_2 related to the two players, which take on values 1 and 0. Actually any other two values will yield exactly the same result, the product moment correlation being independent under a linear transformation of variables. The formula for the correlation of two random variables taking on either of two given values is

$$\rho_0 = \frac{(CC)(DD) - (CD)(DC)}{\sqrt{(CC + CD)(CC + DC)(DD + CD)(DD + DC)}}. \qquad (10)$$

This index can be calculated for each pair of players. The Pure Matrix Conditions are the most suitable for this purpose, since when the players play the same game all the way through, the value of ρ_0 can be attributed entirely to the interaction between them and not to some extraneous variables such as payoffs, which may be affecting both players in the same way and thus contributing to a positive bias for ρ_0.

The values of ρ_0 among the seventy pairs of the Pure Matrix Condition are overwhelmingly positive (sixty-two out of seventy pairs). There is also a positive bias in the Pure No Matrix Condition, although a weaker one. The positive bias in the Block Matrix Condition is even stronger than in the Pure Matrix Condition.

Table 4 shows the average values of ρ_0 in the several conditions.

TABLE 4

Condition	Pure Matrix	Block Matrix	Mixed Matrix	Pure No Matrix	Mixed No Matrix
Average ρ_0	.46	.56	.47	.28	.34

Note that the average values of ρ_0 are smaller in both No Matrix Conditions: in the absence of the matrix the interactions are apparently weaker. The correlation is highest in the Block Matrix Condition, where the same pair plays all seven games and where one can therefore expect the two players to vary together from game to game.

The coefficient ρ_0 does not actually reflect play-to-play interactions precisely. An interaction of this sort is a response of a player to what the other player did on the immediately *preceding* play. In order to get a measure of this interaction, we should define the states *CC*, *CD*, *DC*, and *DD* in such a way that one of the pair of responses represents the preceding play by the other player. This can be easily done if the protocols are "shifted" by one play. In fact this can be done in two ways by having the first player or the second player lag by one play. Each protocol then yields two "shifted" protocols, both representing a correlation coefficient which we designate by ρ_1.

We expect ρ_1 to show a larger positive bias than ρ_0, because the positive interaction will be more precisely reflected in the former. Generalizing the idea of shifting the protocol, we can define analogously ρ_2, ρ_3, ρ_4, etc. Each of these will measure the degree of interaction of a player's response to the responses of the other 2, 3, 4, etc., plays ago. We would expect the strength of the interaction to decay with the interval, and, if it does, we can get an idea of the "memory" component of the interaction. The values of the ρ's in all the conditions are shown in Table 5.

TABLE 5

Condition	ρ_0	ρ_1	ρ_2	ρ_3	ρ_4	ρ_5	ρ_6
Pure Matrix	.46	.51	.46	.42	.40	.38	.36
Block Matrix	.56	.59	.56	.52	.51	.49	.46
Mixed Matrix	.47	.34	.31	.30	.31	.30	.29
Pure No Matrix	.37	.47	.40	.33	.32	.32	.32
Mixed No Matrix	.34	.22	.22	.23	.21	.21	.20

Note that the value of ρ_1 is largest, as expected, except in both mixed conditions. These exceptions are also understandable, since in the Mixed Matrix Condition, the next play in general involves a different game. Evidently "not only what the other did last" but also the game payoffs play a part in influencing the response, and so the effect of imitating the other's last response is obscured in these conditions.

The Lock-in Effect

The strength of interaction can be very clearly seen in the "lock-in" effect. Consider a fifty-play block as a unit of analysis. Each such unit can be characterized by a fraction of times a given state occurs in it, for example *CC*. Thus a number is assigned to each fifty-play block—the fraction of *CC* responses contained in it. We can now examine the distribution of fifty-play blocks with regard to this index. If the distribution were of a type resembling the normal distribution, the mode (i.e., the index represented by the largest number of blocks) would be near the mean value of the index. The plot would have a peak somewhere near the middle and would taper off at the ends, i.e., would exhibit a "bell-shaped" curve. The plots of the *CC* distributions for the Pure and the Block Matrix Conditions are shown in Figures 4 and 5. We note that the picture is exactly the opposite of the one expected from a normal-type distribution. The concentrations are at the ends rather than in the middle.

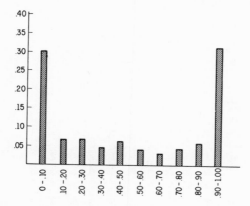

Figure 4. Horizontal: fraction of *CC* responses in a block of fifty plays. Vertical: fraction of fifty-play blocks corresponding to each fraction of *CC* responses (Pure Matrix Condition).

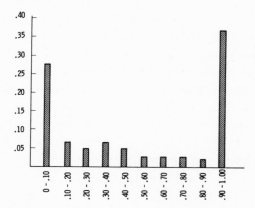

Figure 5. Horizontal: fraction of *CC* responses in a block of fifty plays. Vertical: fraction of fifty-play blocks corresponding to each fraction of *CC* responses (Block Condition).

This effect is not as apparent when the *DD* fractions are plotted, because of the relative paucity of almost total *DD* blocks in the Pure and in the Block Matrix Conditions. However, in the No Matrix Conditions, where the *DD* blocks are plentiful, a similar bi-modal distribution is observed with respect to the fraction of *DD* responses (cf. Figure 6).

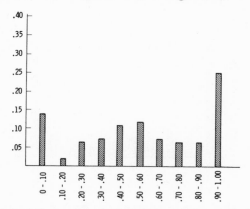

Figure 6. Horizontal: fraction of *DD* responses in a block of fifty plays. Vertical: fraction of fifty-play blocks corresponding to each fraction of *DD* responses (Pure No Matrix Condition).

The study of interaction effects indicates that these effects are very strong. They tend to make the members of a pair behave like each other. Later, when we examine the time course of these effects, we shall find that they become progressively stronger as the session continues. Moreover, the interaction effects tend to throw the performance toward one or the other extreme. The sessions tend to become either predominantly cooperative or predominately uncooperative. Of course the payoff matrix contributes to the outcome: the "mild" games (Games I, II, and IV) tend toward the cooperative extreme; the "severe" games (Games III and V) tend to the uncooperative extreme. Also the condition contributes to the outcome. When the matrix is displayed, more performances tend toward the cooperative extreme. In the No Matrix Conditions, the opposite is the case. However, both the extremes are found in all games and in both conditions. This leads to the conclusion of the inherent *instability* of the Prisoner's Dilemma situation. "Compromises" are comparatively rare. The pair will be thrown either toward a tacit collusion, which remains rather stable, or toward the *DD* trap, also rather stable.

There is no a priori reason why a pair should go to the one extreme rather than to the other since both are "rationalizable." The *DD* trap appears as an eminently reasonable "solution," since neither player can justify a departure toward cooperation on rational grounds. "If I cooperate," he can well say, "the other will simply take advantage of it and secure the big gain for himself." But also the *CC* tacit collusion is justifiable. If the pair have locked-in on it, either can justify refraining from defecting by pointing out that a defection will only break up the collusion: the other is also sure to defect, and the end result will be a lock-in in the *DD* trap to the disadvantage of both. Although this argument also sounds eminently reasonable, it is well to keep in mind that it is demolished by the game-theoretical prescription of the totally uncooperative strategy $D^{(n)}$, when n is known and finite.

Table 6 shows the fractions of pairs in each condition who have locked-in on CC and on DD respectively. Our criterion of a lock-in is 23 or more CC (DD) responses out of the last 25.

TABLE 6

Condition	L_{CC}	L_{DD}	Total Fraction Locked in
Pure Matrix	.53	.17	.70
Block Matrix	.56	.07	.63
Mixed Matrix	.43	.43	.86
Pure No Matrix	.16	.43	.59
Mixed No Matrix	.20	.40	.60

L_{CC}: Fraction of pairs locked-in on CC in the last twenty-five plays.
L_{DD}: Fraction of pairs locked-in on DD in the last twenty-five plays.

The predominance of the CC lock-ins in the favorable conditions shows that our subjects are not sufciently sophisticated game-theoreticians to have figured out that $D^{(n)}$ is the only strategically defensible strategy. Apparently this lack of strategic sophistication allows many of them to find the commonsense solution, namely the tacit collusion, and so to win money instead of losing it.

Summary of Chapter 3

The interaction effect in repeated plays of Prisoner's Dilemma is strong and positive. In the single sessions, a pronounced tendency is observed of each player to imitate the other. The product moment correlation of the frequencies of cooperative responses of paired subjects is in many cases very nearly plus one.

Chapter 4
The Contingent Propensities

We have seen that in repeated plays of Prisoner's Dilemma positive interaction effects are operating. The strongest manifestation of those effects is in the correlations between the frequencies of cooperative choices of the two players. It is fairly clear, therefore, that a search of individual personality correlates of this frequency will not be rewarding. How can we get at indices of performance which are less dependent on interaction effects and therefore more suitable as possible indicators of personal propensities? We shall now describe our attempts to get at such indices.

The Response-Conditioned Propensities

Consider the four conditional probabilities defined as follows:

ξ_1: the probability that player 1 responds cooperatively following player 2's cooperative response on the preceding play.

η_1: the probability that player 1 responds cooperatively following his own cooperative response on the preceding play.

ζ_1: the probability that player 1 responds cooperatively following his own defecting response on the preceding play.

ω_1: the probability that player 1 responds cooperatively following player 2's defecting response on the preceding play.

The conditional probabilities ξ_2, η_2, ζ_2, and ω_2 are defined analogously with the roles of players 1 and 2 reversed.

It is clear that these probabilities are components of the C's. Thus, by definition of the conditional probabilities, we must have the following equations satisfied:

$$\xi_1 C_2 + \omega_1(1 - C_2) = C_1; \tag{11}$$

$$\eta_1 C_1 + \zeta_1(1 - C_1) = C_1; \tag{12}$$

$$\eta_2 C_2 + \zeta_2(1 - C_2) = C_2; \tag{13}$$

$$\xi_2 C_1 + \omega_2(1 - C_1) = C_2. \tag{14}$$

If we solve Equations (12) and (13) for C_1 and C_2 respectively, we obtain

$$C_1 = \frac{\zeta_1}{1 + \zeta_1 - \eta_1}; \tag{15}$$

$$C_2 = \frac{\zeta_2}{1 + \zeta_2 - \eta_2}. \tag{16}$$

If we now substitute these values into Equations (11) and (14), we obtain

$$\frac{\xi_1 \zeta_2 + \omega_1(1 - \eta_2)}{1 + \zeta_2 - \eta_2} = \frac{\zeta_1}{1 + \zeta_1 - \eta_1}; \tag{17}$$

$$\frac{\xi_2 \zeta_1 + \omega_2(1 - \eta_1)}{1 + \zeta_1 - \eta_1} = \frac{\zeta_2}{1 + \zeta_2 - \eta_2}. \tag{18}$$

Thus two constraints are imposed upon our eight conditional probabilities. Consequently, only six of them are mathematically independent. In the symmetrical case, when $\xi_1 = \xi_2$; $\eta_1 = \eta_2$, etc., relations (17) and (18) reduce to

$$\frac{(1 - \eta)}{(1 - \xi)} = \frac{\zeta}{\omega} \tag{19}$$

and so instead of four independent parameters, we have only three. In the C's, we had two independent parameters in the general case and only one in the symmetric case (since $D = 1 - C$). Thus in either case, we have trebled the number of independent parameters and so have refined our indices to that extent.

Let us now see how these conditional probabilities are correlated across pairs. Tables 7 and 8 show the values of the paired conditional probabilities in the Pure Matrix Condition and in the Pure No Matrix Condition, as well as the correlations between the paired indices. We see that the interaction effect on the conditional probabilities is still large, but it is not as large as the effect on C.

Let us now interpret ξ, η, ζ, and ω psychologically and make appropriate conjectures. We shall call these indices *response-conditioned propensities*. From its definition ξ appears to be a propensity to respond cooperatively to the other's cooperative response. The conditional probability η, on the other hand, is the propensity to "respond" cooperatively to one's own cooperative choice, in other words to *continue* to respond cooperatively. We note from Tables 7 and 8 that

TABLE 7

Mean values of response-conditioned cooperative propensities and correlations between paired values in the Pure Matrix Condition. The last column shows correlations between paired C frequencies for comparison.

Game	ξ	η	ζ	ω	ρ_ξ	ρ_η	ρ_ζ	ρ_ω	ρ_C
I	.88	.89	.36	.36	.93	.98	.61	.84	1.00
II	.89	.87	.41	.34	.86	.98	.17	.01	.99
III	.65	.67	.19	.19	.82	.68	.83	.71	.98
IV	.84	.84	.24	.26	.81	.84	.83	.69	.98
V	.57	.59	.12	.15	.85	.83	.91	.75	.96
XI	.82	.88	.22	.25	.93	.70	.93	.36	.92
XII	.68	.74	.21	.24	.85	.93	.90	.72	.91
Mean	.76	.78	.25	.26	.87	.85	.74	.58	.96

the values of ξ and η are quite close to each other. Since the bulk of cooperative responses, at least in the Pure Matrix Condition comes from the locked-in runs CC, a great many cooperative responses following the other's cooperative responses coincide with the coop-

TABLE 8

Mean values of response-conditioned cooperative propensities and correlations between paired values in the Pure No Matrix Condition. The last column shows correlations between paired C frequencies for comparison.

Game	ξ	η	ζ	ω	ρ_ξ	ρ_η	ρ_ζ	ρ_ω	ρ_C
I	.55	.58	.21	.23	.87	.81	.94	.96	.96
II	.52	.57	.29	.31	.87	.89	.27	.23	.83
III	.46	.56	.12	.15	.77	.79	−.09	−.37	.62
IV	.64	.65	.22	.22	.50	.64	.82	.76	.89
V	.40	.47	.12	.14	.54	.63	.63	.16	.90
XI	.56	.63	.11	.12	.99	.77	.96	.94	.98
XII	.45	.55	.18	.22	.63	.65	.60	.26	.23
Mean	.51	.57	.18	.20	.74	.74	.59	.42	.77

erative responses following one's own cooperative responses. There is thus a large overlap in the two sets of responses with respect to which ξ and η are calculated. To a certain extent this is true also of noncooperative responses, since the bulk of these comes from the locked-in DD runs. Therefore we would expect the values of ζ and ω also to be close to each other, which they are.

Let us now interpret ζ and ω. It is more instructive to look at their complements $1 - \zeta$ and $1 - \omega$. The former appears from its definition to be a measure of the persistence in the D response; the latter is related to the propensity to respond noncooperatively to the other's defecting response (i.e., a measure of "vengefulness"). Now on the basis of the high correlations of ξ and η and the comparatively lower correlations of ζ and ω observed in both conditions we can make the following conjectures with respect to the response-conditioned propensities.

1. The two players tend to become like each other with respect to a propensity to respond cooperatively to self's and other's cooperative responses.

2. To a lesser degree the two players tend to become like each other with respect to a propensity to respond noncooperatively to self's and other's defecting responses.

The second statement is a consequence of the fact that the correlations between $1 - \zeta_1$ and $1 - \zeta_2$ and between $1 - \omega_1$ and $1 - \omega_2$ must be equal respectively to those between ζ_1 and ζ_2 and between ω_1 and ω_2.[13] Incidentally, it is clear from this argument that the high correlations between ξ_1 and ξ_2 and between η_1 and η_2 are not consequences of the persistently high values of these variables, since the values of $1 - \zeta$ and $1 - \omega$ are also persistently high, while the correlations between those paired variables are considerably lower. A conclusion is therefore warranted that high interaction effects are operating on the propensities to respond cooperatively to self's and other's cooperative responses but not as much on the propensities to respond noncooperatively to self's and other's defecting responses. The latter propensities are in themselves high but are apparently not subjected to quite as strong interaction effects as the former.

The State-Conditioned Propensities

Next we introduce four other conditional probabilities, which we shall call the *state-conditioned propensities*. These are:

x: the probability that a player will choose cooperatively, following a play in which he chose cooperatively and received R (i.e., following a play in which both players chose cooperatively).

y: the probability that a player will choose cooperatively following a play in which he chose cooperatively and received the sucker's payoff S (i.e., following a play in which he was the lone cooperator).

z: the probability that a player will choose cooperatively following a play on which he defected and received T (i.e., following a play on which he was the lone defector).

w: the probability that a player will choose cooperatively following a play on which he defected and received P (i.e., following a play on which both defected).

Like the response-conditioned propensities, the state-conditioned propensities are defined for player 1 and for player 2. Unlike the former, however, all eight of the latter are mathematically independent (four in the symmetric case). Thus we have in the state-conditioned propensities a still more refined set of indices.

The propensity x indicates a willingness to continue the tacit collusion (implied, by definition, to have been achieved on the previous play). This willingness is associated with a willingness to resist the temptation to defect, which is always present. It therefore suggests something like "trustworthiness."

The propensity y indicates a willingness to persist in cooperating, even though one has been "betrayed." It therefore suggests either "forgiveness" or "martyrdom" or a strong faith in teaching by example, or, perhaps, stupidity, depending on the ethical views of whoever evaluates this behavior.

The propensity z indicates a willingness to stop defecting in response to the other's cooperative choice. It may indicate "repentance" or "responsiveness."

Finally w indicates a willingness to *try* cooperating as a way of breaking out of the DD trap. Clearly this action is justifiable only if a certain amount of trust in the responsiveness of the other exists in the initiator of cooperation. Hence w suggests "trust."

As we have said, the conditional propensities x, y, z, and w are refinements of the gross cooperative index C, and so one reason for examining them is to look at the data with greater resolving power, as it were. The other reason, as already stated, is derived from our search for indices relatively unaffected by the interaction process, since such independence makes an index a more suitable variable which one might try to associate with personality traits or with experimental conditions.

We shall give a mathematical argument for the conjecture that x, y, z, and w may be less affected by interaction than C. If this is true, it will be reflected in weaker correlations of x_1 vs. x_2, y_1 vs. y_2, etc., than we have observed in C_1 vs. C_2. We shall not attempt to derive general conditions under which this situation obtains, but will confine ourselves to a very special case, where it is shown to obtain and hence establishes such a possibility.

The Two Simpletons

Imagine Prisoner's Dilemma played by two simpletons, or, if you prefer, by two automata with exceedingly simple reactions to reinforcements. By and large, these simpletons or automata are characterized by an aversion to negative payoffs. Thus, whenever one of them has made an unreciprocated cooperative choice, he is certain to defect the next time. Also, when both have defected (and therefore received negative payoffs), both change their responses, so that the next response is inevitably CC. If the simpletons were equally consistent with regard to positive payoffs, i.e., if they always repeated their choice whenever they got a positive payoff, then, it can be easily seen that the two would "lock-in" on the CC response after at most two plays. For if the first play happened to be CC, it would remain so thereafter. If the first play happened to be DD, it would change to CC and remain so. If the first play happened to be CD or DC, the cooperator would defect on the following play, while the defector would continue to defect (having got a positive pay-off, T). But this would lead to DD and therefore to CC next. For these two simpletons, Prisoner's Dilemma is not a dilemma. They always achieve tacit collusion almost immediately.

We shall, however, introduce a temptation into our simpletons' psyches. When they are in the CC state, each, we shall assume, is tempted to defect. He defects only at times, namely with probability $1 - x$. It follows that he sticks to the tacit collusion with probability x, the same conditional probability, which we have already defined as one of our conditional propensities, namely "trustworthiness." For the rest, we see that the other conditional propensities of our simpletons must be assigned the following values: $y = 0$, $z = 0$, $w = 1$. This is a consequence of the way we have defined their reactions to the payoffs. To summarize, the only variable in the psychological makeups of our simpletons is described by a single parameter, x—the propensity for repeating a rewarded cooperative choice. We shall suppose that this propensity is distributed in some way throughout the population of simpletons, from which we recruit our subjects, whom we then pair randomly and let play Prisoner's Dilemma some large number of times.

Since the pairs are matched randomly, it follows that the correlation of x_1 vs. x_2 in the population will not vary significantly from zero. Let us see what will be the case with C_1 and C_2.

The cooperative response frequencies C_1 and C_2 can be computed from the x's. In fact, if we suppose that x_1 and x_2 are probabilities of independent events, the resulting process can be viewed as a four-state Markov chain, whose transition probabilities are compounded from x_1 and x_2 and their complements (some transition probabilities being zero or one). If we solve for the steady-state distribution of states in this stochastic process, we obtain the following values of the asymptotic state probabilities:[14]

$$C_1 C_2 = \frac{1}{2 + x_1 + x_2 - 3 x_1 x_2}; \tag{20}$$

$$C_1 D_2 = \frac{x_1 (1 - x_2)}{2 + x_1 + x_2 - 3 x_1 x_2}; \tag{21}$$

$$D_1 C_2 = \frac{x_2 (1 - x_1)}{2 + x_1 + x_2 - 3 x_1 x_2}; \tag{22}$$

$$D_1 D_2 = \frac{1 - x_1 x_2}{2 + x_1 + x_2 - 3 x_1 x_2}. \tag{23}$$

Now $C_1 = C_1 C_2 + C_1 D_2$, while $C_2 = C_1 C_2 + D_1 C_2$. We can therefore, write

$$C_1 = \frac{1 + x_1 - x_1 x_2}{2 + x_1 + x_2 - 3 x_1 x_2}; \tag{24}$$

$$C_2 = \frac{1 + x_2 - x_1 x_2}{2 + x_1 + x_2 - 3 x_1 x_2}. \tag{25}$$

We wish to exhibit a situation in which x_1 and x_2 are not correlated, while C_1 and C_2 are positively correlated. Consider a population of pairs in which the members designated as "player 1" all have the same x_1, while those designated as "player 2" have different values of x_2. Clearly, in this population sample, x_1 and x_2 will be uncorrelated. However, under certain conditions, C_1 and C_2 will be positively correlated. To see this, consider the partial derivatives[15] of C_1 and C_2 with respect to x_2. We have

$$\frac{\partial C_1}{\partial x_2} = \frac{2 x^2 - 1}{(2 + x_1 + x_2 - 3 x_1 x_2)^2}; \tag{26}$$

$$\frac{\partial C_2}{\partial x_2} = \frac{1 + 2 x_1 - x_1^2}{(2 + x_1 + x_2 - 3 x_1 x_2)^2}. \tag{27}$$

From these equations, we see that $\partial C_1 / \partial x_2$ is positive when $x_1 > .707$, while $\partial C_2 / \partial x_2$ is always positive.

Therefore if $x_1 > .707$, both C_1 and C_2 increase if x_1 remains constant and x_2 increases, and both decrease if x_1 remains constant and x_2 decreases. But this is precisely the situation in our hypothetical sample, where the x_1's are all equal and the x_2's vary. If, therefore, the x_1's in our sample are sufficiently large, C_1 and C_2 will be positively correlated even though the correlation of x_1 and x_2 is zero.

This admittedly very special case was offered as an illustration of how a positive correlation can be found among the gross cooperative frequencies even though the underlying conditional propensities which give rise to these frequencies may be uncorrelated.

Generalizing the argument, it is conceivable to have weak positive correlations between the paired state-conditioned propensities and stronger positive correlations among the paired C frequencies. Turning the argument around, we can expect under similar circumstances to find weaker correlations among the propensities than we observe among the C frequencies. But this is precisely what we are seeking—indices of performance which lie "deeper" and so are less subjected to interaction effects than the gross indices of overt performance.

We turn to our data to examine the values of the state-conditioned propensities and of the correlations among them in the Pure Matrix Conditions. These are shown in Tables 9 and 10.

From Tables 9 and 10 we see that although the correlations ρ_x are predominantly positive, their mean is smaller than that of ρ_ξ (cf. Tables 7 and 8) which in turn are lower than that of ρ_C. The ρ_w are also positive and are still smaller. As for ρ_y and ρ_z, they oscillate rather wildly, and so their significance is open to question. We shall not pursue a rigorous investigation of

TABLE 9

Mean values of state-conditioned cooperative propensities and correlations between paired values in the Pure Matrix Condition. The last column shows correlations between paired C frequencies for comparison.

Game	x	y	z	w	ρ_x	ρ_y	ρ_z	ρ_w	ρ_C
I	.92	.45	.45	.30	.99	.61	−.61	.96	1.00
II	.93	.42	.53	.32	.66	−.01	.08	.16	.99
III	.83	.35	.34	.15	.91	.02	−.44	.91	.98
IV	.91	.42	.40	.18	.68	−.15	−.45	.48	.98
V	.71	.28	.25	.05	.96	−.39	−.34	.14	.96
XI	.85	.43	.39	.20	.98	−.35	.63	.59	.92
XII	.79	.44	.33	.20	.36	−.46	−.61	.15	.91
Mean	.84	.40	.38	.20	.79	−.10	−.25	.48	.96

TABLE 10

Mean values of state-conditioned cooperative propensities and correlations between paired values in the Pure No Matrix Condition. The last column shows correlations between paired C frequencies for comparison.

Game	x	y	z	w	ρ_x	ρ_y	ρ_z	ρ_w	ρ_C
I	.66	.36	.25	.14	.47	−.04	.51	.69	.96
II	.70	.34	.28	.25	.76	−.26	.26	.29	.83
III	.68	.37	.20	.09	.88	.24	.13	−.18	.62
IV	.75	.33	.32	.22	.54	−.22	.02	.60	.89
V	.67	.33	.24	.08	.44	.29	.11	.26	.90
XI	.72	.34	.34	.16	−.09	−.74	.38	.64	.98
XII	.69	.40	.22	.11	.52	−.72	−.25	.54	.23
Mean	.70	.35	.26	.15	.50	−.21	.17	.41	.77

the level of significance of our correlations but will rely instead on a rough argument.

Consider the complete table of (mean) correlations among all the state-conditioned propensities, x_1, x_2, $y_1 \ldots w_2$, as shown in Table 11.

Note that of the 28 correlations in Table 11, 24 can be matched into 12 pairs, where one member of the pair can be obtained from the other by interchanging

TABLE II

The correlation matrix of the state-conditioned propensities in the Pure Matrix Condition.

	x_1	y_1	z_1	w_1	x_2	y_2	z_2	w_2
x_1	1.000	.201	.236	.194	.745	.034	.261	.271
y_1	.201	1.000	− .120	.083	.051	− .146	.329	.026
z_1	.236	− .120	1.000	.444	.028	.150	− .189	.537
w_1	.194	.083	.444	1.000	.197	.272	.099	.556
x_2	.745	.051	.028	.197	1.000	.116	.382	.162
y_2	.034	− .146	.150	.272	.116	1.000	.078	.125
z_2	.261	.329	− .189	.099	.382	.078	1.000	.052
w_2	.271	.026	.537	.556	.162	.125	.052	1.000

subscripts 1 and 2. Thus designating the correlations by ρ with appropriate subscripts, we can match them as follows: $\rho_{x_1 y_2}$ with $\rho_{x_2 y_1}$; $\rho_{x_1 z_2}$ with $\rho_{x_2 z_1}$, etc. The significance of the matching is that in any reasonably large population the two members of each pair ought to be nearly equal. This follows from the random assignment of designation 1 or 2 to the players, i.e., from the fact that we ought to consider our population of players 1 identical with our population of players 2, if the labeling of the players makes no difference. Hence the correlation $\rho_{x_1 y_2}$ ought to be nearly equal (except for statistical fluctuations) to correlation $\rho_{x_2 y_1}$, $\rho_{x_1 z_2}$ to $\rho_{x_2 z_1}$, etc.

From the actual differences between these pairs we can estimate (very roughly) the limits of the statistical fluctuations of the ρ's.

Another way to obtain an idea about the significance of these correlations is to treat the several conditions as replications. If a given correlation varies widely among the conditions, this may be due to either statistical fluctuations or to the differences in the conditions. But if a correlation has a consistently large value in all or in most of the conditions, this is an indication of its "reality" and relative independence of the varied conditions.

Table 12 shows the correlations in all the conditions. The correlations appear twice in each condition showing the values when *i* and *j* are interchanged. The differences between these paired correlations are the strongest indicators of the expected magnitude of their statistical fluctuations.

TABLE 12

The entries shown for $\rho_{x_iy_i}$ designate $\rho_{x_1y_1}$ and ρ_{x_2,y_2}; the entries shown for $\rho_{x_iy_j}$ designate ρ_{x_1,y_2} and ρ_{x_2,y_1}, etc. Apparently anomalous values (those which show rather large discrepancies from their paired values) are boxed.

Condition	Pure Matrix	Pure No Matrix	Block Matrix	Mixed Matrix	Mixed No Matrix
$\rho_{x_1x_2}$	.745	.430	.563	.232	.635
$\rho_{y_1y_2}$	−.146	−.156	−.360	−.372	.687
$\rho_{z_1z_2}$	−.189	.148	.161	.002	.434
$\rho_{w_1w_2}$	.556	.630	.181	.966	.909
$\rho_{x_iy_i}$	.201; .116	.230; .336	.264; .125	.702; .666	.373; .338
$\rho_{x_iz_i}$	.236; .382	.236; .013	.102; −.123	.218; .493	−.180; $\boxed{.442}$
$\rho_{x_iw_i}$	.194; .162	.046; .125	−.013; .048	.179; .177	.088; .117
$\rho_{y_iz_i}$	−.120; .078	.124; −.051	−.111; $\boxed{.331}$	−.085; $\boxed{.734}$	.432; .249
$\rho_{y_iw_i}$	.083; .125	.115; .112	.085; .135	−.160; .231	.785; .592
$\rho_{z_iw_i}$	.444; .052	.475; .234	.276; .100	.849; .366	.826; .743
$\rho_{x_iy_j}$	.034; .051	.030; −.039	−.320; −.105	−.254; −.312	.330; .068
$\rho_{x_iz_j}$	.261; .028	.201; −.019	.025; −.123	.241; .224	.405; .193
$\rho_{x_iw_j}$	.271; .197	.204; −.034	−.094; −.187	.323; .237	.028; .145
$\rho_{y_iz_j}$	.329; .150	−.051; −.135	.045; .194	.190; .125	.364; .597
$\rho_{y_iw_j}$	.026; .272	.129; −.107	.057; .087	.052; .230	.629; .841
$\rho_{z_iw_j}$	$\boxed{.537}$; .099	.321; .254	−.085; .232	.781; .209	.809; .518

From the table we can make reasoned guesses about the nature of the correlations.

From the entries for $\rho_{x_1x_2}$ and $\rho_{w_1w_2}$ we can assume that the *x*'s and the *w*'s are still positively correlated. That is to say, the tendency of one player to lock-in on *CC* or on *DD* elicits a similar tendency in the other.

Next, we may assume that the "true" correlations $\rho_{y_iz_i}$, $\rho_{x_iy_i}$ and possibly $\rho_{x_iw_i}$ are probably near zero, because of the more or less symmetric distributions of these correlations around zero. The remaining correlations show a weak positive bias, which shows that they represent overall linked tendencies to cooperate or not to cooperate in the two players. The one exception is $\rho_{y_1y_2}$, which is negative in four of the conditions. If it were not for the large positive value of this correlation in the Mixed No Matrix Condition, we could surmise that a forgiving (martyr) inclination on the part of one player tends to inhibit a similar inclination in the other, which would be an interesting finding. Unfortunately, this result does not hold up in the Mixed No Matrix Condition. On the other hand, the correlations are on the whole more strongly positive in this condition than in any other.

A comparison of the means of all the correlations in each of the conditions is shown in Table 13.

TABLE 13

Condition	Pure Matrix	Pure No Matrix	Block	Mixed Matrix	Mixed No Matrix
$\bar{p}$	.18	.14	.05	.26	.44

The differences are very likely larger than can be accounted for by statistical fluctuations. However, an explanation of the differences does not easily occur. We cannot surmise that more "mixing" tends either to increase or to decrease the correlations, because the "mixing" is medium in the Block Condition, while the mean value of the correlations is lowest. Nor can we say that the displayed matrix tends to increase or to decrease the correlations, for these effects are opposite in the Pure and in the Mixed Matrix Conditions.

Only one conclusion seems justified: the state-conditioned propensities are still positively correlated, like the C frequencies, but not nearly as strongly as the latter. The most pronounced correlations are those between the x's and the w's. Doubtless these reflect the lock-in effect. The remaining correlations are rather low, except for several in the Mixed No Matrix Condition, an effect which we have not attempted to explain.

An interesting negative result should be mentioned. On a priori grounds, we might expect the correlations $\rho_{y_iz_i}$ to show a negative bias. Such a bias would indicate a tendency on the part of the unilaterally defecting player to exploit the unilaterally cooperative player. However, the bias, if any, of this correlation is in the positive direction, as is the case with almost all the others. That is to say, a "forgiving" attitude of one elicits (if anything) a relenting attitude in the other. The effect is admittedly slight.

In summary, we have in the state-conditioned propensities indices of performance which show more promise as indices of individual characteristics, because they are less subject to interaction effects than the gross frequencies of cooperative choices.

Comparison of the Propensities

We see that in passing from the unconditional cooperative propensities (C) to the response-conditioned propensities $(\xi, \eta, \zeta, \omega)$, to the state-conditioned propensities (x, y, z, w) we get indices of performance progressively more "immune" to interaction effects, hence presumably more stable propensities, possibly reflecting deeper psychological traits. We see also that in the case of at least two state-conditioned propensities, namely x and w, we have not yet attained our goal of getting an index independent of interaction. We could go to still "higher" (or deeper) indices by defining conditional probabilities of still higher order (e.g., the probability of responding cooperatively after exactly one, exactly two, etc., CC responses).

There is, of course, the usual price to pay for this, namely a greater complexity of the appropriate analytical apparatus and the need for more massive data to cut down the fluctuations. We shall therefore not pursue this road at this time. Instead we shall examine the indices ξ, η, ζ, ω, and x, y, z, w for their own sake. We have already proposed psychological interpretations for these indices. Now we shall draw some inferences from their magnitudes and the relations among them.

We compare the magnitudes of ξ, η, ζ, and ω in each of the seven games (cf. Tables 7 and 8). We find that in the Pure Matrix Condition, the inequality

$$\eta \geq \xi \geq \omega \geq \zeta \tag{28}$$

is satisfied in all cases with two exceptions: in Game II $\zeta > \omega$ and, $\xi > \eta$. In the No Matrix Condition, there are no exceptions.

Our interpretation of inequality (28) is the following. One's own cooperative choices have a slightly greater tendency to make one's subsequent responses cooperative than the other's cooperative responses and similarly for noncooperative responses. In other words, while it is true that one is more likely to respond cooperatively to the other's cooperative response than to the other's defecting response ($\xi > \omega$), one is still more likely to continue one's own cooperative responses ($\eta > \xi$) and also one's own noncooperative responses ($\zeta < \omega$).

We now introduce the complements of ζ and ω, namely $1 - \zeta$ and $1 - \omega$. These are, of course, the tendencies to respond noncooperatively to one's own and to the other's defecting response respectively. In the Pure Matrix Condition, these satisfy the following inequalities in each of the games:

From these we see that in the games where cooperation is lowest (III, XII and V) the tendency to respond

TABLE 14

Game I	$\eta > \xi > 1 - \omega \geq 1 - \zeta$
Game II	$\xi > \eta > 1 - \omega > 1 - \zeta$
Game III	$1 - \zeta \geq 1 - \omega > \eta > \xi$
Game IV	$\eta \geq \xi > 1 - \zeta > 1 - \omega$
Game V	$1 - \zeta > 1 - \omega > \eta > \xi$
Game XI	$\eta > \xi > 1 - \zeta > 1 - \omega$
Game XII	$1 - \zeta > 1 - \omega > \eta > \xi$

noncooperatively to the other's noncooperative response $(1 - \omega)$ is greater than the tendency to respond cooperatively to the other's cooperative response (ξ). In the games with the most cooperation (I, II, IV and XI) the tendency to respond cooperatively to the other's cooperative response is greater than the tendency to retaliate.

In the No Matrix Condition, the corresponding inequalities are as shown on Table 15.

TABLE 15

Game I	$1 - \zeta > 1 - \omega > \eta > \xi$
Game II	$1 - \zeta > 1 - \omega > \eta > \xi$
Game III	$1 - \zeta > 1 - \omega > \eta > \xi$
Game IV	$1 - \zeta \geq 1 - \omega > \eta > \xi$
Game V	$1 - \zeta > 1 - \omega > \eta > \xi$
Game XI	$1 - \zeta > 1 - \omega > \eta > \xi$
Game XII	$1 - \zeta > 1 - \omega > \eta > \xi$

Here in all cases without exception the tendency to retaliate and to persist in defection is stronger than the tendency to respond cooperatively and to persist in cooperation.

We turn to the corresponding results on the state-conditioned propensities x, y, z, and w (cf. Table 9).

With only a few exceptions, the following inequality is satisfied:

$$x > y > z > w. \tag{29}$$

When we compare x, y, $1 - z$, and $1 - w$ in the Pure Matrix Condition, we have the inequalities as shown in Table 16:

TABLE 16

Game I	$x > 1 - w > 1 - z > y$
Game II	$x > 1 - w > 1 - z > y$
Game III	$1 - w > x > 1 - z > y$
Game IV	$x > 1 - w > 1 - z > y$
Game V	$1 - w > 1 - z > x > y$
Game XI	$x > 1 - w > 1 - z > y$
Game XII	$1 - w > x > 1 - z > y$

Note that the propensities x, y, $1 - z$, and $1 - w$ represent the tendencies to repeat the previous response in each of the four states respectively, CC, CD, DC, and DD (taking the point of view of player 1). Let us see how these tendencies relate to the payoffs associated with the four states. These are (to player 1) R, S, T, and P respectively. Taking into account the inequality $T > R > P > S$, we see that according to certain assumptions made in stochastic learning theory,[16] we could expect the corresponding inequality

$$1 - z > x > 1 - w > y. \tag{30}$$

Inequality (30) implies six paired comparison inequalities, namely (a) $1 - z > x$; (b) $1 - z > 1 - w$; (c) $1 - z > y$; (d) $x > 1 - w$; (e) $x > y$; (f) $1 - w > y$. Now violation of (a) indicates a greater propensity to cooperate than one would expect from the payoffs, while violation of (d) indicates a greater propensity to defect than one would expect from the payoffs. Violation of (b) is ambivalent, because both $1 - z$ and $1 - w$ are propensities to defect. The interpretation of the remaining violations is unnecessary, since they have never been observed. In Table 17 we observe the inequalities violated in the Pure Matrix Condition. The picture is clear. The "cooperative bias" vio-

TABLE 17

Game	Violation
Game I	a, b
Game II	a, b
Game III	a, b, d
Game IV	a, b
Game V	b, d
Game XI	a, b
Game XII	a, b, d

lation of (a) is present in all except the most uncooperative Game V. The "defecting bias" violation of (d) is present only in the three least cooperative Games XII, III, and V. The ambivalent violation of (b) is present in all games. It indicates that fear of receiving S rather than hope of receiving T is the more important factor in persisting D responses. In short, the mild games are mild because the players tend to respond cooperatively to the other's initiation of cooperation (i.e., they do not persist in unilateral defection). The severe games are severe because the players tend to persist in the DD state—the trap set by Prisoner's Dilemma.

The same analysis of the Pure No Matrix Condition yields the inequalities shown in Table 18.

TABLE 18

Game I	$1 - w > 1 - z > x > y$ (violation of b, d)
Game II	$1 - z > 1 - w > x > y$ (violation of d)
Game III	$1 - w > 1 - z > x > y$ (violation of b, d)
Game IV	$1 - w > x > 1 - z > y$ (violation of a, b, d)
Game V	$1 - w > 1 - z > x > y$ (violation of b, d)
Game XI	$1 - w > 1 - z > x > y$ (violation of b, d)
Game XII	$1 - w > 1 - z > x > y$ (violation of b, d)

Here the picture is even simpler. The reversal $1 - w > 1 - z$ (violation of b) is present in all games (except II). The defecting bias violation of (d) is also present in all games. Only in Game IV (which shows the most cooperation in this condition) do we see the cooperative bias violation of (a). In short, without the matrix displayed, the tendency to persist in the defecting response is greater than would be expected on the basis of a stochastic theory which predicts a rank order of response propensities corresponding to the rank order of the associated reinforcements.

Summary of Chapter 4

The response-conditioned cooperative propensities ξ, η, ζ, and ω and the state-conditioned propensities, x, y, z, and w reveal a more detailed picture of the pressures operating in the Prisoner's Dilemma game. The correlations among the paired indices ξ_i, η_i, ζ_i, and ω_i are lower than those among the C_i, and those among the x_i, y_i, z_i, and w_i are still lower, indicating that these indices are less subject to interaction effects. From the latter, moreover, we gain a picture of how the tendencies to persist in a given response depart from those expected on the basis of comparing the associated payoffs. Specifically, in the Pure Matrix Condition two biases are operating, namely a tendency not to persist in the rewarded defecting response (a cooperative bias) and a tendency to persist in the punished defecting response (a noncooperative bias). In the mildest games (where most cooperation is observed) only the cooperative bias seems to be operating in the Pure Matrix Condition. In the most severe game (where least cooperation is observed) only the noncooperative bias seems to be operating. In the intermediate games, both biases are observed.

In the Pure No Matrix Condition, the noncooperative bias is observed in all seven games, and the cooperative bias only in the mildest game.

Chapter 5
The Time Courses

So FAR ALL THE INDICES of performance we have examined
were derived from entire sessions of 300, 350, or 700 responses. We differentiated among the performances in
different games and under different conditions, but did
not inquire into the dynamics of the process, that is,
into the changes exhibited by performances during the
course of a session. We shall now examine these changes.
Consistent trends in changes of behavior are attributed
to learning; or, to put it another way, learning is usually
defined by experimental psychologists as consistent discernible trends in behavior change, especially when
manifested in changed responses to presumably similar
stimuli. Accordingly, we can attribute any consistent
trends in performance in repeated plays of Prisoner's
Dilemma to learning.

The first question which naturally occurs is whether
the subjects learn to cooperate or, on the contrary, learn
to defect. Neither answer can be supported on a priori
grounds, or, perhaps, both answers can be supported by
argument. On the one hand, the structure of Prisoner's
Dilemma is such that the defecting response, when it is
positively reinforced, is reinforced more strongly (assuming reinforcements measured by the payoffs) than the
positively reinforced cooperative response. Also, the
cooperative response, when it is punished, is punished
more strongly than the punished defecting response. On
these grounds learning ought to go in the direction of
decreasing cooperation. This argument is even more
compelling when one keeps in mind that a decrease in
cooperation of one player can be expected to induce more

defection in the other, and so a vicious cycle operates which ought to drive both players to defection.

On the other hand, one can argue that since the double-defecting state is punishing to both players, while the double-cooperative state is rewarding, the latter ought to be fixated, rather than the former. This argument attains even greater plausibility when one remembers that once the *CC* state is established, defecting from it is not likely to "pay" because of the likelihood of retaliation. "Learning" may well be a realization by both players that they are in the same boat, as it were, and hence may lead to the persistence of the *CC* response.

At any rate the problem is a complex one, as we shall see when we extend the stochastic model of rote learning applied to the interaction situation represented by Prisoner's Dilemma. Analysis of data shows that it will be useful to distinguish two phases of the process, namely a short range phase and a long range phase. The trends in the two phases are different.

First we shall examine the values of *C* in the first two responses. Since the gross time trend is our object of attention, we shall not differentiate between games but only between the two conditions, where the matrix is displayed and where it is not. We do this in the interest of having a larger sample, especially since a cursory examination reveals that at this early state the games are not well differentiated by the subjects.

Table 19 shows the comparison of the four categories of responses on the first and second plays observed in groups of ten pairs in the Matrix Conditions (Pure, Block, and Mixed). The first seven relate to the seven games in the Pure Condition, the second seven to the same seven games in the Block Condition, and the last to the group of ten pairs of the Mixed Condition. It is apparent that the tendency on the second move is to cooperate less than on the first move. We might ask whether this tendency is a reaction to betrayed trust or the result of yielding to temptation. Evidence for the second conjecture would be a decrease of *CC* responses on the second play compared with the first. Evidence for the first conjecture would be an increase of *DD* responses at the expense of the unilateral responses on the second play. Table 19 shows that both conjectures are corroborated.

TABLE 19

	1st Move					2nd Move					Change From 1st to 2nd Move
Game	CC	CD	DC	DD	%C	CC	CD	DC	DD	%C	Sgn Δ
Pure											
I	4	4	2	0	70	5	1	2	2	65	—
II	1	6	1	2	45	2	5	2	1	45	o
III	2	4	1	3	45	2	2	3	3	45	o
IV	1	4	3	2	45	1	3	3	3	40	—
V		2	2	3	50	2	2	1	5	35	—
XI	3	1	3	3	50	2	5	1	2	50	o
XII	3	3	2	2	55	4	1	1	4	50	—
Block											
I	5	3	0	2	65	4	4	0	2	65	o
II	3	3	4	0	65	3	3	1	3	50	—
III	1	5	3	1	50	1	4	1	4	35	—
IV	5	1	2	2	65	3	1	4	2	55	—
V	4	0	2	4	50	0	2	3	5	25	—
XI	2	2	4	2	50	3	2	2	3	50	o
XII	1	3	3	3	40	0	2	1	7	15	—
Mixed	4	1	2	3	65	2	3	3	2	50	—
Total	42	42	34	32	53	34	40	28	48	45	—

As control, we can use the No Matrix Condition. Since the first response gives no information to the subjects about the relative advantages or disadvantages of choosing Right or Left, we would expect that in the No Matrix Condition there would be no discernible difference between the cooperative frequencies on the first and second plays. From Table 20 we see that this is indeed the case.

TABLE 20

	1st Move					2nd Move					Change From 1st to 2nd Move
Game	CC	CD	DC	DD	%C	CC	CD	DC	DD	%C	Sgn Δ
I	2	4	0	4	40	0	3	5	2	40	0
II	4	3	0	3	55	5	4	0	1	70	+
III	3	5	1	1	60	6	3	1	0	80	+
IV	5	2	3	0	75	3	3	2	2	45	−
V	3	2	2	3	50	3	2	1	4	55	+
XI	4	1	2	3	45	2	4	3	1	55	+
XII	2	4	0	4	40	1	4	1	4	35	−
Mixed	1	2	4	3	40	2	4	0	4	40	0
Total	24	23	12	21	52	22	27	13	18	52	0

Looking with a "smaller resolving power" at grosser effects, we observe the "running average" of C in the Pure Matrix and No Matrix Conditions. These are shown in Figures 7-11. The running average represents

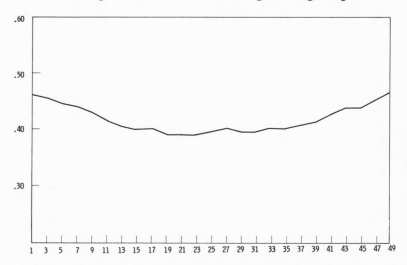

Figure 7. Pure Matrix Condition. Horizontal: Responses 1–15, 3–17, etc. Vertical: Frequency of C Responses.

an average of 15 responses by each pair of players. Accordingly, the point "1" on the horizontal axis represents the average of responses 1–15, point "3" the average of responses 3–17, etc. We see that in the Matrix Conditions (Figures 7, 8, and 9) the first total effect is

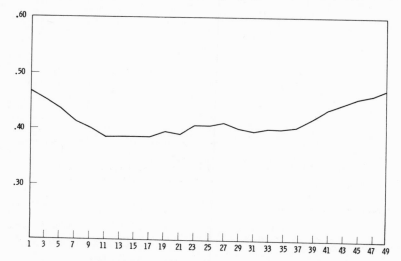

Figure 8. Block Condition. Horizontal: Responses 1–15, 3–17, etc. Vertical: Frequency of *C* Responses.

that of continuing decrease of cooperative choices. Somewhere between the twentieth and the thirtieth responses a recovery appears to set in. The downward trend is observed also in the No Matrix Conditions, but no recovery (Figures 10 and 11).

We now separate the responses into three classes, *CC*, *DD*, and the combined class *CD* + *DC* (the unilaterals) in order to see what changes are responsible for the observed initial downward trend and for the subsequent recovery where it occurs (Figures 12–16). We observe that *DD* initially increases in all the conditions. The trend is reversed after about the thirtieth response in the Matrix Conditions but apparently not in the No Matrix Conditions. The trend in *CC* is at first slightly

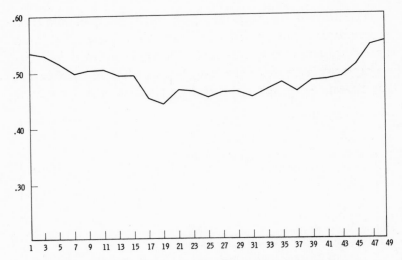

Figure 9. Mixed Matrix Condition. Horizontal: Responses 1–15, 3–17, etc. Vertical: Frequency of C Responses.

downward in the Matrix Conditions but is reversed quite soon. In the No Matrix Conditions, there is no such recovery of *CC*. As for the unilateral responses, they continue to decrease in both conditions.

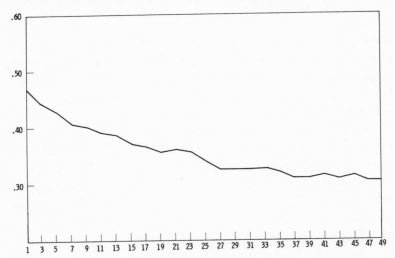

Figure 10. Pure No Matrix Condition. Horizontal: Responses 1–15, 3–17, etc. Vertical: Frequency of C Responses.

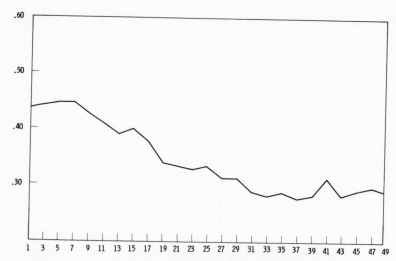

Figure 11. Mixed No Matrix Condition. Horizontal: Responses 1–15, 3–17, etc. Vertical: Frequency of *C* Responses.

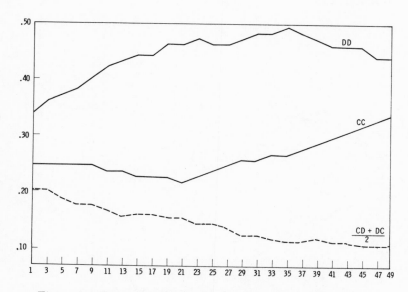

Figure 12. Pure Matrix Condition. Horizontal: Responses 1–15, 3–17, etc. Vertical: Frequencies of *CC*, *DD*, and Unilateral Responses.

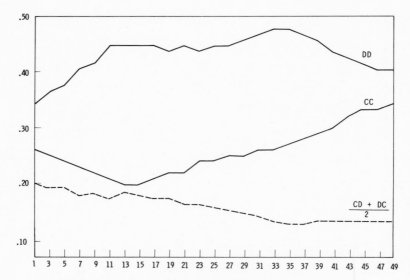

Figure 13. Block Condition. Horizontal: Responses 1–15, 3–17, etc. Vertical: Frequencies of *CC*, *DD*, and Unilateral Responses.

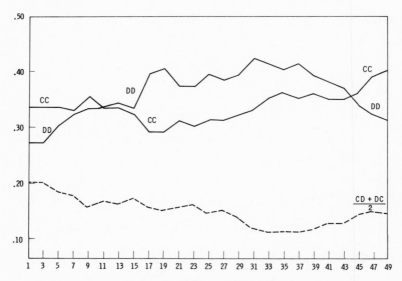

Figure 14. Mixed Matrix Condition. Horizontal: Responses 1–15, 3–17, etc. Vertical: Frequencies of *CC*, *DD*, and Unilateral Responses.

In short, the trends in the first fifty plays are the following. The unilateral responses tend to disappear. Initially they become predominantly *DD* responses both when the matrix is displayed and when it is not. Eventu-

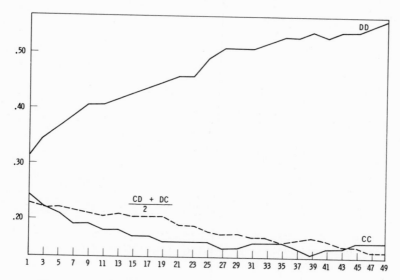

Figure 15. Pure No Matrix Condition. Horizontal: Responses 1–15, 3–17, etc. Vertical: Frequencies of *CC*, *DD*, and Unilateral Responses.

ally, however, if the matrix is displayed, the unilateral responses tend increasingly to become *CC* responses (i.e., attempts to initiate cooperation become more successful). If the matrix is not displayed, on the other hand, this does not occur; the unilateral responses continue to be absorbed into *DD* responses. It appears that we have pinned down the role of the displayed matrix as a reminder to the subjects that a tacit collusion is possible. Evidently on the whole they tend to attain this tacit collusion in an increasing measure after about the thirtieth response, if the matrix is displayed, but not in the absence of the matrix.

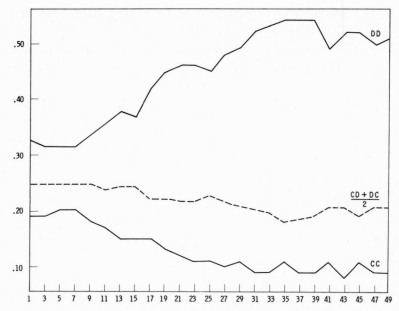

Figure 16. Mixed No Matrix Condition. Horizontal: Responses 1–15, 3–17, etc. Vertical: Frequencies of *CC*, *DD*, and Unilateral Responses.

To see what happens after the fiftieth play, we examine successive fifteen play averages to the end. The comparison of *C* in the successive fifteen play blocks is shown in Figures 17–21. The comparison of state time courses is shown in Figures 22–26.

The trend in the Pure and the Block Matrix Conditions is clear. After the initial drop (shown "blown up" in Figures 7 and 8), *C* increases, appearing to reach an asymptotic value of about .65–.70 on about the 150th play in the Pure Condition and on about the 200th play in the Block Condition. In Figures 22 and 23 we see the breakdown, namely a steady increase of *CC* and decrease of *DD* after the initial trend is reversed. Note that the reversal of *DD* comes somewhat after the reversal of *CC* in both conditions.

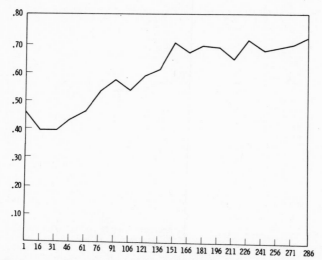

Figure 17. Pure Matrix Condition. Horizontal: Responses 1–15, 16–30, etc. Vertical: Frequencies of *C* Responses.

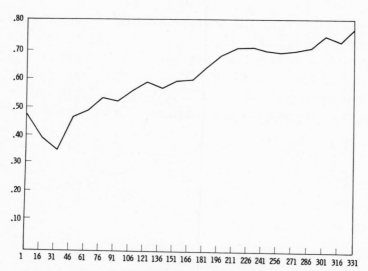

Figure 18. Block Condition. Horizontal: Responses 1–15, 16–30, etc. Vertical: Frequencies of *C* Responses.

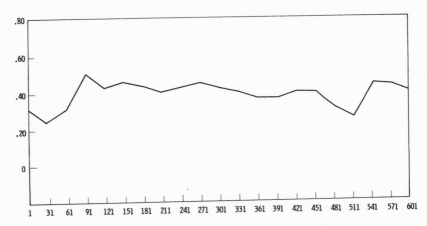

Figure 19. Mixed Matrix Condition. Horizontal: Responses 1–15, 31–45, etc. Vertical: Frequencies of *C* Responses.

In the Pure No Matrix Condition the upward trend of *C* and *CC* comes much later (Figures 20 and 25), on about the 180th play and is very weak.

The picture in the Mixed Conditions is not clear (Figures 24 and 26). This is doubtless due to the fact that only ten protocols are averaged in each of the Mixed Conditions, so that the statistical fluctuations are not smoothed out and tend to mask the gross trends. Still the data support the conjecture that a steady state

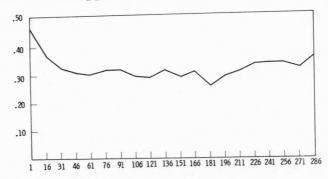

Figure 20. Pure No Matrix Condition. Horizontal: Responses 1–15, 16–30, etc. Vertical: Frequencies of *C* Responses.

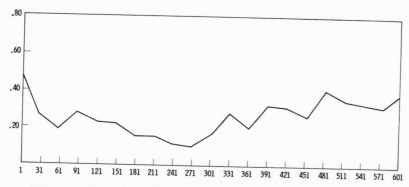

Figure 21. Mixed No Matrix Condition. Horizontal: Responses 1–15, 31–45, etc. Vertical: Frequencies of *C* Responses.

is reached on about the ninetieth play in the Mixed Matrix Condition (Figure 24), that is considerably earlier than in either the Pure or the Block Conditions. Our conjecture is that the Mixed Condition inhibits differentiation between the games and so drives the

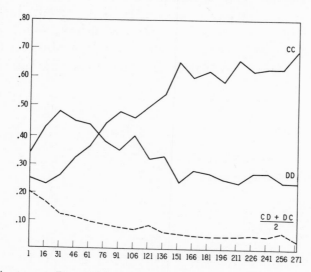

Figure 22. Pure Matrix Condition. Horizontal: Responses 1–15, 16–30, etc. Vertical: Frequencies of *CC*, *DD*, and Unilateral Responses.

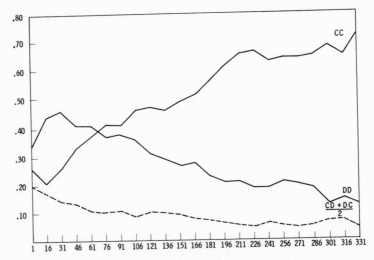

Figure 23. Block Condition. Horizontal: Responses 1–15, 16–30, etc. Vertical: Frequencies of *CC*, *DD*, and Unilateral Responses.

players earlier to a decision as to whether or not to cooperate. The steady state, we recall, represents largely an average of extremes—the pairs who have practically locked-in on *CC* and those who have locked-in on *DD*.

In the Mixed No Matrix Condition the characteristic

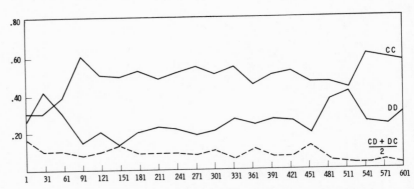

Figure 24. Mixed Matrix Condition. Horizontal: Responses 1–15, 31–45, etc. Vertical: Frequencies of *CC*, *DD*, and Unilateral Responses.

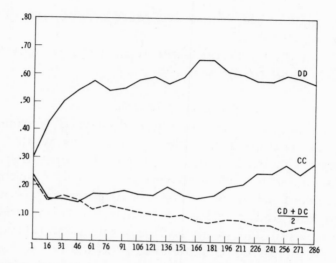

Figure 25. Pure No Matrix Condition. Horizontal: Responses 1–15, 16–30, etc. Vertical: Frequencies of *CC*, *DD*, and Unilateral Responses.

long decline, seen in the Pure No Matrix Condition, is also observed, as well as the eventual slow recovery. The latter seems to start on about the 200th play in the Pure No Matrix Condition (Figure 20) but only on about the

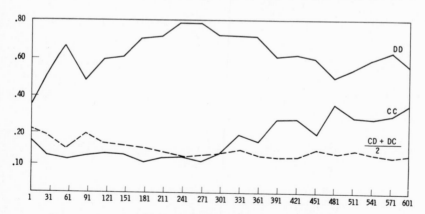

Figure 26. Mixed No Matrix Condition. Horizontal: Responses 1–15, 31–45, etc. Vertical: Frequencies of *CC*, *DD*, and Unilateral Responses.

270th play in the Mixed No Matrix Condition (Figure 21).

As for the unilateral states, these decline slowly but steadily in all conditions.

Summary of Chapter 5

The initial gross trend in repeated plays of Prisoner's Dilemma is toward more defection. After a while "recovery" sets in, and the frequency of cooperative responses increases. This recovery is relatively quick and pronounced when the matrix is displayed but comes much later and is relatively weak when the matrix is not displayed. The steady decline of the unilateral states, i.e., the increasing predominance of *CC* and *DD* states, is evidently responsible for the fact that paired players become more and more like each other in repeated plays of Prisoner's Dilemma.

Part II

Mathematical Theory

Chapter 6
General Remarks

IN THIS PART, we shall be constructing some mathematical models of the processes we have been describing. The task will remain unfinished, since the aim of a mathematical model ought to be to raise more questions than it answers. The value of such models is not confined to their explanatory power (of which some models have much and some little) but extends also to the theoretical leverage which these models provide. The nature of theoretical leverage will, we hope, become clear in a few illustrative examples.

One of the earliest numerical descriptions of a sequence of events is given in Genesis, where the vital statistics of the descendants of Adam are listed.

". . . . And all the days of Seth were nine hundred and twelve years; and he died.

"And Enoch lived ninety years and begat Kenan. . . . And all the days of Enoch were nine hundred and five years; and he died.

"And Kenan lived seventy years and begat Mahalel. . . ."

One can easily represent this account as a graph with the generations on the horizontal axis and longevity of the patriarchs on the vertical. However, one would not call the resulting graph a mathematical model, because it lacks theoretical leverage. No regularity is discernible in the numbers of years lived by the lineal descendants of Adam. At first it seems as if both longevity and the age of begetting the first son are diminishing, but this hypothesis is refuted almost immediately by Jared and again by Methuselah.

To be sure, the number of generations being finite, we could contrive to find a formula for passing a curve through all the ages. But such a curve would have as many free parameters as there are points to go through.[17] Again there would be no theoretical leverage, that is, no additional questions to be asked, except whether the formula continues to predict, which it probably does not.

At the other end of the scale are the classical physical laws, for example, the law of universal gravitation, the conservation laws, etc. Such laws are examples of models with very high explanatory power. The expression of these laws is terse; the consequences are extremely far-reaching.

A progression from purely descriptive models to models with high explanatory power often proceeds by reducing the freedom of the parameters used in the model. A good example would be such a progression in the development of the law of falling bodies, as it might have happened if the history of science confirmed more strictly our expectations in retrospect.

As is well known, Galileo established the law of motion for bodies undergoing constant acceleration, for example sliding down frictionless inclined planes. The distance traveled, s, is related to the time elapsed, t, by the formula

$$s = at^2 \tag{31}$$

where a is constant. The constant is in this context a free parameter. Its value can be determined experimentally, and it has to be adjusted for every new inclined plane. The theoretical leverage of the model at this stage resides in this free parameter. For it soon becomes apparent that the magnitude of this parameter depends on the inclination of the plane. In fact, we are led to another law, namely

$$a = \tfrac{1}{2}g \sin \alpha \tag{32}$$

where α is the angle between the inclined plane and the plumb line. Now g appears as a free parameter. The model still has some theoretical leverage, because investigations can proceed to determine relations between g and other variables. We now know that g depends on the distance from the center of the earth. The law of this dependence yields still another free parameter, namely K, the universal gravitational constant, which in turn can be investigated in the light of the current cosmological theories.

This idealized picture of progressive clarification suggests how one might proceed with the building of a theory, so that its succeeding stages are reached in the process of development. The method suggests also a scale of "strength" for models: the fewer free parameters a model has and the greater the range of situations to which it applies, the stronger it is.

Looking back now on the model proposed in Chapter 1 which purports to predict the relative frequencies of cooperative responses from the payoff matrices, we see that it is a rather weak one. It contains two free parameters and predicts only the rank order of games. However, the model is not totally devoid of theoretical leverage. It could be put to a test in any number of additional games, specifically constructed to test the model further. In particular, if the predicted positions of the games on the cooperative scale were checked out in the range examined, we could inquire about the limits of the range where the model remains valid, etc. Still, even in the most favorable circumstances, i.e., even if the predictions checked out in a large range, the model would still remain an extremely limited one.

We have seen that besides certain regularities in the relations between the C frequencies and the payoffs, there are also certain discernible time trends and certain correlations between members of pairs. Our game-index model implies nothing about these regularities. Clearly, if these are to be included in a theory, we need a model of the *process*, i.e., a dynamic model.

It stands to reason that interactions between the players exert important effects on the process, and it is these interactions which ought to be incorporated into a mathematical model. The derived consequences of the model ought to be statements about our variables as functions of time (i.e., of the number of plays) and about the way the variables are correlated.

Deterministic and Stochastic Models

Two broad classes of dynamic models can be distinguished, the deterministic (classical) and the stochastic. Each has certain advantages and certain disadvantages. The classical models are convenient, because they admit of well-known and established methods of classical analysis. Typically these models are represented by systems of differential equations.[18] It is easy enough to see how equations of this sort could be postulated for the process of repeated Prisoner's Dilemma games: they can represent the relations between the rates of change of the variables and their momentary values. When Lewis F. Richardson (1960) developed his dynamic theory of arms races, he did just that, namely, he assumed that the existing level of armaments of one nation acts as a stimulant to the rate of growth of armaments of a rival nation. Adding to these effects also some inhibitory terms to reflect the economic burden of armaments, and some constant terms to represent the chronic "grievances" of the nations against each other, Richardson derived for the case of two rival blocs a pair of differential equations with the interesting property that for certain values of the parameters the resulting system was stable while for certain other values it was unstable. The former kind of system could conceivably attain a balanced state of armament levels. The latter kind could only go to extremes, that is, it could either escalate into a runaway arms race or go into reverse toward complete disarmament. We could apply a similar conceptualization to the process we are studying.

An important shortcoming of the classical dynamic model is that it does not take into account the probabilistic features typical of behavioral phenomena. These features represent not merely compromises with our ignorance, as is always the case when determinate causes of events are not known. The probabilistic description of behavioral events is inherent in the very method of quantification of these events.

There is a fundamental distinction between mathematicized physical science and mathematicized behavioral science. In the former, the quantities appearing in equations refer typically to results of physical measurements, e.g., masses, velocities, concentrations, temperatures, etc. Also the early extension of physical science methods to psychology depended heavily on the isolation of appropriate physically measurable quantities of behavior. Such were, for example, reaction times, intensities of response reflected in physiological variables, etc. The gap between these measureable quantities and the usual descriptions of behavior is enormous, but the discrepancy does not necessarily have to do with whether behavioral events are described vaguely or precisely. There may be nothing vague about the statements "The rat passed a lever" or "Smith bought a car" or "player 1 played *C*" in the sense that independent observers will have no difficulty in agreeing on whether the event did or did not take place. Yet it is next to impossible to specify such events in terms of physically measured variables or to describe them minutely in terms of specific physical responses.

The objectivity of behavioral data depends on consensus among independent observers about what took place, not on the possibility of reducing the data to physically measurable variables. Once the objective nature of a unit event (e.g., a choice among specified alternatives) is established, a quantification of such events immediately suggests itself, namely in terms of their relative frequencies. Such a quantification lends itself admirably to mathematical treatment, first because frequencies can be objectively measured and second because a relative frequency is a pure number, independent of units. R. D. Luce (1959) has shown how the latitude of our choice of mathematical models depends vitally on the sort of scale used in the measurements. The weaker the scale, the more restricted is the class of models at our disposal. Relative frequencies are measured on an absolute scale, that is, a scale of pure numbers. This scale offers the widest possible range of possibly appropriate models.[19]

Now the relative frequency of an event can be operationally defined only with respect to a population of events. It cannot be defined with respect to a single event. A conceptual extension of the relative frequency notion to apply to a single event is one of the definitions of probability. The probability of a single event is thus a theoretical construct, never an observable. To be translated into observables, probabilities must first be transformed into frequencies.

A stochastic model of a process is concerned with the relations among various probabilities, particularly with the changes which such probabilities suffer as results of interactions of events.

Consider, for example, a sequence of events, such as a protocol of an individual's performance in Prisoner's Dilemma. Such a protocol will be a sequence of C's and D's. A stochastic model of this process would consist of some postulates about how the probability of a C

response depends on what responses have been given before the play in question, including, generally, the responses of the other player. Consequently, the probability of a C response is treated in such a model as a variable, not a constant. It follows that this probability cannot be estimated from the relative frequency of C responses over a stretch of time, as could be done if this probability were constant. Such a probability could conceivably be estimated only if we had several "realizations" of this process, for example, if the game were played by several "identical" pairs of players (in the sense of obeying the "laws" of the same model). But even in this case, the estimation of the probability of a response would not be simple. For example, one could not simply take the relative frequency of C on the t-th response in a population of players as an estimate of the probability of the C response associated with "the" player. Even though the players of our hypothetical population may be "identical," they may have had different *histories* prior to the t-th response in the several realizations of the process, because the responses themselves were probabilistically determined, and consequently the probabilities of a response on a given play may all be different in the different "representations" of the player.

The matter is relatively simple if the probability of a response depends not on previous probabilities but on previous *events*. Suppose, for example, that the probability of a C depends only on what actually happened on the previous play, namely CC, CD, DC, or DD. If we have a large population of identical players, we can on a given play subdivide them into four subpopulations, namely those following a CC response, those following a CD response, etc. Each of these four subpopulations now has an identical "history" (since the history stretches no farther back than one previous play) and the probability of the *C* response can be estimated from its relative frequency in each subpopulation.

Clearly, the farther back the dependence on previous responses goes, the more such subpopulations have to be examined. Specifically their number grows exponentially with the length of the relevant "history." Very soon even enormously large populations of "identical" subjects become insufficient, because they have to be broken up into more subpopulations than there are individuals.

We have pointed out the difficulties involved in putting a stochastic model to a test—the difficulty of translating probabilities into frequencies, when the probabilities themselves depend on the realization of the stochastic process.

In short, the main difficulty in the use of stochastic models of behavior is in the fact that probabilities (which are the variables in such models) are elusive quantities. One never "measures" probabilities; one only estimates them. Typically the problems of estimating probabilities and the parameters governing the changes of probabilities become exceedingly involved in stochastic models where interactions occur.

Interactions are the very essence of the Prisoner's Dilemma played repeatedly; consequently the stochastic models of this process become exceedingly involved. We shall propose some models of this sort, but we shall not put them to tests by the usual method of estimating parameters and comparing predicted with observed results. Instead we shall content ourselves with trying to reproduce some of the gross characteristics of our data by simulation, i.e., postulating players governed by the models to whom some arbitrarily selected values of the parameters are ascribed.

We shall also propose some classical (deterministic) models, which have lately passed out of fashion in mathematical psychology. We shall make no claim for the adequacy of such models. Our purpose in introducing them will be merely to see whether we can derive some gross features of our data and, if so, whether we can draw some suggestive hypotheses about the psychology of the process from the way the theoretically derived results depend on the parameters.

Chapter 7
Markov Chain Models

THE FIRST MODELS we shall examine will be Markov chains. In these models it is assumed that the system under consideration can be at any given time in any of a finite number of states. Let this number be n. When a system is in a given state, say s_i, it can pass to another state, say s_j, with a certain transition probability α_{ij}. Consequently, there are n^2 quantities α_{ij} ($i, j = 1, 2 \ldots n$) which can be put into a square matrix of order n. The transition probability α_{ij} is the entry in the i-th row and the j-th column of this matrix. Some of the α_{ij} may be zero, which means that the system never passes from the particular state s_i to the particular state s_j. Some may be equal to 1, which means that whenever the system is in some particular state s_i it always passes from it to the particular state s_j, etc.

If some α_{ii} equals 1, then the system, once it finds itself in s_i will stay in it forever. Such a state is called an *absorbing state*. In a later chapter we shall be concerned with Markov chains in which there are absorbing states, but for the time being we shall be concerned only with chains in which it is possible to pass from any state to any other state at least via intermediate states. Clearly, such chains have no absorbing states.

More specifically, we shall be first concerned with ergodic chains. Roughly, an ergodic chain is one in which ultimately the system will "visit" each of the states with a certain constant frequency (but not strictly periodically). This frequency is independent of the initial probability of finding the system in any state.

Time, in the context of Markov chains, is quantized. That is, the moments of time are represented by the transition steps from state to state, and so the time variables take on discrete values: $t = 0,1,2 \ldots$.

Let $p_j(t)$ represent the probability that at time t the system is in state s_j. Then clearly

$$p_j(t + 1) = \sum_{i=1}^{n} \alpha_{ij} p_i(t) \quad (j = 1,2 \ldots n). \tag{33}$$

Equation (33) describes the time course of the probability distribution $p_j(t)$. If the initial probability distribution $p_j(0)$ is known, then the fate of the system is determined with respect to the probabilities that the system is in one of the possible states at any future time but, of course, not with respect to the actual sequence of states to be traversed. The actual time course will be a "realization" of any one of the possible sequences of which there are a great many.

If the chain is ergodic, the distribution $p_j(t)$ tends to a limiting distribution $p_j(\infty)$. This means that after a sufficiently long time, the system will be "visiting" each of the states s_j with relative frequency $p_j(\infty)$. These limiting frequencies can be obtained by setting $p_j(t + 1) = p_j(t)$ in Equation (33) and solving for the p_j $(j = 1 \ldots n)$.[20] For the time being, we shall be concerned only with these equilibrium distributions, the so-called *steady states* of Markov chains.

Let the probability of a cooperative response of a player depend only on what happened on the previous play. The dependence can be (1) on what the player in question did, (2) on what the other player did, or (3) on what both of them did. If the dependence is only on what the player in question did, clearly our conditional probabilities η and ζ are the relevant parameters (cf. p. 67). If the dependence is only on what the other player did, then the relevant parameters are ξ and ω. If the dependence is on what both did, we must use $x, y, z,$ and w as our parameters (cf. p. 71).

Of these three cases, the first is not interesting. If the response probabilities of each player are determined only by what he himself has been doing, there is no interaction between the two. The essence of Prisoner's Dilemma is in the interactions between the pair members. To be sure, the noninteractive model cannot be discarded on a priori grounds alone. However, since we have already seen how strong positive interactions are reflected in the data (cf. Chapter 3), we can dismiss the models governed by η and ζ alone. We already know that they are inadequate to describe the results of our experiments.

We turn to a model which supposes that the process is governed by ξ and ω. We wish to examine the simplest possible types first in order to see what interesting features of the process, if any, are reflected already in the simplest models.

The most drastic simplification of a (ξ, ω) model would result if one left only one of these parameters free and assigned an extreme value, zero or one, to the other. However, some of these models are immediately revealed as trivial, as we shall now show.

Let ξ be arbitrary and $\omega = 0$. This means that in response to the other's defection, a player always defects, and in response to the other's cooperation he responds cooperatively with probability ξ. Since $0 < \xi < 1$, a double defection is bound to occur sometime. Further, because $\omega = 0$, this double defection will be immediately fixated and will persist thereafter.

A similar argument reveals the triviality of the model where $0 < \omega < 1$ and $\xi = 1$, since in that case a CC response will be certainly fixated.

On the other hand, the two models represented by

o $< \xi <$ 1; $\omega =$ 1 and by o $< \omega <$ 1; $\xi =$ o lead to nontrivial steady states which depend on the respective variable parameters. Let us consider each of these in turn.

Case: o $< \xi <$ 1; $\omega =$ 1.

In this situation, each player responds cooperatively whenever the other defects and with respective probabilities ξ_1 and ξ_2 whenever the other cooperates. This assumption may seem unrealistic, but can be rationalized. When the other player defects, the player in question tries to induce him to cooperate, hence he himself cooperates. When the other cooperates, the player in question sometimes cooperates (with probability ξ_i) but is sometimes tempted to defect (with probability $1 - \xi_i$). In any case, the realism of this assumption will not be of concern to us in these preliminary theoretical explorations.

The Markov equations are now the following:

$$(CC)' = CC\xi_1\xi_2 + CD\xi_2 + DC\xi_1 + DD, \qquad (34)$$

$$(CD)' = CC\xi_1(1 - \xi_2) + CD(1 - \xi_2), \qquad (35)$$

$$(DC)' = CC(1 - \xi_1)\xi_2 + DC(1 - \xi_1), \qquad (36)$$

$$(DD)' = CC(1 - \xi_1)(1 - \xi_2), \qquad (37)$$

where the primed quantities represent the probabilities of the corresponding states on the play following the play in question.

To see this, denote (CC) by s_1, (CD) by s_2, (DC) by s_3, and (DD) by s_4. Observe that the transition probability α_{11} is given in the present model by $\xi_1\xi_2$, since when the system is in state s_1 it passes to the same state if and only if both players respond cooperatively, and the conditional probability of this event is $\xi_1\xi_2$ under the assumption that in the absence of communication the responses of the two subjects in any particular play must be independent of each other. Similarly $\alpha_{21} = \xi_2$, since when the system is in state CD (s_2) we have assumed that player 1 will always cooperate (in response to the other's defection, since $\omega = 1$) while the second player will cooperate with probability ξ_2, etc.

The steady state solution of the four categories of responses is given by

$$CC = \frac{\xi_1\xi_2}{(\xi_1 + \xi_2)^2 + \xi_1\xi_2(\xi_1\xi_2 - 2\xi_1 - 2\xi_2)}; \quad (38)$$

$$CD = \frac{\xi_1^2(1 - \xi_2)}{(\xi_1 + \xi_2)^2 + \xi_1\xi_2(\xi_1\xi_2 - 2\xi_1 - 2\xi_2)}; \quad (39)$$

$$DC = \frac{\xi_2^2(1 - \xi_1)}{(\xi_1 + \xi_2)^2 + \xi_1\xi_2(\xi_1\xi_2 - 2\xi_1 - 2\xi_2)}; \quad (40)$$

$$DD = \frac{\xi_1\xi_2(1 - \xi_1)(1 - \xi_2)}{(\xi_1 + \xi_2)^2 + \xi_1\xi_2(\xi_1\xi_2 - 2\xi_1 - 2\xi_2)}. \quad (41)$$

It is easily verified that CC tends to 1 and all the other states to zero as ξ_1 and ξ_2 tend to one. When ξ_1 and ξ_2 vanish, the expression becomes indeterminate, but limits can be evaluated if the way in which each ξ_1 approaches zero is specified.[21] In particular, if $\xi_1 = \xi_2$ as both approach zero, the limiting distribution is $CC = CD = DC = DD = \frac{1}{4}$, as can be seen intuitively, for in that case, if the players happen to start in either CD or DC, they will remain in that state, and if they happen to start with either CC or DD, they will oscillate between these two states.

This model has one feature which immediately removes it from consideration. In the steady state, the correlation coefficient ρ_0 (cf. p. 67) must vanish, regardless of the values of ξ_1 and ξ_2. This is so because the numerator of the expression denoting ρ_0 [Equation (10) of Chapter 3] vanishes when the expressions (38-41) are substituted for the four states.

Case: $\xi_1 = \xi_2 = 0$; $0 < \omega_1 < 1$; $0 < \omega_2 < 1$.

In this case, the Markov equations for the steady state become

$$CC = DD\omega_1\omega_2; \tag{42}$$

$$CD = CD\omega_1 + DD\omega_1(1 - \omega_2); \tag{43}$$

$$DC = DC\omega_2 + DD\omega_2(1 - \omega_1); \tag{44}$$

$$DD = CC + CD(1 - \omega_1) + DC(1 - \omega_2) +$$
$$DD(1 - \omega_1)(1 - \omega_2). \tag{45}$$

Proceeding exactly the same way, we get the steady-state distribution:

$$DD = \frac{(1 - \omega_1)(1 - \omega_2)}{(1 - \omega_1)(1 - \omega_2)(1 + \omega_1\omega_2) + \omega_1(1 - \omega_2)^2 + \omega_2(1 - \omega_1)^2}; \tag{46}$$

$$DC = \frac{\omega_2(1 - \omega_1)^2}{(1 - \omega_1)(1 - \omega_2)(1 + \omega_1\omega_2) + \omega_1(1 - \omega_2)^2 + \omega_2(1 - \omega_1)^2}; \tag{47}$$

$$CD = \frac{\omega_1(1 - \omega_2)^2}{(1 - \omega_1)(1 - \omega_2)(1 + \omega_1\omega_2) + \omega_1(1 - \omega_2)^2 + \omega_2(1 - \omega_1)^2}; \tag{48}$$

$$CC = \frac{\omega_1\omega_2(1 - \omega_1)(1 - \omega_2)}{(1 - \omega_1)(1 - \omega_2)(1 + \omega_1\omega_2) + \omega_1(1 - \omega_2)^2 + \omega_2(1 - \omega_1)^2}. \tag{49}$$

Here DD tends to one as ω_1 and ω_2 tend to zero. As ω_1 and ω_2 tend to one (while $\omega_1 = \omega_2$), the system again tends toward equal distributions of states. Again we see that $\rho_0 = 0$ for any values of ω_1 and ω_2. Hence this model also fails to account for the observed predominantly positive ρ_0.

We could go on to a general model of this sort with arbitrarily chosen values of the eight parameters (subject, of course, to the constraints noted on p. 34). However, the expressions become unwieldly in the general case, and we shall not develop these types of models further. Instead, we turn our attention to models based on the state-conditioned propensities, x, y, z, and w.

Case:

$$0 < x_1 < 1; \quad 0 < x_2 < 1; \quad y = z = 0; \quad w_1 = w_2 = 1.$$

This will be recognized as the case of the two tempted simpletons (cf. p. 85). The simpletons always change their responses when the payoff is negative and stay with the same response when the payoff is positive except that following a *CC* response, each may defect with probability $1 - x_i (i = 1, 2)$. Consequently, the *CD* and the *DC* responses are always followed by *DD*, which, in turn is always followed by *CC*. However, the *CC* response can be followed by any of the other three.

The steady-state Markov equations for this case are (cf. Note 14)

$$CC = CCx_1x_2 + DD; \tag{50}$$

$$CD = CCx_1(1 - x_2); \tag{51}$$

$$DC = CCx_2(1 - x_1); \tag{52}$$

$$DD = CC(1 - x_1)(1 - x_2) + CD + DC. \tag{53}$$

The steady-state distribution is (cf. p. 75)

$$CC = \frac{1}{2 + x_1 + x_2 - 3x_1x_2}; \tag{54}$$

$$CD = \frac{x_1(1 - x_2)}{2 + x_1 + x_2 - 3x_1x_2}; \tag{55}$$

$$DC = \frac{x_2(1 - x_1)}{2 + x_1 + x_2 - 3x_1x_2}; \tag{56}$$

$$DD = \frac{1 - x_1x_2}{2 + x_1 + x_2 - 3x_1x_2}. \tag{57}$$

Let us now compute the numerator of the expression for ρ_0. This is

$$(CC)(DD) - (CD)(DC)$$
$$= (1 - x_1x_2) - (x_1x_2 - x_1^2x_2 - x_1x_2^2 + x_1^2x_2^2)$$
$$= 1 - 2x_1x_2 + x_1^2x_2 + x_1x_2^2 - x_1^2x_2^2. \tag{58}$$

Consider now the polynomial on the right side of (58) which we shall call $F(x_1, x_2)$. We shall show that the value of this polynomial for all values of x_1 and x_2 in the interval $(0 < x < 1)$ is positive and consequently that ρ_0 is positive for all values of x_1 and x_2 in that interval.

First observe that the partial derivatives of $F(x_1,x_2)$ with respect to x_1 and x_2 are both negative in the interval $(0 < x < 1)$. For

$$\frac{\partial F}{\partial x_1} = -2x_2 + 2x_1x_2 + x_2{}^2 - 2x_1x_2{}^2$$

$$= x_2[(x_1 - 1)(1 - x_2) + x_1 - 1 - x_1x_2] < 0; \quad (59)$$

$$\frac{\partial F}{\partial x_2} = -2x_1 + x_1{}^2 + 2x_1x_2 - 2x_1{}^2x_2$$

$$= x_1[(x_2 - 1)(1 - x_1) + x_2 - 1 - x_1x_2] < 0, \quad (60)$$

if $0 < x_1 < 1; 0 < x_2 < 1$. This means that $F(x_1,x_2)$ increases as either x_1 or x_2 decreases when x_1 and x_2 are in the interval $(0,1)$. But $F(1,1) = 0,$[22] $F(0,0) = 1$. Therefore $F(x_1,x_2) > 0$ in the interval $(0 < x < 1)$, and so is ρ_0.

We have now shown how a positive correlation of C responses (and therefore of D responses) is a consequence of the simplest interactive model, based on the conditional probabilities x, y, z, and w (namely the very special case where $y = z = 0; w = 1$). We therefore select this model for further treatment.

The Four-State Markov Model, *General Case*

We now assume that x_i, y_i, z_i, and w_i $(i = 1, 2)$ can assume arbitrary values in the interval $(0,1)$. The complete set of Markov equations is now given by

$$(CC)' = CCx_1x_2 + CDy_1z_2 + DCy_2z_1 + DDw_1w_2, \quad (61)$$

$$(CD)' = CCx_1\tilde{x}_2 + CDy_1\tilde{z}_2 + DCy_2\tilde{z}_1 + DDw_1\tilde{w}_2, \quad (62)$$

$$(DC)' = CC\tilde{x}_1x_2 + CD\tilde{y}_1z_2 + DC\tilde{y}_2z_1 + DD\tilde{w}_1w_2, \quad (63)$$

$$(DD)' = CC\tilde{x}_1\tilde{x}_2 + CD\tilde{y}_1\tilde{z}_2 + DC\tilde{y}_2\tilde{z}_1 + DD\tilde{w}_1\tilde{w}_2, \quad (64)$$

where we have written $\tilde{x}$ for $1 - x$, $\tilde{y}$ for $1 - y$, etc.

The steady-state equations are derived in the same way as previously, namely by setting $(CC)' = CC$, $(CD)' = CD$, etc., and by solving the resulting system for the four states. The solution is extremely unwieldly and is omitted here. The special case where $x_1 = x_2$, $y_1 = y_2$, etc., is shown below.

$$(CC) = \frac{w^2(1 - y\tilde{z} - \tilde{y}z + 2w\tilde{w}) - 2w\tilde{w}(w^2 - yz)}{(1 - y\tilde{z} - \tilde{y}z + 2w\tilde{w})(1 - x^2 + w^2) - 2(w^2 - yz)(w\tilde{w} - x\tilde{x})}, \tag{65}$$

$$(CD) = \frac{w\tilde{w}(1 - x^2 + w^2) - w^2(w\tilde{w} - xx)}{(1 - y\tilde{z} - \tilde{y}z + 2w\tilde{w})(1 - x^2 + w^2) - 2(w^2 - yz)(w\tilde{w} - x\tilde{x})}, \tag{66}$$

$$(DC) = (CD), \tag{67}$$

$$(DD) = 1 - (CC) - 2(CD). \tag{68}$$

Equations (61)-(64) constitute the four-state Markov chain model. To put such a model to a test one needs to estimate the parameters x_i, y_i, z_i, and w_i, as well as the initial probability distribution of the four states. If such estimates can be obtained, statistical predictions can be made to be compared with the statistics obtained from the data. As we have already pointed out, the task of estimating the parameters is by no means easy. Besides, a single set of estimates will enable us to test the model only in a single situation. As a consequence, even if the test corroborates the model we shall still be in the dark concerning the generality of its applicability. Therefore, rather than investigate a single model in detail, we shall develop a variety of models. Our aim is to indicate many different approaches and to postpone the question which of them, if any, is fruitful. In what follows, therefore, we shall describe other mathematical models of Prisoner's Dilemma which seem reasonable to us. When we finally undertake the problem of testing the models it will be only with respect to certain general features of the data with a view of demonstrating the sort of questions which naturally arise in the light of the mathematical models. In this book no definitive argument will be made in favor of any of the models, although evidence for and against some of the models we have constructed will be offered.

Markov Model with Absorbing States

An absorbing state is one from which there is no exit. Once a system enters this state, it remains in it thereafter. Such states are well known in nature, for example the end states of irreversible chemical reactions, death, considered as a state of an organism, etc. In our contexts, absorbing states would be introduced if we supposed that at times one or both players make a decision to play exclusively cooperatively or exclusively uncooperatively, no matter what happens. However, as we shall see, absorbing states can be introduced also under a weaker assumption.

A successful application of an absorbing state model was made by Bernard P. Cohen (1963) in another experimental context. Cohen's experiments were variants of Asch's experiments on conformity under social pressure.

The essential feature of the situation examined by Asch and Cohen is that a single subject is required to make judgments (about comparative lengths of line segments) following the expressed judgments of several pseudo-subjects, who are actually confederates of the experimenter. These pseudo-subjects make deliberately false judgments about the relative lengths of lines, which ordinarily would be easily judged correctly. This presumed social pressure frequently induces the bonafide subject to make incorrect judgments also.

Cohen's model of the process is a Markov chain with four states, two of which are absorbing states. The states are:

s_1: if the subject is in this state, he will give the correct response on the next trial and correct responses thereafter.

s_2: if the subject is in this state, he will give the correct response on the next trial but may give wrong responses on subsequent trials.

s_3: if the subject is in this state, he will give the wrong response on the next trial but may give correct responses on subsequent trials.

s_4: if the subject is in this state, he will give the wrong response on the next trial and on every trial thereafter.

The confederates are instructed always to give the wrong response following the first two trials (on which correct responses are given "to establish confidence" that the lengths are indeed being compared).

Consequently, a decision on the part of the subject to give wrong responses is behaviorally equivalent to a decision to conform to the judgment of the group. Similarly, a decision to give correct responses is equivalent to a decision to ignore the judgment of the group. If a subject makes either of these commitments, he passes into one of the two absorbing states (s_1 or s_4).

Now a Markov chain with two absorbing states will eventually pass into the one or into the other. If it is possible to pass into either of the two absorbing states from an arbitrary nonabsorbing state, there is no way of knowing with certainty in which of the absorbing states the system will end up. Such a process is non-ergodic. This means roughly that a given realized history of the system will not exhibit the same relative frequencies of states independent of initial conditions (as is the case with ergodic processes). It follows that the process described by Cohen's model is not an ergodic process. Any realization of it (a protocol) is bound to end up in one or in the other of the absorbing states. However, the probability of ending up in one or the other can be determined from the initial condition (which Cohen assumes with justification to be s_2) and from the transition probabilities. The latter must be estimated from the data.

The circumstance which led Cohen to postulate a model with absorbing states was the fact that several of the subjects did end up in uninterrupted runs of correct or incorrect responses. Thus Cohen observed essentially the same sort of lock-in effect which we observed in repeated Prisoner's Dilemma. Drawing the statistical inferences from the resulting stochastic model, Cohen got good agreements with several of the important statistics of the process (though not all).

Let us now construct a Markov model with absorbing states for Prisoner's Dilemma. The relevant "decisions" immediately suggest themselves, namely a decision on the part of a subject henceforth to cooperate or a decision henceforth not to cooperate. Theoretically, these decisions could be made unconditionally, namely to cooperate no matter what the other does or not to cooperate regardless of what the other does. Our situation, however, speaks against such a hypothesis. We must remember that we have here two minds, not one. Therefore each of the subjects can make his decision independently of the other. If we supposed that one subject makes a decision to cooperate no matter what the other does, and the other makes an opposite decision, we would observe sessions ending in runs composed exclusively of *CD* or *DC*. Now long runs of unilateral cooperation are sometimes observed, but they are rather rare, and the ending of a session in such a run almost never occurs. We can, however, easily exclude the possibility of the state in which one of the players has decided irrevocably to cooperate while the other has decided irrevocably to defect. We need only assume that passage to the absorbing states, i.e., the irrevocable decision, is possible only when the system is in the *CC* state (in which state one or both of the players may decide to cooperate from then on) or in the *DD* state (in which state one or both may decide not to cooperate from then on). It follows that opposite decisions cannot be made. Obviously they cannot be made simultaneously. Nor can they be made on different occasions. For suppose player 1 has already made the decision to cooperate. Then the *DD* state will never occur, and consequently, by our hypothesis player 2 cannot make the irrevocable decision to defect. Similarly, if one player decides always to defect, the *CC* state will never occur; consequently, the other player cannot make the opposite decision.

We shall now construct a matrix of transition probabilities for one of the players. The entries in this matrix, however, will be not single transition probabilities but pairs of such, because what the subject is prone to do depends not only on what he himself has just done but also on what the other player did on the previous play. Let the states of the single player be as follows:

Γ: if the player is in this state, he will henceforth play only *C*.

C: if the player is in this state, he will play *C* but may play *D* on succeeding plays.

D: if the player is in this state, he will play *D* but may play *C* on succeeding states.

Δ: if the player is in this state, he will henceforth play only *D*.

Matrix 14 shows the transition probabilities. The first of each pair denotes the transition probability in case the other player has played *C*; the second, in case he has played D. Note that the transition probabilities cannot depend on the *state* of the other player. His state is known only to himself. His partner can observe only his choice on the preceding play.

	Γ	C	D	Δ
Γ	1,1	0,0	0,0	0,0
C	γ,0	x,y	$1 - x - \gamma,\ 1 - y$	0,0
D	0,0	z,w	$1 - z,\ 1 - w - \delta$	0,δ
Δ	0,0	0,0	0,0	1,1

Matrix 14.

	ΓΓ	ΓC	ΓD	ΓΔ	CΓ	CC	CD	CΔ	DΓ	DC	DD	DΔ	ΔΓ	ΔC	ΔD	ΔΔ
ΓΓ	1	0	0	0	0	0	0	0	0	0	0	0	0	0	0	0
ΓC	γ	x	$\tilde{x}$	0	0	0	0	0	0	0	0	0	0	0	0	0
ΓD	0	z	$\tilde{z}$	0	0	0	0	0	0	0	0	0	0	0	0	0
ΓΔ	0	0	0	0	0	0	0	0	0	0	0	0	0	0	0	0
CΓ	γ	0	0	0	x	0	0	0	$\tilde{x}$	0	0	0	0	0	0	0
CC	γ^2	γx	$\gamma\tilde{x}$	0	γx	x^2	$x\tilde{x}$	0	$\tilde{x}\gamma$	$\tilde{x}x$	$\tilde{x}^2$	0	0	0	0	0
CD	0	0	0	0	0	yz	$y\tilde{z}$	0	0	$\tilde{y}z$	$\tilde{y}\tilde{z}$	0	0	0	0	0
CΔ	0	0	0	0	0	0	0	y	0	0	0	$\tilde{y}$	0	0	0	0
DΓ	0	0	0	0	z	0	0	0	$\tilde{z}$	0	0	0	0	0	0	0
DC	0	0	0	0	0	zy	$z\tilde{y}$	0	0	$\tilde{z}y$	$\tilde{z}\tilde{y}$	0	0	0	0	0
DD	0	0	0	0	0	w^2	$w\tilde{w}$	$w\delta$	0	$\tilde{w}w$	$\tilde{w}^2$	$\tilde{w}\delta$	0	δw	$\delta\tilde{w}$	δ^2
DΔ	0	0	0	0	0	0	0	w	0	0	0	$\tilde{w}$	0	0	0	δ
ΔΓ	0	0	0	0	0	0	0	0	0	0	0	0	0	0	0	0
ΔC	0	0	0	0	0	0	0	0	0	0	0	0	0	y	$\tilde{y}$	0
ΔD	0	0	0	0	0	0	0	0	0	0	0	0	0	w	$\tilde{w}$	δ
ΔΔ	0	0	0	0	0	0	0	0	0	0	0	0	0	0	0	1

Matrix 15.

Assuming identical players, we can now construct the matrix of transition probabilities for the pair. This is shown in Matrix 15.

Matrix 15 constitutes the Markov chain model with absorbing states. As we see, it turns out to be a fourteen-state Markov chain if transitions to the absorbing states can be made only from *CC* and *DD*. (Otherwise there are sixteen states.)

Here $\tilde{y}$ and $\tilde{z}$ denote $1 - y$ and $1 - z$ as usual, but $\tilde{x}$ and $\tilde{w}$ denote $1 - x - \gamma$ and $1 - w - \delta$ respectively. Tests of this model by simulation methods will be discussed in Chapter 12.

Chapter 8
Equilibrium Models with Adjustable Parameters

So far we have been examining models in which the parameters represent fixed propensities of the subjects. Whatever dynamics emerge in these models is a consequence of interaction among probabilistically determined events, the laws of interaction being determined by the fixed parameters. Now we shall consider models in which the parameters themselves undergo changes.

As a simplest example consider two subjects characterized by a single pair of parameters C_1 and C_2, these being, as before, the probabilities of responding cooperatively in a Prisoner's Dilemma game. Assume now that each subject is able to adjust his own parameter and that he seeks to adjust it so as to "maximize his expected gain." From the nature of Prisoner's Dilemma, we see that if each makes calculations based on the payoffs, then each player will set his C equal to zero, because the D response is "better" against either response of the other player. Suppose, however, that the players are sentient but not calculating beings, that is, they are governed by a homeostatic type process in which the behavioral parameters seek the most favorable gradient with respect to the resulting payoffs averaged over some interval of time.

To fix ideas, assume that C_2 is held constant and that player 1 seeks to adjust his C_1 in the way just mentioned. Player 1 will try some value of C_1 for a while, note the average payoff that accrues to him, then try another value $C_1' > C_1$. If the resulting average payoff is larger, he will increase C_1 still more on the next trial. If the resulting average payoff is smaller, he will try an adjustment in the opposite direction, i.e., will adopt $C_1'' < C_1$. In this way, he goes through a search procedure which will ultimately carry him to an optimal value of C_1 (given a specified constant value of C_2). This value will be optimal in the sense that it will correspond to at least a local maximum in the average payoff accruing to player 1.

In the meantime, player 2 will be going through the same procedure. We would expect that this type of search-and-fix adjustment would carry both C_1 and C_2 to zero. Let us show this formally. Call the expected payoff of the two players respectively G_1 and G_2. Then, in view of the payoffs R, T, S, and P associated with the four states, we have the following equations:[23]

$$G_1 = (CC)R + (CD)S + (DC)T + (DD)P, \qquad (69)$$

$$G_2 = (CC)R + (CD)T + (DC)S + (DD)P. \qquad (70)$$

In these equations the four states now represent *instantaneous probabilities*, not overall frequencies. Since in the absence of communication, we must assume the responses of the two players *at a given moment* to be independent, we may equate CC to $(C_1)(C_2)$, CD to $(C_1)(D_2)$, etc.

To find an extremum, we take the partial derivatives of G_1 and G_2 with respect to C_1 and C_2 respectively. This gives, in view of the fact that $D_i = 1 - C_i$,

$$\frac{\partial G_1}{\partial C_1} = (R - T)C_2 + (S - P)D_2, \qquad (71)$$

$$\frac{\partial G_2}{\partial C_2} = (R - T)C_1 + (S - P)D_1. \qquad (72)$$

But by definition of Prisoner's Dilemma, $R < T$ and $S < P$. Hence the partial derivatives are negative for all positive values of $C_i (i = 1,2)$, and so this "adjustment model" must lead to the stable result $C_1 = C_2 = 0$, i.e., to the persistence of the DD state.

The situation is different if the *conditional* probabilities (the propensities) are adjustable. Already the simplest yields an interesting result instead of a trivial one.

Consider two subjects with propensities x_1 and x_2 between o and 1, while $y_1 = y_2 = z_1 = z_2 = 0$; $w_1 = w_2 = 1$. We are again dealing with our two tempted simpletons (cf. p. 73). For simplicity of computation, we shall suppose that they are playing a game in which $S = -T$, $P = -R$ (e.g., Games III, IV or V of our experiments). From Equations (54)-(57), we now have the following expected payoffs:

$$G_1 = \frac{Rx_1x_2 + T(x_2 - x_1)}{2 + x_1 + x_2 - 3x_1x_2}, \tag{73}$$

$$G_2 = \frac{Rx_1x_2 + T(x_1 - x_2)}{2 + x_1 + x_2 - 3x_1x_2}. \tag{74}$$

The partial derivatives of G_1 and G_2 with respect to x_1 and x_2 respectively are:

$$\frac{\partial G_1}{\partial x_1} = \frac{x_2^2(3T + R) + 2x_2(R - T) - 2T}{(2 + x_1 + x_2 - 3x_1x_2)^2}, \tag{75}$$

$$\frac{\partial G_2}{\partial x_2} = \frac{x_1^2(3T + R) + 2x_1(R - T) - 2T}{(2 + x_1 + x_2 - 3x_1x_2)^2}. \tag{76}$$

If an equilibrium exists, it must be where the numerators of both expressions (75) and (76) vanish. Both the numerators[24] represent the same parabola, which crosses the horizontal axis at

$$x = x^* = \frac{T - R \pm \sqrt{R^2 + 7T^2}}{3T + R}. \tag{77}$$

For this value to have meaning in our context, we must have $0 \le x \le 1$. Hence only the positive square roots need to be considered. Furthermore, we must have:[25]

$$T - R + \sqrt{7T^2 + R^2} \le 3T + R, \tag{78}$$

$$7T^2 + R^2 \leq [2(T + R)]^2, \qquad (79)$$

$$7T^2 + R^2 \leq 4T^2 + 8TR + 4R^2, \qquad (80)$$

$$3T^2 - 8TR - 3R^2 \leq 0. \qquad (81)$$

Inequality (81) holds if and only if $T \leq 3R$.

Our first conclusion, therefore, is that an equilibrium state will exist between 0 and 1 if and only if $T \leq 3R$.[26]

Next we observe that this equilibrium value of x^* is the larger, the larger the magnitude of T. To see this, differentiate (77) partially with respect to T:

$$\frac{\partial x^*}{\partial T} = \frac{4RQ + 7RT - 3R^2}{Q} \qquad (82)$$

where we have denoted $\sqrt{7T^2 + R^2}$ by Q. Since $7RT > 3R^2$, $\partial x^*/\partial T > 0$.

It seems strange at first that the equilibrium value of x^* should increase with T inasmuch as we intuitively associate larger values of T with *smaller* frequencies of cooperative responses, while the latter increase with both x_1 and x_2. A closer look at the nature of the equilibrium dispels our doubts concerning the intuitive acceptability of this result. Observe that the equilibrium obtains where the parabola represented by the numerators of expressions (75) and (76) has its *larger* root (cf. Figure 27). Moreover, the parabola is concave upward, since the coefficient of its squared term is positive. It follows that as, say, x_1 increases to a value larger than x^*, the partial derivative $\partial G_1/\partial x_1$ becomes positive and the conditional probability x_1 is adjusted to a still larger value. Mutatis mutandis, if x_1 falls below x^*, $\partial G_1/\partial x_1$ becomes negative, and so the parameter will be adjusted to a still lower value. Hence, not homeostasis but a positive feedback is operating in this system. The equilibrium at x^* is unstable and cannot persist. The value x^* is, in fact, a

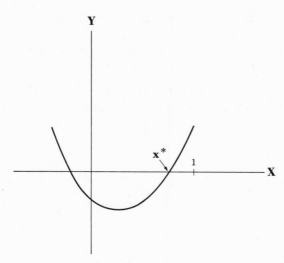

Figure 27. The parabola $y = (3T + R)X^2 + 2X(R - T) - 2T$, where $T < 3R$.

point on a "watershed" in $(x_1 x_2)$-space. When x_1 and x_2 fall short of this watershed, they tend to become smaller: the system tends toward noncooperation. If x_1 and x_2 pass over the "hump," they will tend to become still larger: the system will tend toward cooperation.

Now it is clear why x^* increases with T. The larger the temptation, the more it takes to push the system "over the hump" toward increasing cooperation. If $T > 3R$, it is altogether impossible to do so. In this case $x^* > 1$, hence it is nonexistent as a probability, and the system will go toward noncooperation whatever are the values of x_1 and x_2.

Note that in this very special case $x_1 = x_2 = 0$, $C_1 = C_2 = \frac{1}{2}$. This can be seen from Equations (54) and (57). The reason for this is the high value of w ($w = 1$), which insures that every time our two simpletons find themselves in the DD state, they cooperate on the next play. The restriction was applied solely in the interest of simplifying the mathematics, since we are using this model for illustrative purposes only.

In summary, we have described a model which generates a "Richardson Effect," i.e., an unstable situation in which both the tendency to cooperate and to defect are "self-propelling," governed by a positive feedback.

Chapter 9
Stochastic Learning Models

THE BASIC ASSUMPTION underlying this class of models, developed by Estes (1950), Bush and Mosteller (1955), is that the probability of a response changes by an increment (positive or negative) which is a linear function of the response probability, namely

$$p(t + 1) = \alpha p(t) + (1 - \alpha)\lambda, \quad 1 \geq \alpha, \quad \curlyvee \geq 0. \quad (83)$$

The right-hand side of (83) is viewed as an operator acting upon $p(t)$. Clearly, this operator is determined by two parameters, α and λ.[27] The magnitude of these parameters depends on the outcome of the response. In particular, if the outcome is "rewarding" to the subjects we may have $\lambda = 1$, in which case $p(t)$ will tend toward 1 (certainly) as the response is repeated. That is to say, the response will be ultimately fixated. If the outcome is "punishing," we may have $\lambda = 0$, in which case the response will become extinguished. Intermediate values of λ are also possible, in which case the probability of the response in question will tend to some limiting value ($0 \leq p \leq 1$). The rate of learning is reflected in α. The smaller the magnitude of this parameter, the more quickly $p(t)$ will approach its limiting value. In the extreme cases, if $\alpha = 0$, the limiting value of λ is reached at once; if $\alpha = 1$, $p(t)$ remains constant.

If there are two choices of response, we need to consider only one probability, for the other is clearly the complement. However, if each choice leads to a different outcome, there will be generally two operators, each associated with one of the outcomes. Both operators may be affecting $p(t)$ in the same direction. For example, both the success associated with the "correct" choice and the failure associated with the "wrong" choice may cause $p(t)$, the probability of the correct response to increase, but the rates of increase may be different. For example, the effect of rewarding the correct response may be greater than the effect of punishing the wrong response or vice versa.

The outcome of the subject's response may not be unique. Suppose for example that each of his responses is sometimes rewarded and sometimes punished, the probabilities of the rewards and punishments being fixed for each response. If the rewards can be reduced to a common utility scale, then the "rational solution" of the problem (essentially a decision under risk) is always to make the choice associated with the greatest expected gain. However, the subject (especially if he is not human) may be ignorant of rational decision theory or the rewards may not be reducible to a common utility scale. In this case, it is conceivable that neither response will be either fixated or extinguished.

A subject playing Prisoner's Dilemma has two choices of response (C or D). Each of these choices may result in two outcomes. For player 1, C may result in R (if CC occurs) or in S (if CD occurs). For player 2, C may result in R (if CC occurs) or in S (if DC occurs), and similarly for D. Associated with each player, therefore, we have four operators acting on the probability of cooperative response. Thus, assuming $i = 1$ or 2,

$$C_i(t + 1) = \alpha_i^{(1)} C_i(t) + (1 - \alpha_i^{(1)}) \lambda_i^{(1)}, \qquad (84)$$
$$\text{if } CC \text{ occurs;}$$

$$C_i(t + 1) = \alpha_i^{(2)} C_i(t) + (1 - \alpha_i^{(2)}) \lambda_i^{(2)}, \qquad (85)$$

$$\text{if } CD \text{ occurs, when } i = 1 \text{ or}$$
$$\text{if } DC \text{ occurs, when } i = 2;$$

$$C_i(t + 1) = \alpha_i^{(3)}C_i(t) + (1 - \alpha_i^{(3)})\lambda_i^{(3)}, \tag{86}$$

if *DC* occurs, when $i = 1$ or
if *CD* occurs, when $i = 2$;

$$C_i(t + 1) = \alpha_i^{(4)}C_i(t) + (1 - \alpha_i^{(4)})\lambda_i^{(4)}, \tag{87}$$

if *DD* occurs.

Note that C is affected whatever the outcome. This is in consequence of the fact that whenever D is reinforced or inhibited, C is also necessarily inhibited or reinforced, since $C = 1 - D$.

This model, then, contains eight parameters associated with each player or sixteen associated with each pair.

The model can be simplified if we make some commonsense assumptions based on observations. For example, we suspect that the *CC* response is fixated if it is repeated sufficiently many times (at least in the Matrix conditions). Thus we can set $\lambda_i^{(1)} = 1$. Similarly, in view of the virtual extinction of the unilateral cooperative responses, we can set $\lambda_i^{(2)} = 0$.

Successful defection also inhibits the cooperative response. Hence we can set $\lambda_i^{(3)} = 0$. With respect to $\lambda_i^{(4)}$, we are not sure. On the one hand *DD* is a punishing state, so that one might suppose that it would inhibit D (reinforce C) whenever it occurs. On the other hand in the special context of Prisoner's Dilemma, *DD* may be self-enhancing, since it indicates to each player that the other is not to be trusted. We therefore should leave the magnitude of $\lambda_i^{(4)}$ undetermined a priori.

This simplification leaves us with ten parameters, namely $\alpha_i^{(j)}$ ($i = 1, 2; j = 1, \ldots 4$), $\lambda_1^{(4)}$ and $\lambda_2^{(4)}$.

Stochastic Learning Model Superimposed upon the Four-State Markov Chain

As has already been pointed out, the basic idea of the stochastic learning model is that probabilities of responses become modified in a specific way as a result of the responses themselves, whereby the outcome resulting from the response determines the operator acting on the probability in question. In the previous section we have assumed that the probabilities being modified are the unconditional probabilities of cooperative response. We can, however, assume another point of view, namely, that the probabilities being modified are the conditional propensities. If we suppose these to be the state-conditioned propensities x, y, z, and w, then our stochastic learning model expands into the following system of equations:

$$x_i(t + 1) = \alpha_{i1}^{(jk)} x_i(t) + (1 - \alpha_{i1}^{(jk)}) \lambda_{i1}^{(jk)}, \qquad (88)$$

$$y_i(t + 1) = \alpha_{i2}^{(jk)} y_i(t) + (1 - \alpha_{i2}^{(jk)}) \lambda_{i2}^{(jk)}, \qquad (89)$$

$$z_i(t + 1) = \alpha_{i3}^{(jk)} z_i(t) + (1 - \alpha_{i3}^{(jk)}) \lambda_{i3}^{(jk)}, \qquad (90)$$

$$w_i(t + 1) = \alpha_{i4}^{(jk)} w_i(t) + (1 - \alpha_{i4}^{(jk)}) \lambda_{i4}^{(jk)}, \qquad (91)$$

$(i = 1, 2; j, k = 1, \ldots 4)$.

We recall that the operator is determined by the outcome resulting from the last response. In this model the outcome is associated not with a state (like CC) but with a transition from one state to another (as $CC \rightarrow CD$). There are sixteen such transitions, and they are designated in our equations by the double superscripts (jk), where both indices range over the four states.

Thus the system (88)-(91) involves 256 parameters. However, as in the preceding case, we can make some simplifying assumptions. Suppose, for example, the propensity x is affected by experience only if the corresponding transition has just occurred, i.e., only if the transition has been from CC to one of the four states. This is tantamount to setting $\alpha_{ij}^{(jk)} = 1$ for all $j \neq 1$.

We can therefore write

$$x_1(t + 1) = \alpha_{11}^{(k)} x_1(t) + (1 - \alpha_{11}^{(k)}) \lambda_{11}^{(k)} \quad (k = 1 \ldots 4), \qquad (92)$$

$$x_2(t + 1) = \alpha_{21}^{(k)} x_2(t) + (1 - \alpha_{21}^{(k)}) \lambda_{21}^{(k)} \quad (k = 1 \ldots 4). \qquad (93)$$

We can make a similar assumption with regard to the other propensities. This simplification reduces the number of parameters from 256 to 64. We can further reduce the number to 32 if we assume as we did previously that the propensities tend to be either fixated or extinguished, i.e., the parameters λ are either equal to 1 or to 0.

For example, if *CC* were followed only by *CC*, we might expect this transition to be fixated. According to this assumption, we would set $\lambda_{11}^{(1)} = 1$.

On the other hand, if *CC* were always followed by *CD*, we would expect the *C* response following *CC* to be extinguished, both because it would be punishing for the cooperator and because the *D* response would be rewarding to the defector. (Note that the "higher order effects" are being ignored, for example the effect of retaliation for defecting from the *CC* response.) If *CC* is followed by *DD*, this might tend to fixate *x* (the cooperative response following *CC*), since *DD* is punishing for both players.

If we are guided only by these considerations, i.e., whether the immediate response is punished or rewarded, we may reduce all the λ's to either 1 or 0 on the basis of the following assumptions:

(1) If the payoff was positive and remained the same in the succeeding play, the corresponding propensity tends toward fixation.

(2) If the payoff was improved, the corresponding propensity tends to fixation.

(3) If the payoff was worsened, the corresponding propensity tends to extinction.

(4) If the payoff was negative and remained the same, the corresponding propensity tends to extinction.

All of these seem to us to be reasonable hypotheses with two exceptions. According to (4) above, the *D* responses following *DD* when transition $DD \rightarrow DD$

has occurred should be inhibited, since the payoff is negative and remains constant. However, this assumption seems to be contradicted by some of our data. In many cases prolonged sequences of DD seem to enhance the fixation of that response (cf. Chapter 11). The other exception is the transition from DC to CC from the standpoint of player 1. In this transition, player 1's payoff is reduced from T to R. However, assuming some insight into the nature of the game, the shift from D to C by player 1 might have been motivated by "repentance," i.e., by a decision to cooperate in response to the other's unilateral cooperation. If the outcome is CC, it may well be interpreted as rewarding, not punishing, by player 1, in spite of the reduced payoff. If we leave both of these cases open, then the parameters $\lambda_{43}^{(1)}$ and $\lambda_{44}^{(4)}$ cannot be set equal to zero as our assumption (3) above implies and must be left as free parameters. There are thus thirty-six parameters remaining in the simplified stochastic learning model, in which the state-conditioned propensities x, y, z, and w are subject to learning.

The test of this model would involve prodigious calculations. It would be ill-advised to undertake this work in the early stages of constructing a theory. A more promising strategy is to test some models which purport to describe gross features of the situation instead of attempting to determine the fine structure of the process.

Chapter 10
Classical Dynamic Models

CLASSICAL DYNAMIC MODELS are those which are appropriate for describing the behavior of deterministic dynamic systems. The best-known examples of these are the systems examined in celestial mechanics and those related to electromagnetic phenomena. Typically, events of this sort are described by systems of second order ordinary or partial differential equations.[28] Chemical systems, on the other hand, can be frequently described by first order ordinary differential equations, since in these systems the reaction rates (rates of change of concentrations) are directly related to the concentrations of the various reacting substances and of the catalysts. All systems so described are typically deterministic in the sense that a set of initial conditions and the parameters of the equations determine the fate of such a system for all time.

In behavioral science, the present trend is away from deterministic models. The trend is well justified in view of the recognition that it is all but impossible to specify initial conditions and the laws of behavior so exactly as to predict the behavior of a living system for any significant length of time. Stochastic models have been put forward as more appropriate in behavioral contexts. Nevertheless, much can be learned by casting a behavioral situation into a deterministic model. This is done not so much with the view of finding deterministic models adequate for the behavioral systems to be described as for the purpose of revealing some general features of the situation.

Nevertheless, the predictive potential of deterministic models is not always to be discounted in behavioral science. It is sometimes considerable if the behaving systems are large enough. For example, the time course of C averaged in a very large population sample playing a Prisoner's Dilemma game may very well be "determined" in the sense that it could be accurately replicated by another large sample from the same population playing the same game. There is thus a curve describing the time course and therefore a set of dynamic laws from which the equation of the curve can be derived. What one must guard against is jumping to the conclusion that one has discovered *the* dynamic laws once a successful derivation has been made. A corroboration of a model never proves that the model represents reality but only that it can be *taken* to represent the phenomenon studied.

In the models to be presently constructed, we shall not seek an adequate representation of our data, let alone definitive dynamic laws. We merely wish to investigate the consequences of certain assumptions concerning a *possible* dynamic underlying the Prisoner's Dilemma game.

Classical dynamic models are usually represented in the form of systems of differential equations, in which the independent variable is time and the dependent variables are the quantities whose time courses determine the sequence of states through which the system in question passes. Our independent variable will also be time, which is here assumed to be measured by the number of elapsed plays of a game (or games). For our dependent variables we can take either the unconditional propensities for cooperative response, that is C_1 and C_2, or the conditional propensities, x_i, y_i, z_i, w_i. In the former case, we shall speak of first order dynamic models; in the latter case, of second order dynamic models. These models will be either dynamic extensions of the equilibrium models examined in Chapter 8 or deterministic versions of stochastic models examined in Chapter 9.

Recall that in the equilibrium model each subject was assumed to adjust some variable so as to maximize his expected gain. When the adjusted variables are C_1 and C_2, the model leads to the counter-intuitive "strategic" solution of Prisoner's Dilemma, namely to eventual one hundred percent noncooperation (cf. p. 130). We therefore already know where a dynamic extension of this model will lead. We shall, accordingly, bypass this version and pass directly to a deterministic version of the stochastic model. In the stochastic model C_1 and C_2 undergo modifications which result not from attempts to maximize expected gains but rather from immediate reactions to the outcomes. Thus C_1 suffers a positive increment following the outcome C_1C_2, etc. In the classical version the same thing happens. But now the process is described by a deterministic system of differential equations, namely

$$dC_1/dt =$$
$$\alpha_1 C_1 C_2 - \beta_1 C_1(1 - C_2) - \gamma_1 C_2(1 - C_1) + \delta_1(1 - C_1)(1 - C_2),$$
$$(94)$$

$$dC_2/dt =$$
$$\alpha_2 C_1 C_2 - \beta_2 C_2(1 - C_1) - \gamma_2 C_1(1 - C_2) + \delta_2(1 - C_2)(1 - C_1),$$
$$(95)$$

where α_i, β_i, and γ_i are positive constants. The sign of δ_i, however, is ambivalent.

The terms on the right-hand side of (94) and (95) are interpreted as follows. The term involving α_i represents the positive contribution to dC_1/dt due to a double-cooperative outcome. The term involving β_i represents the negative contribution due to an unreciprocated cooperation. The terms involving γ_i represent the negative contribution due to successful defection. As for δ_i, we are not sure of the sign of its contribution. On the one hand, the punished defection may contribute to an increase in the probability of cooperative choices; but on the other hand, repeated double defections may contribute to increased distrust and so may have the opposite effect. Accordingly, the sign of δ_i will remain ambivalent.[29]

Systems like (94) and (95) are frequently studied by means of the so-called phase space. In our case, the coordinates of this space are C_1 and C_2. At each point (C_1, C_2) the magnitudes of dC_1/dt and of dC_2/dt are represented by a vector. One can imagine a particle moving with a velocity whose horizontal and vertical components are represented by the components of that vector, namely dC_1/dt and dC_2/dt. The motion of the particle reflects the time courses of C_1 and C_2 and hence the dynamics of the system.

Let us arbitrarily set $\alpha_i = \gamma_i = 1$; $\beta_i = 2$; $\delta_i = 1$. This reduces Equations (94) and (95) to

$$dC_1/dt = 5C_1C_2 - 3C_1 - 2C_2 + 1, \qquad (96)$$

$$dC_2/dt = 5C_1C_2 - 2C_1 - 3C_2 + 1. \qquad (97)$$

It is apparent that there are two equilibrium points. In fact, these can be obtained directly by setting the right-hand side of Equations (96) and (97) equal to zero and solving for C_1 and C_2.[30] The equilibria turn out to be at

$$C_1 = C_2 = \frac{5 + \sqrt{5}}{10} \text{ and at } C_1 = C_2 = \frac{5 - \sqrt{5}}{10}. \qquad (98)$$

Moreover, it is easily inferred from the appearance of the phase space that the lower equilibrium is stable while the upper one is unstable. Once C_1 and C_2 become sufficiently large, they are driven into the upper right-hand corner of the phase space where $C_1 = C_2 = 1$. Otherwise the C's are driven toward the stable equilibrium point. In other words, this model (with the values of parameters as chosen) predicts that if the players cooperate sufficiently frequently initially, they will eventually lock-in on cooperation. If the initial frequencies of cooperative choices are not large enough, the players will still show a residual amount of co-operation (at the lower equilibrium). The reason for the latter result is not far to seek. Our assumption is that $\delta > 0$ keeps "scaring" the players away from *DD*.

The picture looks different if $\delta < 0$. We now arbitrarily set $\alpha_i = 4; \beta_i = 3; \gamma_i = 2; \delta_i = -1$. Equations (94) and (95) now become

$$dC_1/dt = 8C_1C_2 - 2C_1 - C_2 - 1, \tag{99}$$

$$dC_2/dt = 8C_1C_2 - C_1 - 2C_2 - 1. \tag{100}$$

Now there is only one equilibrium in the region bounded by the unit square, which is the region where C_1 and C_2 have meanings as probabilities. From the appearance of the phase space, we see that here the all-or-nothing Richardson Effect is operating: C_1 and C_2 will be either driven toward 1 or toward 0.

In general if $\alpha_1 = \alpha_2, \beta_1 = \beta_2, \gamma_1 = \gamma_2, \delta_1 = \delta_2$ equilibria will lie on the line $C_1 = C_2$. Let us see how their nature depends on the parameters. We obtain the equilibria by setting dC_1/dt and dC_2/dt equal to zero; this reduces the right-hand side of (94) to

$$F(C) \equiv (\alpha + \beta + \gamma + \delta)C^2 - (\beta + \gamma + 2\delta)C + \delta. \tag{101}$$

The quadratic polynomial has real roots if

$$(\beta + \gamma + 2\delta)^2 \geq 4\delta(\alpha + \beta + \gamma + \delta), \tag{102}$$

which upon expansion and simplification, reduces to

$$(\beta + \gamma)^2 \geq 4\alpha\delta. \tag{103}$$

In summary, we have the following results:

(1) If $\delta > 0$ and if $(\beta + \gamma)^2 < 4\alpha\delta$, the system will be driven unconditionally toward full cooperation;

(2) If $\delta > 0$ and $(\beta + \gamma)^2 > 4\alpha\delta$, then, depending on the initial value of C, the system will be either driven toward complete cooperation or will be stabilized at a certain positive value of $C_1 = C_2$;

(3) If $\delta < 0$, then, depending on the initial value of C, the system will be driven either toward full cooperation or toward full defection.[31]

The method can, of course, be extended to the general case where the parameters of the two players are not the same, but we shall not pursue this generalization here.

A Simplest Second Order Model

By a second order model we mean one where the principal variables are not the probabilities of cooperative choice but the *contingent* probabilities, such as x, y, z, and w. We shall consider the simplest case where $y_i = z_i = 0$; $w_i = 1$ ($i = 1, 2$), so that only x_1 and x_2 are variable. This is the case of the two tempted simpletons (cf. p. 73). We have already examined the statics of that situation. Now let us consider the dynamics.

Suppose the simpletons adjust their x's at a rate proportional to the *gradient* of the expected gain. In other words, if increasing x_1 results in a large positive change in the expected gain of player 1, then he will increase x_1 rapidly; if x_1 results in a small negative change in the expected gain, he will decrease x_1 slowly, etc.

Formally, we represent this by the following equations:

$$\frac{dx_1}{dt} = k_1 \frac{\partial G_1}{\partial x_1}, \tag{104}$$

$$\frac{dx_2}{dt} = k_2 \frac{\partial G_2}{\partial x_2}, \tag{105}$$

where k_1 and k_2 are constants. Substituting for $\partial G_1/\partial x_1$ and $\partial G_2/\partial x_2$ the expressions derived earlier (cf. p. 132), we have, assuming $P = -R$,

$$\frac{dx_1}{dt} = k_1 \frac{x_2^2(3T + R) + 2x_2(R - T) - 2T}{(2 + x_1 + x_2 - 3x_1x_2)^2}, \tag{106}$$

$$\frac{dx_2}{dt} = k_2 \frac{x_1^2(3T + R) + 2x_1(R - T) - 2T}{(2 + x_1 + x_2 - 3x_1x_2)^2}. \tag{107}$$

Equations (106) and (107) constitute the dynamics of the system.

The numerators of the right sides of Equations (106) and (107) represent the same parabola, and the denominators are always positive. Hence the signs of dx_1/dt and dx_2/dt are determined entirely by the signs of the numerators. If $T < 3R$ the parabola has a single root in the unit interval, namely (cf. p. 133)

$$x = \frac{T - R + \sqrt{R^2 + 7T^2}}{3T + R} = x^*. \tag{108}$$

Therefore the unit square is divided into four quadrants, in which the signs of the derivatives are as follows:

where $x_1 > x^*$; $x_2 > x^*$, $dx_1/dt > 0$; $dx_2/dt > 0$;

where $x_1 > x^*$; $x_2 < x^*$, $dx_1/dt < 0$; $dx_2/dt > 0$;

where $x_1 < x^*$; $x_2 > x^*$, $dx_1/dt > 0$; $dx_2/dt < 0$;

where $x_1 < x^*$; $x_2 < x^*$, $dx_1/dt < 0$; $dx_2/dt < 0$.

Figure 28 shows a schematic representation of this dynamic system.

Once the motion of a point in (x_1, x_2) space is determined, the motion of a point in (C_1, C_2) space is also determined, since every pair of values (x_1, x_2) "maps" upon a pair of values (C_1, C_2) according to Equations (24) and (25). The model is deterministic with respect to the motion of a point in (C_1, C_2) space. However, the position of a point (C_1, C_2) does not determine a particular outcome, since in the present context C_1 and C_2 are only probabilities of choosing C. At most a pair of probabilities (C_1, C_2) determine the corresponding frequencies in a population of "identical players." Recall, however, that we have assumed that x_1 and x_2 are adjusted with reference to corresponding expected payoffs, i.e., with reference to C_1 and C_2 viewed as probabilities.

How these probabilities are *instantaneously* estimated by the players is an embarrassing question for the theory.

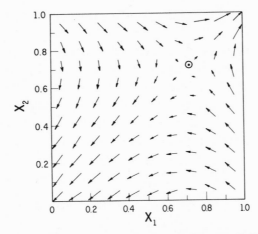

Figure 28. The dynamics of playing Prisoner's Dilemma by adjusting x so as to maximize expected gain. For purely esthetic reasons the game represented here was chosen as the limiting case where $R = T$. Also $P = -R$ and $S = -T$. The fixed parameters are $y = z = 0$; $w = 1$.

The circled point represents the (unstable) equilibrium at $x_1 = x_2 = x^* = \sqrt{2}/2$, which obtains in this case. If the initial values of x_1 and x_2 are the coordinates of the tail of any of the arrows, the direction of the arrow represents the direction of motion of the point (x_1, x_2) while the length of the arrow represents the speed of the motion. Thus the line inclined 135° to the horizontal drawn through the equilibrium represents a "watershed." All the motion above and to the right of this watershed will be toward the upper right-hand corner $(x_1 = x_2 = 1)$, and all the motion below and to the left will be toward the lower left-hand corner $(x_1 = x_2 = 0)$.

After all, the players do not have access to a "population of identical players," in which the probabilities can be observed as frequencies.

The only possible way in which the adjustment model can be realized in practice is for the players to make their adjustment extremely slowly, waiting until the values accruing to them become good estimates of their expected payoffs before making the next adjustment. This involves waiting until each new equilibrium is established (i.e., the steady state determined by the Markov chain involving the newly adjusted value of x) and then waiting until the steady state has been maintained long enough to estimate the new expected payoff. During all this time, moreover, the player must remember the average payoff determined by the value of x used previously, in order to compare it with the present value, so as to know in which direction the next adjustment should be made. In the meantime the other player must bide his time until it is his turn to go through this process.[32]

When we recall that all this insures the adjustment of only one pair of parameters, not four pairs contained in the general model of this type, we see even more clearly the tremendous gap that separates a formal model from what can be reasonably expected in "real life," and "real life" in this case denotes only the laboratory situation, not real "real life."

The situation would be utterly discouraging if one expected the models to be faithful replicas of behavior. The purpose of all models, however, is, or ought to be, quite different. Every model can be expected to represent reality only in an "as if" fashion. The goal of the theoretician working with mathematical models in behavioral science ought to be not detailed prediction but an understanding of what is involved in the phenomenon in question. An understanding is achieved by examining the salient features of the models, then searching for these features (or, perhaps, noting their absence) in what is observed. Thus, a vitally important feature of the model in which state-conditioned propensities are adjusted is the Richardson Effect. The lock-in phenomenon observed in the data seems to be also a manifestation of a similar effect. The problem before us now is to demonstrate the reality of the effect (or to refute it) under various conditions, to search for its psychological underpinnings, etc. The various models serve here as ways of viewing the behavioral situation. A good model is one which suggests ways of bringing out important features of the situation not hitherto considered or understood. Every mathematical model in behavioral science should serve as a point of departure for investigations, not as a conclusive formulation of a theory.

Summary of Part II

We have proposed a number of models, some stochastic, some deterministic of the sort of process which may be governed by the interactions of two players playing Prisoner's Dilemma. The usefulness of the models in constructing a testable theory of the process is severely limited by the quickly increasing number of parameters which must be estimated in order to compare the predictions of the models with empirical results. Nevertheless, an important feature of the experimental results already emerges in some of the models, namely the lock-in effect which drives the players to either of the extremes. This lock-in effect is explicitly built into some of the models we have proposed, for example, the stochastic models with absorbing states. In other models, however, this effect is a consequence of certain assumptions, for example, that players adjust their propensities of response as a result of experience. Even though the specific assumptions of the parameter-adjusting model (namely that the "system" passes through contiguous equilibria as in a reversible thermodynamic process) are not plausible, it is not unlikely that the effect is also a consequence of more general assumptions.

Part III

Discussion and Projection

Chapter 11
Testing the Models

A TEST OF A MATHEMATICAL MODEL is made when the predictions of the model are compared with observed results. When data are quantified, results are obtained as numbers. The model, however, as a rule, predicts the results in the form of mathematical expressions involving variables and parameters. These are designated by letters, not numbers. The expressions are evaluated as numbers when specific values are assigned to the letters. These letters stand for two kinds of quantities, *variables* and *parameters*.

In the classical formula for the distance passed by a falling body, $s = at^2$, t, i.e., time, the independent variable, is given a value, which determines the value of s, i.e., the distance fallen, provided a is also given. The latter quantity is a parameter. Its value is, as a rule, not known when the formula is derived. Therefore, a test of the formula can be put in the form of a question of the following sort: "Of all the parabolas of the form $s = at^2$ (every value of a determines a particular parabola) is there one which fits the observed plot of s against t? If so, what is the value of a which determines it?"

Note that two questions are involved. The first one asks whether the data *can be made* consistent with the theory. We say "can be made consistent," not "are consistent," because in our parameter we still have a degree of freedom left. We *seek* a parabola to fit our data. The second question provides further theoretical leverage. If under different conditions the values of a (which give a fitting parabola) are different, we can go on to the next order of questions, namely on what does a itself depend. For example, if the experiments with falling bodies are performed on inclined planes, a will depend on the inclination of the plane. Specifically $a = \frac{1}{2}g \sin \alpha$, where α is the angle which the plane makes with the plumbline and g is another parameter, which, in turn depends on the geographical location and the altitude of the experimental site. Thus, the investigation need not end with a corroboration of the proposed mathematical model. Corroboration is obtained when the value(s) of the parameter(s) is (are) found which effect agreement between the theoretical formula and the data. But this opens the road to the further development of the theory, namely an *interpretation* of the parameter(s) and questions concerning their dependence on the conditions of the experiment.

All this makes good sense if the parameters are few and easily interpretable. In the case of bodies falling in vacuum, there is only one parameter and it is easily interpretable as twice the acceleration of the body. If, however, there are several parameters, the situation is not so straight forward. The parameters may not be easily interpreted and even if they are, the further development of the theory may become so involved that hardly any clear understanding emerges from it. Most important, the presence of many parameters leaves many degrees of freedom in fitting the theoretical formula to the data. Given enough parameters, the theoretical curve can be "twisted" to fit almost any set of data. But then, many other theoretical curves involving the same number of parameters can be made to fit the same set of data, and so the theory is left ambivalent.

In some of our models of Prisoner's Dilemma we find ourselves in situations of this sort. For example, the "full dress" stochastic learning model of the second order, that is, applied to the state-conditioned propensities, x, y, z, and w involves, as we have seen, 256 independent parameters. Aside from the almost impossible task of estimating this number of parameters from a given set of data, it is probably the case that a set of values can *always* be found to fit the data on hand, because of the tremendous number of degrees of freedom. But there may be a very large number of such sets of values which will give equally good fits. And even if we were able to select the "best" set of values, we would be powerless to continue the development of the theory, i.e., to investigate the dependence of every one of the 256 parameters on experimental conditions, which is the standard next step in a theoretical investigation instigated by a mathematical model.

Therefore, when we speak here of "testing our models," we do not mean it in the strict sense of corroboration or refutation, except in those instances when we shall be in a position to refute a model definitively. We shall go only part of the way in putting some models to tests. Our goal will be to gain some understanding of what *may* be happening in repeated plays of Prisoner's Dilemma. In short, the main purpose of the discussion in Part III will be to generate hypotheses rather than to corroborate or refute them.

The "Two Simpletons" Model (Static)

Consider the model of the two tempted simpletons, who are characterized by $y_i = z_i = 0$; $w_i = 1$ and who adjust their x_i so as to maximize expected gain. The formula for the expected gains given in Chapter 8 [cf. Equations (73) and (74)] applies to the simplified case where $S = -T$, $P = -R$. In our games the first of these relations always holds but not the second. To apply the model to our data we therefore need a generalized formula involving three parameters, T, R, and P. The generalized formulae for expected payoffs are given by

$$G_1 = \frac{R + T(x_2 - x_1) + P(1 - x_1 x_2)}{2 - 3x_1 x_2 + x_1 + x_2}, \qquad (109)$$

$$G_2 = \frac{R + T(x_1 - x_2) + P(1 - x_1 x_2)}{2 - 3x_1 x_2 + x_1 + x_2}. \qquad (110)$$

Setting $\partial G_1/\partial x_1 = \partial G_2/\partial x_2 = 0$ and solving for x_1 and x_2, we have

$$x_1 = x_2 = x^* = \frac{2T - 3R - P \pm \sqrt{28T^2 + 2RP - 3P^2 + 9R^2}}{6T - 2P}. \qquad (111)$$

Only the larger root has meaning. If $P = -R$, formula (111) reduces to (77) of Chapter 8, as, of course, it should.

Let us now evaluate the right-hand side of (111) for each of our seven games. The result is shown in Table 21.

TABLE 21

Game	x^*
I	.857
II	.980
III	1.14
IV	.912
V	1.20
XI	.989
XII	1.06

According to the theory developed in Chapter 10, x_i should be driven unconditionally toward zero in Games III, V, and XII. In the remaining games there is a threshold value of x, so that x will be driven toward one only if that threshold is exceeded. Unless we know the dynamics of the process, we do not know the actual paths of x_1 and x_2 in the phase space and so cannot say anything about the magnitudes of the average values of these variables. It is reasonable to suppose, however, that the larger the magnitude of x^*, the more quickly and certainly will x be driven toward zero. This conjecture applies even in the cases represented by Games III, V, and XII where x^* exceeds one and hence has no real meaning as an equilibrium. On the basis of this conjecture we would assign the following rank order to the games as the inverse of the rank order of their associated x^* values:

$$I > IV > II > XI > XII > III > V. \qquad (112)$$

But this rank order coincides with that prescribed by our Hypothesis 3 (cf. p. 43).

Therefore the model of the two tempted simpletons who adjust their x's to maximize expected gains can be taken as a model underlying Hypothesis 3.

To be sure, the state-conditioned propensities of the simpletons do not at all correspond to those observed in our subjects. First, the x's of the subjects are practically all large, clustering in the 80's and 90's and this is observed even in the most severe games in which, according to our model, the x's ought to tend toward zero. Further, the y's and z's of our subjects, while not large, are seldom near zero. Finally, the w's of our subjects are consistently low, not equal to 1, as they are assumed in the model. This shows that the model is extremely insensitive to the actual values of the propensities. It does, however, predict the rank order of the games roughly consistent with the observed rank order.

The one discrepancy between the rank order given by (112) and that observed in the Pure Matrix Condition is that involving the rank of Game II, which is observed to be first in the Pure Matrix Condition but ought to be third according to the model. It is natural to conjecture that the reason for this discrepancy is the unrealistically high value of w ($= 1$) assumed in the model.[33]

We wish, therefore, to see what happens at the other extreme, when w is very small. We cannot simply set

$w = 0$, because this would make DD an absorbing state. We can, however, examine the behavior of our system as *w approaches* zero.

As before, we set $y = z = 0$ but now leave w free, assuming $w_1 = w_2 = w$. The steady state Equations (65–68) of Chapter 7 now become

$$CC = \frac{w^2}{(1 - x_1x_2)(1 + 2w - 2w^2) + w^2(1 + x_1 + x_2 - 2x_1x_2)};$$
(113)

$$CD = \frac{w^2x_1(1 - x_2) + (1 - x_1x_2)w(1 - w)}{(1 - x_1x_2)(1 + 2w - 2w^2) + w^2(1 + x_1 + x_2 - 2x_1x_2)};$$
(114)

$$DC = \frac{w^2x_2(1 - x_1) + (1 - x_1x_2)w(1 - w)}{(1 - x_1x_2)(1 + 2w - 2w^2) + w^2(1 + x_1 + x_2 - 2x_1x_2)};$$
(115)

$$DD = \frac{1 - x_1x_2}{(1 - x_1x_2)(1 + 2w - 2w^2) + w^2(1 + x_1 + x_2 - 2x_1x_2)}.$$
(116)

Proceeding exactly as before, we calculate G_1 and G_2 and set $\partial G_1/\partial x_1$ and $\partial G_2/\partial x_2$ equal to zero. The parabola corresponding to that given by Equation (75) now becomes

$$w^2[(T + 2w^2T - P)x^2 + (R + 2Rw + P - 2w^2T)x$$
$$+ (w^2T - 2wT - T - P - w^2R)] = 0. \quad (117)$$

Now we see mathematically, as well as intuitively, why we could not set $w = 0$ at the start. If we did, our "parabola" would disappear. As long as $w \neq 0$, we can divide the left-hand side of (117) by w^2 and so obtain the parabola represented by the expression in the brackets. As a check, observe that if $w = 1$, (117) reduces to the numerator of (75).

After dividing by w, we can set $w = 0$, and (117) reduces to

$$(T - P)x^2 + (R + P)x - (T + P) = 0, \quad (118)$$

whose positive root is

$$x^* = \frac{-(R + P) + \sqrt{(R + P)^2 + 4(T^2 - P^2)}}{2(T - P)}. \qquad (119)$$

Inserting the values of T, R, and P from our game matrices, we obtain the results shown in Table 22.

TABLE 22

Game	x^*
I	.61
II	.52
III	.90
IV	.58
V	.98
XI	.74
XII	.73

Now the rank order of the games is the following:

$$II > IV > I > XII > XI > III > V. \qquad (120)$$

Observe that this rank order is exactly that implied by Hypothesis 4 (cf. Chapter 1, p. 43). Thus, we have provided a model for both of our ad hoc hypotheses, from which we had derived the theoretical rank order of the seven games with respect to C. The model is an extremely simple one, involving a trial-and-error adjustment of *one* of the four state-conditioned propensities by each of the players, the other propensities being assumed fixed. The one or the other hypothesis is a consequence of this model depending on the fixed but arbitrary value of w. If w is large, Hypothesis 3 emerges from the model; if w is small, Hypothesis 4 emerges.

It is interesting to observe that the values of x^* are smaller when w is small than when w is large. In other words, x is more likely to be driven to zero when w is large than when w is small. This seems paradoxical at first, since C is positively related to x, and so we have the apparently anomalous result that two "distrusting" players (with low w) will achieve more cooperation than two "trusting" players (with high w). However, this conclusion is unwarranted. Recall that when $w = 1$, there will be fifty percent cooperation even when $x = 0$. When w is near zero, on the other hand, low values of x will induce very large D's. In the last analysis, therefore, players with low w's will also exhibit low C's, as we would expect.

To the extent that the data are in rough agreement with either hypothesis, they are consistent with the model. However, the model cannot be taken seriously as a good representation of the actual situation. First, the hypothesis which is in better agreement with the data, namely Hypothesis 3, is a consequence of the assumption that w is large, whereas in fact w is small. Second, the model implies that in Game V, at least, x is almost certain to be driven to zero whether w is large or small, and this has never been observed. Finally, as has been already pointed out, the fact that the model is of an equilibrium type gives rise to the extremely unrealistic assumption that the players can calculate their expected gains and adjust their conditional probabilities of response accordingly. It does not help to argue that they learn to do so "intuitively," because to get "intuitive" estimates of expected gains and moreover to compare them with average payoffs obtained from previous values of x would require prodigious "intuitive" memories. Therefore, this type of model has at most a heuristic value. It serves as a stage in the trial-and-error process of constructing a theory.

Evidence Against the Four-State Markov Chain

We could view the mass of data yielded by the twenty-one thousand responses in the Pure Matrix Condition as follows: we have here three hundred consecutive responses by each of seventy pairs playing certain (unspecified) versions of Prisoner's Dilemma. Can the massed data be viewed as a realization of a stochastic process to be accounted for by a four-state Markov model? If it can, we shall say that a "composite subject" is playing a "composite game" and is behaving *as if* he were governed by a four-state Markov chain with such and such parameters. If not, we shall look for sources of errors in our assumptions and attempt to construct another model.

The advantage of this deliberately imposed ignorance (pretending that we know nothing about the different subconditions and subpopulations which comprise our total process) is that we can bring in the refinements gradually and stop when we have a model which will have withstood certain specified tests. No model of a real process can withstand *all* tests, and we do not know at this point how far we should go to test our model. It may turn out that a model which is adequate on a certain level will prove to be already sufficiently fruitful in generating interesting hypotheses to serve as the raw materials of a theory on the next level of complexity. This is our principal aim. All models, however refined, will retain an "as if" character. Therefore the level of refinements should correspond to the level of complexity at which the theory becomes fruitful and still remains tractable.

We start with a crude test of the simple Markov model. Suppose we had a population of players each characterized by the same values of the state-conditioned propensities. Our "average player" in the Pure Matrix Condition has the following profile (cf. Table 9): $x = .84$; $y = .40$; $z = .38$; $w = .20$. How would the time courses of the four states look in a population of this sort if they all started out "neutral," i.e., $CC = CD = DC = DD = \frac{1}{4}$? In particular, how long would it take them to reach the steady state?

To see this, we examine a matrix of transition

probabilities, constructed from the state-conditioned propensities, as was described in Chapter 7. The matrix is shown below.

	CC	CD	DC	DD
CC	.71	.13	.13	.03
CD	.15	.25	.23	.37
DC	.15	.23	.25	.37
DD	.04	.16	.16	.64

Matrix 16.

Next we square the matrix, square the result, etc., thus getting successively the fourth, eighth, sixteenth powers, etc. When the columns of the matrix are all identical, steady state has been reached, for then, as can be easily verified, Equations (61)–(64) reduce to $(CC)' = (CC)$; $(CD)' = (CD)$, etc.

According to this model, we expect the steady state to be reached at about the thirtieth play. Actually, however, as we have seen, the steady state is reached by the combined time course in the Pure Matrix Condition at only about the 150th trial. Moreover, the discrepancy does not substantially depend on the initial distribution of the states. Whatever this distribution is, the steady state will be reached when the columns of the transition probability matrix become identical. This happens when the transition probabilities are of the sort we observe, much sooner than is observed in the data.

There are at least two possible sources of error in our model Markov chain. One is in the fact that we have lumped seventy pairs into a single process. Each of the pairs, in fact each of the individuals, may be characterized by a different set of propensities (even assuming these to be constant for each individual). It is mathematically not the case that when the propensities of the individuals are lumped into an "average" propensity, the resulting process will be a population average of the corresponding individual processes.

Another possible source of error is the assumption that the propensities remain constant in time. There is a straightforward test of this assumption. Consider the length of a run in some particular state, say *CC*. If the probability that following a given state the next state will be *CC* depends only on the given state (which is the assumption to be tested), then the probability that a given run of *CC*'s will be ended at any specific play will be independent of the number of *CC*'s in the run. To put it in another way, the probability that a *CC* run will have "survived" for at least *t* plays will be given by

$$p(t) = e^{-mt}, \tag{121}$$

where *m* is the inverse of the average length of a *CC* run.[34]

Consider the exponent of *e*. It is a linear function of *t*. Consider now a generalized form of the negative exponential function, namely $e^{-f(t)}$, where $f(t)$ is a function which is either concave upward, i.e., has a positive second derivative with respect to *t*, or concave downward, i.e., has a negative second derivative. If $f(t)$ is linear, its second derivative is zero. We can now characterize three types of runs corresponding to the three classes of functions $f(t)$ just described. These are (1) runs which are more likely to be terminated the longer they last (if $f''(t) > 0$); (2) runs which are less likely to be terminated the longer they last (if $f''(t) < 0$); (3) runs which have the same probability of terminating regardless of how long they last (if $f''(t) = 0$). The simple Markov model implies that all runs occurring in the process are of the third type.

We can now see how our runs behave in this respect. Plots of $-\ln p(t)$ against *t* for Games II and V in the

Pure Matrix Condition are shown in Figures 29 and 30.[35] The curves are unquestionably concave downward. Therefore $f(t)$ is of the second type: the longer a *CC* run lasts the less likely it is to terminate. The corresponding

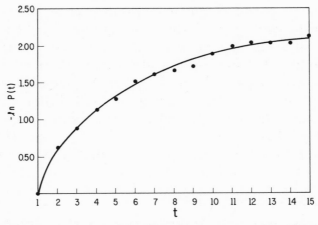

Figure 29. Horizontal: length of *CC* run (t). Vertical: $-\ln p(t)$, where $p(t)$ is the fraction of *CC* runs not yet terminated at t, observed in Game II of the Pure Matrix Condition.

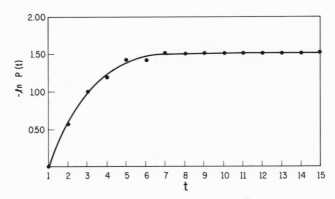

Figure 30. Horizontal: length of *CC* run (t). Vertical: $-\ln p(t)$, where $p(t)$ is the fraction of *CC* runs not yet terminated at t, observed in Game V of the Pure Matrix Condition.

plots of *DD* runs are shown in Figures 31 and 32. The results are similar.

The conclusion that the longer a *CC* run lasts the less likely it is to terminate is an attractive one. It is in accord with our intuitive feeling that continued co-

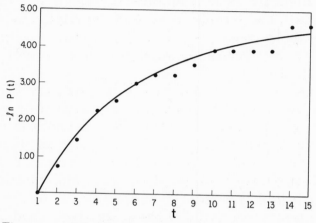

Figure 31. Horizontal: length of *DD* run (*t*). Vertical: −ln *p*(*t*), where *p*(*t*) is the fraction of *DD* runs not yet terminated at *t*, observed in Game II of the Pure Matrix Condition.

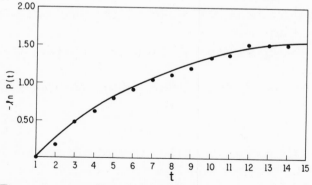

Figure 32. Horizontal: length of *DD* run (*t*). Vertical: −ln *p*(*t*), where *p*(*t*) is the fraction of *DD* runs not yet terminated at *t*, observed in Game V of the Pure Matrix Condition.

operation reinforces the mutual trust of the subjects and so inhibits defection. Likewise, the same conclusion with respect to *DD* runs can be rationalized on the same grounds. Both conclusions are also in harmony with the previously observed lock-in effect (cf. Chapter 3).

Unfortunately, there is another interpretation of this result, which has nothing to do with self-reinforcement of the double cooperative and the double defecting states. This interpretation is an effect akin to the process of natural selection.

Suppose we have a "population" of processes. Each individual process in the population can end with equal probability at any moment of time. But this probability is different in the different individual processes. If we plot the fraction of the processes which have not yet terminated against time, we shall have some function $g(t)$, which we may write $e^{-f(t)}$, where $f(t) = -\log_e g(t)$. We shall now show that $f(t)$ has a negative second derivative. That is to say, $f(t)$ plotted against time is convex upward, and so the combined process gives the appearance of being "self-enhancing"—the longer it lasts, the less likely it is to end. We shall first show this by a formal mathematical argument and then will offer an informal intuitive one.

Consider a population of processes of type 3, i.e., where $f''(t) = 0$.

The probability that a given individual process has not yet terminated at time t is given by

$$p(t) = e^{-\mu t}, \tag{122}$$

where μ is the reciprocal of the expected life span of the process. The parameter μ, therefore, characterizes the "mortality" of the process. The bigger the value of μ the larger the "mortality" or the smaller the "viability."

Now the parameter μ is different for the different processes of our population. Let us assume that this parameter is distributed in accordance with some frequency function $\psi(\mu)$. Then the fraction of the processes in the entire population, which have not yet terminated at time t will be given by

$$\int_0^\infty \psi(\mu)e^{-\mu t}\,d\mu, \tag{123}$$

the function which we have called $g(t)$ or $e^{-f(t)}$. Therefore

$$f(t) = -\log_e\left[\int_0^\infty \psi(\mu)e^{-\mu t}\,d\mu\right]. \tag{124}$$

Let us denote by I the integral (123). Then

$$f'(t) = -\frac{I'}{I}, \tag{125}$$

$$f''(t) = -\frac{(I)(I'') - (I')^2}{I^2}, \tag{126}$$

where the derivatives are with respect to t. We shall have proved our contention if we show that $(I')^2 < (I)(I'')$.

If the frequency distribution $\psi(\mu)$ is reasonably well behaved, differentiation with respect to t can be performed underneath the integral sign. Thus

$$I' = -\int_0^\infty \mu e^{-\mu t}\psi(\mu)\,d\mu, \tag{127}$$

$$(I')^2 = \left[\int_0^\infty \mu e^{-\mu t}\psi(\mu)\,d\mu\right]^2, \tag{128}$$

$$I'' = \int_0^\infty \mu^2 e^{-\mu t}\psi(\mu)\,d\mu. \tag{129}$$

Our inequality can now be written as

$$\left[\int_0^\infty \mu e^{-\mu t}\psi(\mu)\,d\mu\right]^2$$
$$< \left[\int_0^\infty e^{-\mu t}\psi(\mu)\,d\mu\right]\left[\int_0^\infty \mu^2 e^{-\mu t}\psi(\mu)\,d\mu\right]. \tag{130}$$

Now on the right side of (130) we have in the two brackets the averages of $e^{-\mu t}$ and of $\mu^2 e^{-\mu t}$ respectively with respect to the distribution function $\psi(\mu)$. Moreover, the functions $e^{-\mu t}$ and $\mu^2 e^{-\mu t}$ have only nonnegative values. We can therefore assert that

$$\left[\int_0^\infty e^{-\mu t}\,\psi(\mu)\,d\mu\right]\left[\int_0^\infty \mu^2 e^{-\mu t}\,\psi(\mu)\,d\mu\right]$$
$$\geq \int_0^\infty \mu^2 e^{-2\mu t}\,\psi(\mu)\,d\mu,\quad (131)$$

by virtue of the fact that the product of the averages of two functions assuming only nonnegative values is at least as great as the average of the product. We can therefore say that if inequality

$$\left[\int_0^\infty \mu e^{-\mu t}\,\psi(\mu)\,d\mu\right]^2 < \int_0^\infty \mu^2 e^{-2\mu t}\,\psi(\mu)\,d\mu \quad (132)$$

holds, then inequality (130) certainly holds.

Consider now the function $\mu e^{-\mu t}$. The left side of (132) represents the square of its first moment, $M^{(1)}$, with respect to the distribution function $\psi(\mu)$ while the right side represents its second moment $M^{(2)}$. Now the variance of this function is given by

$$\sigma_m^2 = M^{(2)} - [M^{(1)}]^2. \quad (133)$$

This variance, however, must be positive except in the trivial case when all the individual processes in our population have the same μ. In all other cases we must have

$$M^{(2)} > [M^{(1)}]^2, \quad (134)$$

which implies inequality (132) and therefore inequality (130).

This result ought to be intuitively evident. The less viable processes terminate early, and so raise the average viability of the processes which have not yet terminated. The combined process, therefore, gives the impression that it becomes more viable the longer it lasts, but actually the effect is due to a "natural selection" acting on the population.

It follows that if some combined process appears *less* viable, the longer it lasts, it cannot be composed of individual processes, each with a viability independent of time. The best known example of such a compound process is a not too young human population. If we follow this population in time, we see that its overall death rate increases rather than decreases. The common-sense conclusion is that the probability that a particular individual will die at a given moment is not constant but increases with age.

With respect to processes which appear to become more viable, we cannot decide without more evidence whether a process of this sort is a combination of many individual processes with constant but different viabilities or whether for each individual the viability increases (or even decreases) with time. Therefore, all we can say at this point is that the process defined by a run of *CC* or *DD* responses behaves in a way consistent with the hypothesis that for each pair of players the run can terminate at any moment with equal probability. We cannot, however, conclude on the basis of this evidence alone that the hypothesis is true, although we can pursue the consequences of the hypothesis if it is assumed to be true.

Suppose then that our empirical function $g(t)$, i.e., the fraction of runs not yet terminated at time t is actually given by

$$g(t) = e^{-m\sqrt{t}}, \tag{135}$$

which is roughly indicated by the data.[36] If we suppose that the combined process is the result of lumping all the runs, each one of which has a constant viability (this viability being different in different pairs), we can ask the following question: Is there a distribution $\psi(\mu)$ in the population of pairs which insures this result? In other words, we are asking whether the integral equation

$$e^{-m\sqrt{t}} = \int_0^\infty \psi(\mu)e^{-\mu t}\, d\mu \tag{136}$$

has a solution $\psi(\mu)$, which is a density distribution, that is, satisfies

$$\int_0^\infty \psi(\mu)\, d\mu = 1. \tag{137}$$

If we demand also that $\psi(\mu)$ be a continuous function of μ, then we know that (136) has a unique solution. We are not sure, however, whether this solution also satisfies (137). We note that the right side of (136) is the Laplace transform of the $\psi(\mu)$[37]. It turns out that $e^{-m\sqrt{t}}$ does have an inverse Laplace transform which is also a density distribution, namely

$$\frac{m}{2\sqrt{\pi\mu^3}} \exp\left\{-\frac{m^2}{4\mu}\right\}. \qquad (138)$$

The question before us is whether (138) is a "reasonable" density distribution of μ, the "reciprocal" of the "viability" of the runs in our population of pairs.

The question cannot be verified directly, since μ cannot be directly observed. We note, however, that the shape of $\psi(\mu)$, as given by (138), is a "reasonable" one. It resembles a logarithmic normal distribution, which is frequently observed with respect to parameters which cannot assume negative values (as is the case with μ). We conclude, therefore, that the "natural selection" principle can be reasonably invoked to explain the observed distribution of lengths of runs.

Nevertheless, in view of the attractiveness of the self-reinforcement hypothesis, we shall not reject it until we have put it to a further test. We shall examine the distribution of lengths of runs in the protocols of individual pairs. If we still observe the same effect in the distribution of the *individual pairs*, namely that the longer the run lasts the less likely it is to terminate, we have a partial confirmation of the self-reinforcement hypothesis, because the natural selection principle cannot be assumed to operate on a single pair.

We note in the protocol of each pair the number of, say, *CC* runs which are at least one play long, at least two plays long, etc. Call these numbers $N(1)$, $N(2)$, etc. Obviously $N(1) \geq N(2) \geq N(3)$, etc. Consider the ratio

$$r_{cc}^{(i)} = \frac{N(i)}{N(i-1)} \leq 1. \tag{139}$$

This ratio is an estimate of the probability that a run will not end with the $(i - 1)$th play given that it has lasted for $i - 1$ plays. Therefore, the behavior of the $r_{cc}^{(i)}$ averaged over the population of pairs $(i = 1, 2, \ldots)$ will give us an idea of whether the "viability" of *CC* runs increases, decreases, or remains the same on the average in single pairs, i.e., without the operation of "natural selection."

To get the most information, we would like to examine long sequences of the $r^{(i)}$. However, some pairs will not have longer runs, and for these pairs the ratios $r^{(i)}$ will not be defined for $i - 1 > m$, where m is the length of the longest run observed in the pair in question.

We shall therefore resort to the following convention. In the case of *CC* runs and *DD* runs, we shall average the $r^{(i)}$ over all pairs which have runs of this type at least five long. This will give us $r^{(1)}$, $r^{(2)}$, $r^{(3)}$, and $r^{(4)}$. This comprises most but not all of the pairs in our population. Now the pairs which do have, say, *CC* runs at least five plays long are a selected subpopulation of our population. Indeed we would expect these to be the more cooperative pairs. We may find, in fact, that the *CC* runs of these selected pairs do become more "viable" as they become longer.

Next, we adjoin to this subpopulation the pairs that have no *CC* runs at least four plays long. In the combined population we can now estimate only $r_{cc}^{(1)}$, $r_{cc}^{(2)}$, and $r_{cc}^{(3)}$. If the pairs with shorter maximal runs are "less cooperative," we might expect that the increasing viability of the *CC* runs, if it is observed in the originally selected population, becomes weaker in the larger population.

We continue by adjoining the pairs which have no *CC* runs at least three plays long. Now we can estimate only $r_{cc}^{(1)}$ and $r_{cc}^{(2)}$ and expect the "lock-in effect" as reflected in the greater viability of longer CC runs to become still weaker. It may even be reversed, in which case we shall observe $r_{cc}^{(2)} < r_{cc}^{(1)}$.

We shall repeat this procedure with DD runs and with the unilateral runs. In the case of the latter our original selected population will comprise the pairs which have unilateral runs of four or more, which will give us estimates of $r_{CD}^{(i)}$ (or $r_{DC}^{(i)}$) for $i = 1$, 2, and 3 only. There is no point in estimating $r_{CD}^{(i)}$ for $i > 3$, because the pairs which have unilateral runs longer than four plays are too few in number.

The results are shown in Table 23.

TABLE 23

	$r_{CC}^{(1)}$	$r_{CC}^{(2)}$	$r_{CC}^{(3)}$	$r_{CC}^{(4)}$	$r_{DD}^{(1)}$	$r_{DD}^{(2)}$	$r_{DD}^{(3)}$	$r_{DD}^{(4)}$	$r_{CD}^{(1)}$	$r_{CD}^{(2)}$	$r_{CD}^{(3)}$
(5)	.68	.79	.86	.87	.69	.69	.71	.74			
(4)	.66	.78	.80		.68	.67	.68		.34	.39	.32
(3)	.65	.75			.67	.62			.27	.21	

(5): Average over pairs having runs at least five long.
(4): Average over pairs having runs at least four long.
(3): Average over pairs having runs at least three long.

We observe the following. In the selected pairs which have CC runs of five or more plays the lock-in effect is quite pronounced, as evidenced by the steadily increasing $r_{cc}^{(i)}$ ($i = 1$, 2, 3, 4). Moreover, this effect is still strong even when the pairs which have no CC runs longer than 3 are adjoined.

With regard to the DD runs, the picture is different. The lock-in effect is considerably weaker, and is present only in the pairs which have DD runs of five or more plays; further, it disappears when pairs are adjoined with runs not longer than four, and is actually reversed when pairs are adjoined with runs not longer than three.

With regard to the unilateral ("martyr") runs the

picture is again a different one. Even in the pairs having such runs of at least four plays, the lock-in effect is no longer observed. The probability that a unilateral response continues after two such responses is, to be sure, greater than the probability that a single response is repeated, but the probability that a run of three *CD*'s (or *DC*'s) continues is smaller. When pairs are adjoined with no unilateral runs greater than three, the reverse of the lock-in effect is observed.

In summary, then, we have ample evidence that, at least in those pairs which have long runs, the probability that a run ends at any time is not a constant. Especially in the case of *CC*, a lock-in effect seems to operate: the longer such a run lasts the more likely it is to continue. In our opinion it is this effect which is responsible for the failure of the four-state Markov chain to describe the time courses of the states.

Chapter 12
Simulation

To TEST A MATHEMATICAL MODEL means to compare the predictions of the model with observations. If the model contains no free parameters, such predictions are categorical. Usually, however, a model involves one or more parameters which are to be "adjusted" to fit the theory to observations. This adjustment is a straightforward matter if the mathematical laws derived from the model are simple. For example, the law derived from the model which assumes constant acceleration is $s = at^2$. Here a is a free parameter, and it can be estimated by a single reading of s and of the corresponding t, namely $a = s/t^2$. In case the data do not fit the formula exactly, a "best estimate" of a is still a simple problem. For example, we can plot s against t^2 and obtain a value of a so as to minimize the sum of the squared deviations of the data from the (theoretical) straight line.

As the number of parameters increases, the task of estimating them becomes progressively more unwieldy and the criterion for the "best fit" becomes more vague.

In principle, one could by trial and error gradually approach a set of values for the parameters which will generate data to agree with the real data to a greater and greater extent, i.e., with respect to an ever greater number of statistics. If our object were to find the "best" model of Prisoner's Dilemma, we would do just that and, in addition, go through the parameter-adjusting process of several different models. Here the job has been only barely started. In particular we shall obtain simulations from (1) the Markov chain model with fourteen states (including two absorbing states) described on pp. 123 ff; (2) the stochastic learning model of the first order described on pp. 138 ff.

We started each run from the same initial condition (i.e., equiprobable C and D responses) and chose the parameters so as to fit the time course of C averaged for the entire Pure Matrix Condition. We then compared the time courses of the four states (CC, CD, DC, and DD) obtained from the simulation with the data obtained from that condition, and the variance of C obtained from the simulation and that observed in the same data.

The comparison of the time course of C obtained from the Markov model with absorbing states and the data is shown in Figure 33. The parameters x, y, z, w, γ, and δ were adjusted by trial and error until a reasonably good fit was obtained. Note that it has been possible to obtain the initial decline of C and its recovery by this simulation. Evidently what is happening in the simulated process is the following. Because of the small values of γ and δ, hardly any of the simulated pairs pass into either of the absorbing states in the early stage. On the other hand, the values of x, y, z, and w are such that C initially decreases. However, eventually the pairs start to pass into the absorbing states. Since the probability of passing into $\Gamma\Gamma$ is larger than that of passing into $\Delta\Delta$, recruitment into the CC lock-in is more rapid. Since this recruitment is irreversible, a "recovery" is observed in the average C as more pairs get into the $\Gamma\Gamma$ absorbing state. This recruitment is just sufficiently great to offset the downward trend of C due to x, y, z, w, and δ to match the gradual growth of C observed in the data. In this way a fair fit of the time course of C is obtained.

Let us now see how good the resulting fits are for the time courses of the four states. The comparison is shown in Figures 34–36.

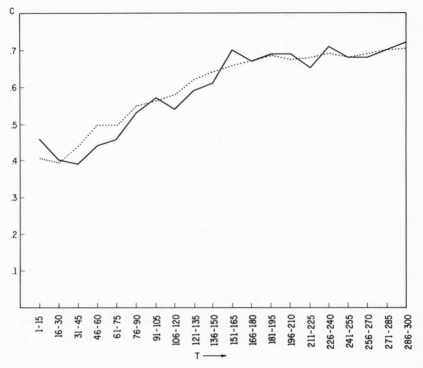

Figure 33. Comparison of observed time course of C in the Pure Matrix Condition (solid line) with that obtained from a simulated Markov model (dotted line) with absorbing states. Parameter values: $x = .6; y = .43; z = .35; w = .30;$ $\gamma = .018; \delta = .0024.$

As we see, the simulated time courses of the four component states show systematic discrepancies when compared with the observed time courses. Specifically, the frequencies of both the CC and the DD responses are too low in the simulation while those of the unilateral responses are too high. This suggests that if we had used higher values of both γ and δ, thus insuring more frequent lock-ins on both *CC* and *DD*, we might have obtained better fits for the three component time

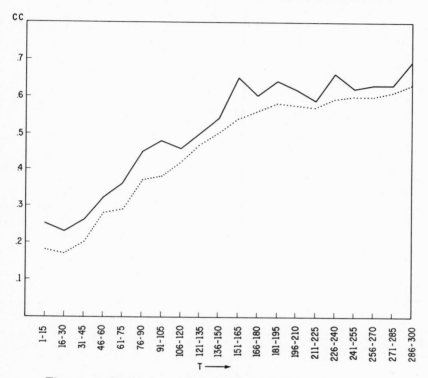

Figure 34. Comparison of observed time course of *CC* in the Pure Matrix Condition (solid line) with that obtained from a simulated Markov model (dotted line) with absorbing states. Parameter values: $x = .6$; $y = .43$; $z = .35$; $w = .30$; $\gamma = .018$; $\delta = .0024$.

courses. However, we followed the policy of stopping the search for the best fitting parameters once the composite (*C*) time course was reasonably well fitted by the simulation and so did not attempt to get better fits for the components by further manipulation of the parameters.

Turning to the first order stochastic learning models, we have the comparisons between simulated and observed time courses shown in Figures 37–40.

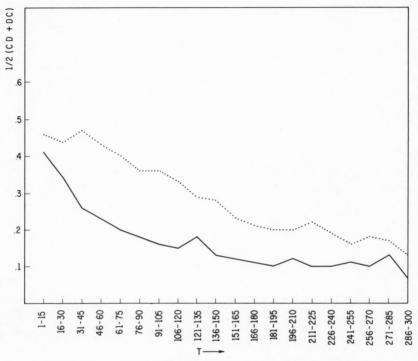

Figure 35. Comparison of observed time course of 1/2 (CD + DC) in the Pure Matrix Condition (solid line) with that obtained from a simulated Markov model (dotted line) with absorbing states. Parameter values: $x = .6$; $y = .43$; $z = .35$; $w = .30$; $\gamma = .018$; $\delta = .0024$.

As is seen from the figures, the fits are reasonably good for all the components although, as before, the parameters were fixed as soon as a good fit was obtained for the composite curve.

Finally we compare the variances of the variables C, CC, CD, DC, and DD as they emerge in the seventy simulated pairs of each model with the variances observed in the seventy real pairs of the Pure Matrix Condition. The comparison is shown in Table 24.

We see that the variances obtained in the simula-

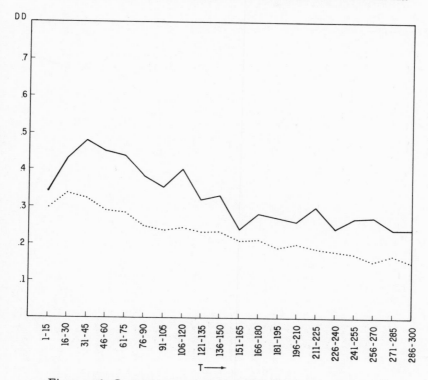

Figure 36. Comparison of observed time course of *DD* in the Pure Matrix Condition (solid line) with that obtained from a simulated Markov model (dotted line) with absorbing states. Parameter values: $x = .6$; $y = .43$; $z = .35$; $w = .30$; $\gamma = .018$; $\delta = .0024$.

TABLE 24

	Var [C]	Var [CC]	Var [CD]	Var [DC]	Var [DD]
Pure Matrix Condition	.091	.110	.006	.006	.080
Markov Model with Absorbing States	.069	.091	.014	.014	.056
First Order Stochastic Learning Model	.094	.134	.004	.004	.060

tions are comparable to those observed in the data, the stochastic learning model showing perhaps somewhat better agreement.

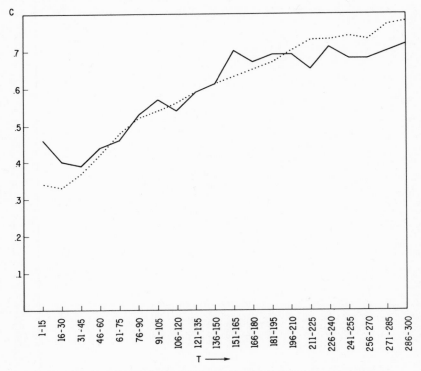

Figure 37. Comparison of observed time course of C in the Pure Matrix Condition (solid line) with that obtained from a simulated first order stochastic learning model (dotted line). Parameter values: $\alpha^{(1)} = .57$; $\lambda^{(1)} = 1$; $\alpha^{(2)} = .4$; $\lambda^{(2)} = 0$; $\alpha^{(3)} = .4$; $\lambda^{(3)} = 0$; $\alpha^{(4)} = .74$; $\lambda^{(4)} = .4$.

Note that the simulated data were obtained from a model in which every "subject" was characterized by the same parameter values. The variances resulted only from the stochastic process itself. This shows that the observed variances need not *necessarily* be ascribed to individual differences among subjects, a point brought out by B. P. Cohen (1963).

We know, of course, that individuals do differ. We know also that the combined data of the Pure Matrix Condition represent the protocols of seven

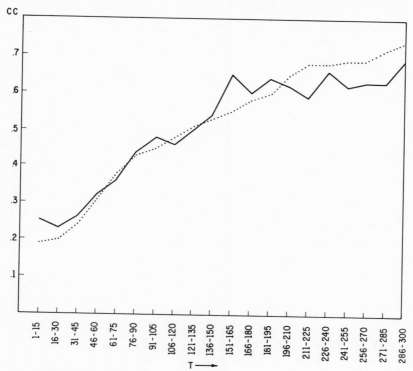

Figure 38. Comparison of observed time course of *CC* in the Pure Matrix Condition (solid line) with that obtained from a simulated first order stochastic learning model (dotted line). Parameter values: $\alpha^{(1)} = .57$; $\lambda^{(1)} = 1$; $\alpha^{(2)} = .4$; $\lambda^{(2)} = 0$; $\alpha^{(3)} = .4$; $\lambda^{(3)} = 0$; $\alpha^{(4)} = .74$; $\lambda^{(4)} = .4$.

different games, among which significant differences in performance have been observed. These credible sources of variance are deliberately ignored in our models. It is important to keep in mind that *every* model is an "as if" representation of reality. Physicists talk, for example, about the "effective volume" of a molecule, meaning not its real volume but the volume of an object with given properties which behaves like the molecule in question in certain contexts.

Similarly the parameters of our simulated models are "effective parameters," i.e., parameters of a hy-

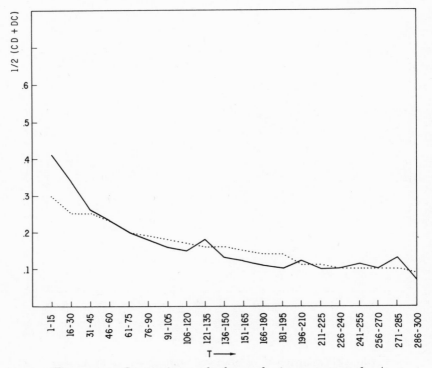

Figure 39. Comparison of observed time course of $1/2$ $(CD + DC)$ in the Pure Matrix Condition (solid line) with that obtained from a simulated first order stochastic learning model (dotted line). Parameter values: $\alpha^{(1)} = .57$; $\lambda^{(1)} = 1; \alpha^{(2)} = .4; \lambda^{(2)} = 0; \alpha^{(3)} = .4; \lambda^{(3)} = 0; \alpha^{(4)} = .74;$ $\lambda^{(4)} = .4.$

pothetical subject "replicated" 140 times who plays Prisoner's Dilemma "stochastically" and whose protocols are reasonable facsimiles of observed protocols.

It is very likely that if the first order learning model, which gave good results as far as it went, were pressed further (for example, if its distributions of lengths of runs or some other statistics were compared with data), it too would eventually fail. This would then call for further refinement. The goal of such an investi-

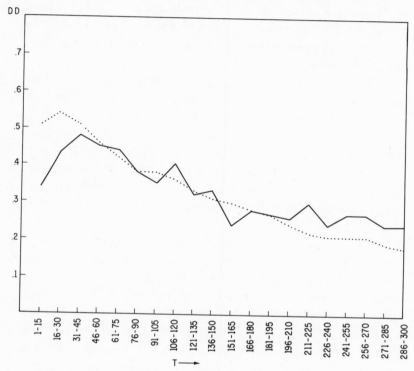

Figure 40. Comparison of observed time course of *DD* in the Pure Matrix Condition (solid line) with that obtained from a simulated first order stochastic learning model (dotted line). Parameter values: $\alpha^{(1)} = .57$; $\lambda^{(1)} = 1$; $\alpha^{(2)} = .4$; $\lambda^{(2)} = 0$; $\alpha^{(3)} = .4$; $\lambda^{(3)} = 0$; $\alpha^{(4)} = .74$; $\lambda^{(4)} = .4$.

gation would be to reach a model good in several important respects and then to declare the parameters in that model to be "effective" parameters which describe a Prisoner's Dilemma experiment under given conditions with a given population as subjects. For example, if we were to declare the first order learning model adequate, the parameters we would be dealing with would be the four learning parameters $\alpha^{(j)}$ $(j = 1 \ldots 4)$ and the parameter $\lambda^{(4)}$, which represents the asymptotic value of the probability of a CC response following a long run of DD responses. A given game, condition, or population would then be scored by the values of these parameters which would give the best fit to its performance.

On the other hand, if the Markov model with absorbing states were declared adequate, then populations or conditions would be scored in terms of x, y, z, w, γ, and δ. The psychological interpretation of these parameters is different from that of the α's and the λ's; consequently the psychological theory that would emerge from the Markov model would also be a different one than one that would emerge from a stochastic learning model.

The direction for future theory construction is thus indicated. One should seek a mathematical model which among many tested models describes most accurately with respect to most variables the behavior of populations playing Prisoner's Dilemma. The parameters of the model, psychologically interpreted, would then become the key concepts of the theory, and the content of the theory would be a collection of statements arrived at by induction or deduction concerning the interrelationships among the parameters, their dependence on manipulable conditions, and their role as characteristics of populations.

Chapter 13
Comparing Populations

OUR FIRST OBJECTIVE in undertaking the experimental program described here has been to gain some understanding of what goes on in long sequences of plays of Prisoner's Dilemma. We have attempted to gain this understanding by postulating a system going through a sequence of states and by attempting to formulate some mathematical models from which the dynamics of the system could be deduced. Once such a model is found, its parameters, properly interpreted, become the key terms in the emerging psychological theory. This strategy can be deemed successful, if the parameters so discovered are independent of the process itself, if they suggest further investigations, and if the further investigations, in turn, lead to a more inclusive theory.

For example, suppose we had found that the parameters x, y, z, and w were independent of the process and that, when the estimated values of these parameters were substituted into the Markov equations, the time courses of the four states were accurately predicted, as well as other important statistics of the process theoretically deduced from the generated stochastic model. Then the values of x, y, z, and w would be *the* parameters of the process. We could then ask questions about how these parameters are affected by, say, the payoffs. A model relating the payoffs to x, y, z, and w would then constitute an extension of the theory. We would also have a solid basis for comparing populations, namely, in terms of the values of these parameters. In the light of the psychological suggestiveness of the propensities x, y, z, and w, we could then say more specifically why there is more cooperation in one population than in another, for example because the one population is more "trustworthy" than another or more "trustful," or both, or perhaps less trustworthy but more trusting to the extent that the latter characteristic more than offsets the former, etc. We might find that two populations exhibit the same gross degree of cooperative behavior, but that their "profiles" in terms of propensities may be quite different. We could then predict a divergence between their behaviors under a different set of conditions.

Further, if extraneous circumstances brought about changes in performance, we could see where (in which parameters) these changes were brought to bear. Or, if extraneous circumstances brought about only transient changes at the start of the performance, we could explain this by pointing out that only the initial conditions were affected by the changes, not the system parameters themselves which govern the ultimate steady state characteristics of the system.

If, on the other hand, one of the adjustable parameter's models were most successful in accounting for the data, a different set of constants would be singled out for attention. These might be the constants of proportionality connecting the rate of adjustment to the gradient in the corresponding expected payoff, or the like. And in these models the positions of the unstable equilibria, rather than steady state equilibria, would be the most important features of the dynamic, as we have shown in Chapter 10.

At this time we cannot single out from the models proposed any one which is best in every respect. As we have seen, the task of comparing the various models, if taken seriously, is one of formidable difficulty, which we did not undertake to accomplish by a tour de force.

In our opinion, data much more voluminous than those we have gathered are required in order to establish confidence in a dynamic model, especially a stochastic one, possessing the degree of complexity which the situation requires.

We therefore will content ourselves with parameters which do not fulfill the requirement of being independent of the process. We shall use, as a basis for comparing populations, all the important variables and parameters which have entered our discussion. That is, we sacrifice parsimony (which would have been served had we been able to isolate the "basic" parameters) in order to get a descriptively "rich" comparison. In doing so, we shall be wary of the confusion which often results when seemingly unrelated statistics are piled up in describing or comparing phenomena. We shall try to avoid such confusion by fitting the indices of comparison into a more or less coherent picture.

1. *The frequency of cooperative responses.* The most natural index is, of course, the total relative frequency of cooperative responses in each of the games. We have seen that this index is very strongly affected by interaction. However, to the extent that we compare populations playing the game under identical conditions, we shall suppose that differences in the total frequency of cooperation found among different populations reflect a difference in some characteristic of the populations, whether the characteristic resides inherently in the individuals comprising each population or in the way these individuals interact. We shall therefore follow the established tradition in evaluating performance in Prisoner's Dilemma in terms of observed values of C, including its time course.

2. *The correlation indices* ρ_i. These indices measure the extent to which one player's choice is an imitation

of the other player's simultaneous choice, his choice on the last play, on the play before that, etc. Thus the ρ_i's form a "profile." We shall compare only values of ρ_0, ρ_1, and ρ_6.

3. *The correlation coefficient $\rho_{C_1 C_2}$ over a population of pairs*. This is a grosser measure than the ρ_i; it measures the overall similarity of pair members with respect to their cooperative frequencies.

4. *The response-conditioned propensities ξ, η, ζ, and ω*. Of these ξ and ω are measures of responsiveness to the other's choices, while η and ζ are measures of "response" to one's own choices. (N.B.: the two pairs are not independent since one's own choices always occur in conjunction with the other's choices [cf. p. 68].)

5. *The state-conditioned propensities x, y, z, and w*. These are propensities similar to the preceding ones but now separated by reference to the four mutually exclusive response categories. It will be useful also to compare x, y, $1 - z$, and $1 - w$ (cf. p. 84), which are measures of persistence in the *same* response in each of the four states.

6. *The ratios $r^{(i)}$ discussed in Chapter 11*. The behavior of the sequences of these ratios $(i = 1, 2, \ldots)$ will tell us something about the lock-in effect, whether it is operating (if the $r^{(i)}$ increase) or not, or whether perhaps an "antilock-in effect" is operating (if the $r^{(i)}$ decrease).

7. Next, there are a few special indices of interest. Consider, for example, the index

$$M = \frac{(1 - y_1)(1 - z_2)}{y_1 z_2} \text{ or } \frac{(1 - y_2)(1 - z_1)}{y_2 z_1}.$$

This index is related to the "martyr" runs (runs of unilateral states). The numerator of M represents the probability that a unilateral state passes to DD, i.e., the "martyr" gives up while the defector continues to defect. The denominator represents the probability that the defector starts to cooperate while the "martyr" continues to cooperate. Thus M represents the ratio of "failures" to "successes" of such runs, that is, the ratio of the number of times such runs turn into double defecting or double cooperative responses.

8. Next we wish to examine the fractions of compared populations choosing C on the very first play $[C(1)]$ and on the second play $[C(2)]$.

9. Finally, we shall examine the fractions of compared populations which have locked in on the CC response (L_{CC}) and on the DD response (L_{DD}) in the last twenty-five plays. Our criterion of lock-in will be arbitrarily taken as twenty-three of twenty-five responses in the category in question.

We shall compare three populations, namely, MM: 70 male pairs; WW: 70 female pairs; MW: 70 mixed pairs.

All the populations played Prisoner's Dilemma in the Pure Matrix Condition. Therefore for our MM population we shall take the one already examined.

In our comparison, games will not be differentiated. Since each population played under identical conditions we shall be concerned only with the gross indices averaged over each of the entire populations of seventy pairs.

In the MM and WW populations the individual players in a pair (i.e., the players labeled 1, 2) will not be differentiated. In the MW population they will be. Thus in Table 25 the row MW contains indices pertaining to men playing opposite women, while row WM contains indices pertaining to women playing against men. For example, the CD in MW represents cooperation by the man and defection by the woman, while in WM it represents cooperation by the woman and defection by the man. Obviously, sym-

TABLE 25

	CC	CD	DC	DD	C	$\rho_{C_1C_2}$	p_0	p_1	p_6	ξ	η	ζ	ω	x	y	z	w	$\rho_{x_1x_2}$	$\rho_{y_1y_2}$	$\rho_{z_1z_2}$	$\rho_{w_1w_2}$
	1	2	3	4	5	6	7	8	9	10	11	12	13	14	15	16	17	18	19	20	21
MM	.51	.08	.09	.32	.59	.97	.46	.51	.36	.76	.78	.25	.25	.85	.40	.38	.20	.79	−.10	−.25	.48
MW	.40	.10	.09	.41	.50	.91	.35	.39	.28	.68	.71	.24	.25	.80	.40	.33	.21	.58	.12	.02	.72
WM	.40	.09	.10	.41	.48	.91	.35	.35	.24	.65	.69	.22	.27	.78	.44	.29	.22	.58	.12	.02	.72
WW	.23	.11	.11	.55	.34	.87	.31	.34	.22	.55	.60	.17	.19	.75	.37	.26	.15	.34	−.29	−.20	.46

		$r_{CC}^{(1)}$	$r_{CC}^{(2)}$	$r_{CC}^{(3)}$	$r_{CC}^{(4)}$	$r_{DD}^{(1)}$	$r_{DD}^{(2)}$	$r_{DD}^{(3)}$	$r_{DD}^{(4)}$	$r_{CD}^{(1)}$	$r_{CD}^{(2)}$	$r_{CD}^{(3)}$	M	C(1)	C(2)	L_{CC}	L_{DD}
		22	23	24	25	26	27	28	29	30	31	32	33	34	35	36	37
MM	1)	.68	.79	.86	.87	.69	.69	.71	.74	.34	.39	.32	2.4	.53	.48	.57	.13
	2)	.66	.78	.80		.68	.67	.68		.27	.21						
	3)	.65	.75			.67	.62										
MW	1)	.74	.75	.85	.85	.64	.70	.71	.79	.31	.40	.35	3.7	.63	.56	.39	.21
	2)	.68	.69	.74		.62	.69	.67		.32	.28						
	3)	.64	.62			.60	.65										
WM	1)	.74	.75	.85	.85	.64	.70	.71	.79	.41	.39	.23	2.6	.63	.54	.39	.21
	2)	.68	.69	.74		.62	.69	.67		.36	.25						
	3)	.64	.62			.60	.65										
WW	1)	.69	.66	.73	.68	.69	.71	.72	.73	.33	.37	.27	4.8	.53	.49	.17	.30
	2)	.68	.61	.64		.68	.71	.71		.30	.25						
	3)	.63	.53			.68	.70										

1) Average over pairs having runs at least five long.
2) Average over pairs having runs at least four long.
3) Average over pairs having runs at least three long.

metric indices like CC or $\rho_{x_1 x_2}$ will be identical in both these rows.

We turn to the results.

First we examine the distributions of the four states. The most striking difference is between the male and the female populations. There is a clear indication that males cooperate more than females, as can be seen directly by comparing the respective C's.[38]

However, when men play against women there is no perceptible difference between them with respect to the total frequency of cooperative choices. The one percent difference in favor of the men observed in the unilateral responses cannot be significant in view of the fact that a difference of this magnitude is observed also between CD and DC responses of the all-male population, where it must reflect only a statistical fluctuation, since here the difference is only between players labeled 1 and 2.

Next we compare the performance of men playing against men with that of men playing against women and also the performance of women playing against women with that of women playing against men. We find that women are "pulled up" when playing against men, that is, they play more cooperatively against men than against women. Men, on the contrary, are "pulled down" when playing against women as compared with their performance against players of their own sex. However, the men are not pulled down as much as the women are pulled up. In general, the performance of mixed groups is squarely between the performances of the men and of the women, rather nearer that of men.

Next we note that this difference between the sexes is not observed at all at the very beginning of the process. (Columns 34 and 35 show the fraction of subjects choosing C on the first and second plays respectively.) The behavior of men and of women is practically identical both in the homogeneous pairs and in mixed pairs. Therefore, we cannot say that the pronounced difference in the performances is due to some *initial* difference in the propensities to cooperate. We must look for the roots of the difference in the interaction effects.

Accordingly, we examine next the conditional propensities, ξ, η, ζ, ω, x, y, z, and w. Throughout we observe the same effect: the women's propensities are brought up when they play against men; the men's propensities are brought down when they play against women. When men play against women, the propensities are practically equal when averaged over the entire session.

Comparing $1 - \omega$ with ξ we see that men playing men are somewhat more likely to respond cooperatively to the other's cooperative choice than to retaliate against the other's defecting choice ($\xi > 1 - \omega$). However, women playing against women are much more likely to retaliate against the other's defecting response than to respond cooperatively against the other's cooperative response ($\xi < 1 - \omega$). When men play against women, the retaliating tendency is slightly greater than cooperative responsiveness in both.

Next we examine the correlation measures. The ρ's of the men (playing against men) are consistently higher than those of the women (playing against women), which is to say that the men tend to imitate each other more than the women. The values of the ρ's in the mixed groups indicate that there men tend to imitate women more than women tend to imitate men (columns 8 and 9). In short, men are inclined to play tit-for-tat more than women.

From column 18 we conjecture that men tend to become more like each other with regard to the propensity x (to cooperate following CC) than women. Here the value of $\rho_{x_1 x_2}$ in the mixed groups is again intermediate between that in the male and in the female pairs. With respect to $\rho_{w_1 w_2}$, however, the tendency to become like each other is strongest in the mixed groups. We shall not venture to interpret this result.

Next we look at the dynamics of the state-conditioned propensities. We have already seen (cf. Chapter 11) that the mean probability of continuing a given state is not necessarily a constant (as implied by the four-state Markov model) but appears to be a function of the number of times the state in question has just occurred. In particular, we conjecture that the lock-in effect is due primarily to the fact that the more times in succession the CC or the DD state occurs, the more likely it is to be repeated at least in the pairs in whose protocols sufficiently long runs occur. This effect, if it occurs, is shown in columns 22 through 25. Comparing the probabilities of the continuation of CC runs, we see that in the male pairs these steadily increase and that the increase is still seen even when the pairs without runs longer than three plays are included. In the female pairs this effect is not observed. Even in the pairs where CC runs at least five plays long occur, r_{CC} actually declines. This is to say, when women play women the average probability of a CC response following two consecutive CC's is actually less than the average probability of a CC response following a single CC. This indicates that the lock-in effect on CC does not operate in the average female pair. In mixed pairs, the lock-in effect is observed in pairs containing CC runs of at least five. It is still observed when pairs with runs not longer than four are included and is lost when pairs are included which contain no runs longer than three.

With regard to DD runs, the picture is reversed.

In the male pairs, the lock-in effect is observed only in the selected pairs with DD runs at least five long, is lost as soon as pairs with no runs longer than four are included, and is actually reversed when pairs with runs no longer than three are included. In the female pairs, on the other hand, the effect is observed even when pairs with runs no longer than three are included. The mixed pairs behave like the male pairs with respect to the DD runs. We conjecture that women become more prone than men to lock-in on DD as a DD run continues.

With respect to r_{CD} the picture is about the same throughout. In general $r_{CD}^{(2)} > r_{CD}^{(1)} > r_{CD}^{(3)}$ (with the curious exception of women against men), when pairs with "martyr runs" of at least four are included. When pairs are included with runs no longer than three, $r_{CD}^{(2)} < r_{CD}^{(1)}$. On the whole, this means that following two unilateral cooperative plays the probability of the next such play *decreases* (an antilock-in effect), although it increases in pairs which have unilateral runs longer than three. Even in these pairs the probability of the fourth unilateral cooperative choice decreases markedly.

Turning to our index $M = (1 - y)(1 - z)/yz$, which, we recall, is a measure of the extent to which "martyr runs" fail, we see another striking difference between men and women. Martyr runs of men playing against men end in failure about two and one-half times more frequently than in success (column 33). Martyr runs of women playing against women end in failure almost five times as frequently as in success. Looking at the MW population we see that with respect to this index the difference between men and women is still pronounced (although it is erased in most other respects). The martyr runs of *women* playing against men end in failure about two and a half times more frequently than in success.[39] That is to say, a man gets "converted" by a woman's martyr run with about probability .28 (a value close to .29, the probability of his being converted by a man's martyr run). But a woman gets converted by a man's martyr run with probability of only .21. This is a larger probability than .17 with which a woman gets converted by a woman's martyr run but still significantly smaller than .28.

However, we cannot on this basis alone lay a greater blame for the failures of martyr runs on the woman. For the failure of a martyr run can be ascribed as much to the martyr's giving up his unilateral cooperation as to the defector's failure to respond. Indeed, comparing the y's of men and women in mixed pairs we see that women's are greater, indicating a greater persistence in the martyr runs. Also the women's ω is slightly higher than men's, indicating a higher overall propensity to respond cooperatively to man's defection. The slightly higher value of w in the woman (playing against a man) indicates a slightly higher propensity to break out of DD, i.e., to *initiate* a martyr run. In short, the greater frequency of failures of men's martyr runs is as much due to the fact that the man is somewhat more prone to give up as to the fact that the woman is somewhat less prone to switch from successful defection to cooperation, both tendencies being a reflection of man's greater propensity to give tit-for-tat.

Turning to the final lock-ins (columns 36 and 37), we see that seventy percent of the male pairs end the sessions locked in, and that of these over four times as many pairs have locked in on CC than on DD. Of the female pairs less than fifty percent end the sessions locked in and of these almost twice as many have locked in on DD than on CC. The mixed pairs are again in between: sixty percent have locked in and of these twice as many end the sessions cooperatively rather than uncooperatively.

Finally we look at the values of *C* on the first and second plays (columns 34 and 35). Here we see no sig-

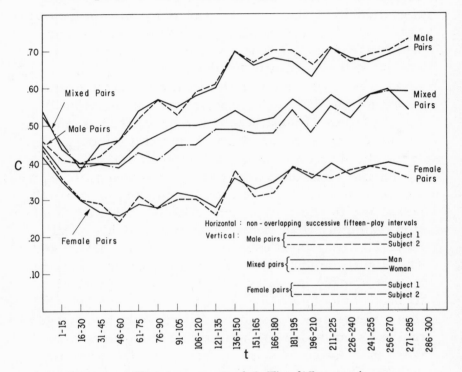

Figure 41. The time course of *C*. The differences between subjects 1 and 2 in the male and female pairs are evidently due to statistical fluctuations. In the case of mixed pairs, the higher values of *C* in men seem to be fairly consistent. These are, however, numerically small. For evaluation of significance, see Appendix III.

nificant differences between men and women either when they play against partners of the same sex or of the other.

We see, however, a remarkable result in the initial high value of *C* when men play against women. The difference between .53 and .63 in a population sample of 140 individuals is about five standard deviations (assuming the largest value of a standard deviation of C binomially distributed when $C = D = .5$). An interesting conjecture suggests itself that the *initial* propensity to cooperate is greatest in mixed pairs. The fact that the overall cooperative level attained by mixed pairs is below that of the male pairs must therefore be attributed to interaction effects.

All in all, when men play opposite women, in the long run the women are pulled up toward the men's levels of cooperation and in the amount of interaction (as reflected in the various interaction indices) while the men are slightly pulled down on both counts. These effects are easily seen in graphical representation as shown in Figure 41.

Chapter 14
Summary of Results

In our results, we have been principally interested in the coalescence of the performances of paired players. Whatever individual differences exist among the players (and it is difficult to believe other than that they exist) tend to be ironed out in the course of the interactions between them. The clearest manifestation of this effect is in the high values of $\rho_{C_1C_2}$ (cf. p. 59). Other correlation measures, e.g., ρ_i, $\rho_{x_1x_2}$, etc., while not as large as $\rho_{C_1C_2}$ are nevertheless overwhelmingly positive and point to the same effect.

The "cause" of this emerging similarity between the paired players (if one can speak of causes in this context) is the universally observed elimination of the unilateral responses. If no unilateral responses occurred, the players of a pair would be exactly like each other, because their protocols would be identical. It is only through the unilateral responses that the two members of a pair are distinguished. When these responses decline in frequency, the similarity of the players emerges.

Therefore the next question to ask is why the unilateral responses are eliminated. The answer which immediately suggests itself is that the payoff S is unbearable to the lone cooperator. He tends to switch from C to D upon receiving this payoff, and so regardless of what the other does (except when he happens to switch simultaneously from D to C) the unilateral response is eliminated. Of course, the unilateral response vanishes also when the defector is "converted," which happens much less frequently, but not too rarely, as indicated by the values of z.

This is not the whole story, however, since the unilateral responses could well appear as frequently as they disappear. A unilateral response could result from a player's defection from CC (in response to temptation) or from a player's attempt to escape from DD. These effects, however, are weak, as we see by examining the typical values of $1 - x$ and of w, which are the propensities associated with the events just mentioned. These values are both low. Consequently, not only are the unilaterals "killed" soon after they appear, but their "birthrate" is also low because of the lock-in on both CC and DD.

Typically, toward the end of the sessions over ninety percent of the responses are matched. It is this which accounts for the consistent similarity between paired players.

Therefore it makes sense to take the pair, rather than the individual, as the unit of a population. Variance among pairs is rather large; even within games (cf. Chapter 12). We have strong reason to believe, however, that much of this variance is accounted for not by the inherent propensities of the players to cooperate or not to cooperate, but rather by the characteristic instabilities of the dynamic process which governs the interactions in Prisoner's Dilemma. We have seen in Part II how these instabilities emerge as consequences of several mathematical models which we have proposed. To be sure, we cannot claim that any of these models has been corroborated, but our results are consistent with several of their aspects and we venture to suggest that the dynamics of interaction is of a somewhat similar sort as that inherent in our models.

Besides, our data provide evidence that the quality of interaction rather than inherent propensities is the important factor in the process. A case in point is the comparison between men and women. Whether playing against partners of their own or of the opposite sex, the paired men and women exhibited exactly the same average value of C on the first play, that is, before any interaction took place (cf. Table 25, column 34). The value of C on the second play (column 35) is still practically the same in men and women. Namely, it drops slightly less in WW than in MM and slightly more in WM than in MW. However, the protocols of MM and WW are widely different, whereas the protocols of MW and WM are quite similar. All this points to the interaction effects as being the chief determinants of the protocols.

The interaction effects are reflected in the time courses. The most typical feature of the time course of a Prisoner's Dilemma protocol is the initial decline in cooperation, followed eventually by a recovery. The time of onset of the recovery and its extent is the chief determinant of the overall amount of cooperation which will be observed. Thus the great difference between the Matrix Conditions and the No Matrix Conditions (cf. Chapter 2) is a result of the fact that in the latter the recovery comes much later and proceeds much more slowly than in the former. The same can be said for the difference between the MM and the WW populations.

We are thus led to the general conclusion about the psychological factors operating in the dynamics of Prisoner's Dilemma. There is initially either a reservoir of good intention or a lack of appreciation of the strategic structure of the game. At any rate the expectation that DD will predominate is not borne out on the first play. The fraction of cooperative responses is over fifty percent in all cases where the subjects see the matrix and is as high as sixty-three percent in pairs of mixed sex.

Thereafter this initial goodwill (or naïveté) decreases. The *DD* responses increase at the expense of the *CC* responses and especially of the unilateral responses whose initial rate of decline is typically the largest. This initial period, therefore, is a "sobering" period in which the "hard realities" of the Prisoner's Dilemma game become impressed on the players. However there is no percentage in *DD*, and sooner or later the players recognize this. Accordingly a recovery sets in. Typically the frequency of *CC* increases at the expense of the unilaterals. Hence, to put it another way, while in the beginning of the process the unilaterals tend to turn into *DD*'s (the cooperator defects), toward the end they tend to turn into *CC*'s (the defector cooperates). Thus learning goes both ways in Prisoner's Dilemma. First the subjects learn not to trust each other; then they learn to trust each other.

Payoffs have the expected effect on performance. As one would surmise by common sense, by and large the cooperation seen is related to the payoffs. However, the finer points of these effects have not yet been established. We do not know on the whole whether the reward for *CC* or the punishment for *DD* plays the more important role in eliciting cooperation. The consistently higher cooperation observed in Game XI compared with Game XII suggests that *R* is more important than *P*. However this is not borne out (nor contradicted) in the comparison between Games I and II.

It should be possible, in our opinion, to construct a mathematical model which would predict a greater effect of *P* when the magnitudes of *R* and *P* are large (as in Games I and II respectively) and a greater effect of R when these magnitudes are smaller (as in Games XI and XII respectively). This would account for the results in the Pure Matrix Condition. However the value of such a model would become manifest only if, in addition, it predicted also other characteristic peculiarities observed in the data.

This brings us to what we have already said is the principal valuable result of the investigation. The structure of the process generates questions of psychological interest and suggests the aspects of the data to be further examined to answer the questions. Many of the conjectures we have made cannot be substantiated without at least establishing the statistical significance of the results. But if the questions are of sufficient interest, motivation is provided to put the results to more severe tests.

For example, the differences between men and women in mixed pairs are all quite small (and probably statistically insignificant in relation to the sizes of the populations) but highly suggestive. We have conjectured, for example, on the basis of comparing ρ_1, ξ, and ω that men are more prone to give tit-for-tat than women. Two players who *always* give tit-for-tat would produce only three types of protocol, namely (1) all CC; (2) all DD; (3) all alternating CD and DC. However an *insight* into the fact that tit-for-tat is always given would invariably result in all-CC protocols, since these give the largest payoff to both. The other two types can be easily changed into an all-CC protocol by just one shift of phase from an alternating CD-DC protocol and just two shifts of phase from an all-DD protocol. Hence we would expect greater cooperation in a population of players more prone to give tit-for-tat, and this may be the principal reason why men cooperate more. At any rate, questions of this sort can be answered in principle thanks to the theoretical framework provided by a detailed structural analysis of the statistics generated by the data.

The opportunity of developing and refining such methods with a view of applying them broadly in experimental social psychology are, accordingly, offered as the principal result of our efforts.

Chapter 15
Concluding Remarks

WE HAVE SUMMARIZED our experimental work on Prisoner's Dilemma through the end of 1963 and have given the rather sketchy outlines of a mathematical theory purporting to deal with the process consisting of repeated plays. As is frequently the case, the work did not follow a strict predesigned plan. To a great extent, lines of investigation were stimulated by some (to us) interesting results of an experiment just completed; certain lines were discontinued as too costly of time and of subjects. The depletion of the subject pool was a constantly threatening limitation. Once we decided to use naïve subjects, we had to restrict ourselves to using each subject only once. In the studies reported here 740 subjects were used. The switch to female subjects was made partly in order to tap a "virgin" population. But when the first "returns" began to come in, we quickly decided to utilize this opportunity of a cross-population comparative study.

As a rule, ideas for experiments forced themselves on our attention much more rapidly than experiments could be performed. Going at a normal pace, we could run two pairs per day during the five-day week. Thus, to complete one of our conditions typically took seven weeks.

In this final chapter, we shall outline some experiments, which, we feel, ought to be performed and which we intend to perform, but not soon enough to warrant further delays in publishing the results already obtained.

The Strategy as an Independent Variable

In our experiments we were not able to use the strategy of one player as an independent variable with which to ascertain the behavior of the other player. Obviously this could not be done as long as both players were freely-choosing subjects. A controlled experiment using one player's strategy as an independent variable can be performed only if that player is a confederate of the experimenter. The use of stooges in experimental psychology has certain disadvantages. Questions of ethics have been raised with regard to this practice. Quite aside from the ethical issue (if any), however, the use of stooges has certain practical drawbacks, an obvious one being the need for secrecy and the ever-present danger that the subject population will "get wise" to the ruse and so block an entire avenue of exploration.

In experiments such as ours the use of stooges does not present quite so serious a problem. For one thing, it may not even be necessary to conceal the fact that one of the players is "programmed" to play a certain way. For example, the experimenter himself may take the role of the other player. There are several degrees of knowledge that the subject can have about the other player's role. For example, he may not only be told that the other player is to play a prescribed strategy but even informed of the strategy that the other player will play. In this case, then, there is clearly a normative theory (that of simply maximizing one's own payoffs) with which the behavior of the subject can be compared. (Of course, if it is consistently found that the players do in fact maximize their payoffs when they know the other's strategy, the experiments cease to be psychologically interesting.) Next, the subject can be told that the other player has a preassigned strategy but not what it is. This situation is no longer a simple maximization problem for the subject, and therefore the theory cannot be confined to a simple normative one: it must include psychological components. The disadvantage of this situation is that some subjects may design their choices so as to "experiment" in order to find out the strategy of the other player. Such trial-and-error explorations would be expected to mask the motivations we are interested in. It seems that the most suitable condition is the one in which the subject believes that the other player is also a bona fide subject, and so a certain amount of deception is unavoidable. However, the deception in this case is not "severe": the experiment is not something entirely different from what it purports to be. If word gets around that the "other player" is a confederate of the experimenter, this still does not make the experiment pointless, as it does in other situations with deception. For in our case the subject's problem is still to play as well as he can.

Assume, then, that the subject believes the other player to be a bona fide subject. We can now use the programmed strategy of our stooge as the independent variable. In particular consider the following class of strategies.

1. *The stooge always plays C.* One would expect that many subjects, perhaps the majority, will take advantage of such a player and exploit him. In other words, we may expect the response to a fully cooperative strategy to be mostly an uncooperative one.

2. *The stooge always plays D.* Here we can expect even with greater confidence that the subject will play mostly D. For to play C against D consistently takes an altogether ardent dedication to cooperation. At any rate, while "martyr runs" are seen to occur in

repeated games of Prisoner's Dilemma, very long such runs are quite rare.

3. *The stooge randomizes his choices*, playing a variable proportion of C. This proportion is then our independent variable. The two pure strategies mentioned above are special cases with $C = 1$ and $C = 0$.

If we are right in our conjecture that cooperation in response to both $C = 1$ and against $C = 0$ will be minimal,[40] it follows that maximal cooperation will be elicited by some intermediate value of C. It would be interesting to see what this optimum mixture (optimum in the sense of eliciting maximum cooperation) is. On the other hand, a mixture may be optimal in the sense of maximizing the payoff of the "mixer" (i.e., of the stooge) and this optimizing strategy may not be identical with the one which maximizes the subject's frequency of cooperative responses.

4. *The stooge plays a tit-for-tat strategy*. As the name implies, a tit-for-tat strategy is one which apes the other player: one plays whatever the other played the last time.[41] By convention we can agree that the first choice of this strategy is C. Departures can now be made from the tit-for-tat strategy in either the direction of greater cooperation or in the direction of greater defection. In the former case one always responds cooperatively to the other's C and, in addition, to a certain fraction of the other's D's. This fraction is now the independent variable. Deviating in the direction of defection, one always responds by defecting to the other's defection, and also to a certain fraction of the other's cooperative responses. This fraction is then the corresponding negative value of our variable. The tit-for-tat strategy is the special case where the value of this variable is zero.

5. An important class of strategies is one in which

the results of the first trials become the principal independent variable. For example, suppose one cooperates for the first N trials and thereafter plays a tit-for-
tat strategy. Here N is the independent variable. Or
suppose one defects for the first N trials and thereafter
plays the tit-for-tat strategy. How large must N be
for the tit-for-tat strategy to become ineffective in
eliciting cooperation (we assume the one hundred
percent tit-for-tat strategy will elicit cooperation
rather effectively)? The initial N cooperative responses
can also be combined with a subsequent completely
defecting strategy in order to see how long the initial
impact of cooperation takes to wear off. It is assumed
that *initially* the one hundred percent cooperative
strategy tends to induce cooperation, although not
in the long run. Or one may ask, how large does the
initial totally defecting run have to be in order for subsequent "therapy" (either cooperative or tit-for-tat)
to become futile.

False Information about the Payoff Matrix

Somewhat more serious deception is involved when
wrong information is given to the subjects about the
payoffs. Obviously such wrong information can be
given only about the payoffs of the other player. We
have performed one experiment of this sort. Consider
the game shown in Matrix 17.

	C	D
C	1,1	−2,50
D	2,−50	−1,−1

Matrix 17.

Here the game is no longer symmetric. For $S_1 \neq S_2$
and $T_1 \neq T_2$. In fact it appears to the first player that
the second player's temptation parameter and the mag-

nitude of his sucker's payoff are very much greater than his own. In our experiment, both players had the same impression, i.e., they were shown a game matrix like Matrix 17, in which they were both supposed to be the row-chooser. In reality, however, the subjects were playing our Game IV (Matrix 10, p. 37). Thus it only appeared to each of them that the other's S and T were both much larger numerically than his own. To carry out this deception, the procedure had to be somewhat changed. The payoffs could not now be announced orally following each play of the game, since if this were done, the players would see the discrepancy between the announced payoffs of the other and the payoffs entered in the matrix. Consequently, the outcomes were announced by specifying which choice was made by each player, L (which corresponds to our C choice) or R (which corresponds to our D choice). After this announcement, the players presumably looked up the payoffs for that outcome in the game matrix.

The apparent matrix of this game, which we shall call IV-F, is apparently a mixture of our Games IV and V (cf. Matrices 10, 11). In fact, each player believes that he himself is playing Game IV while the other is playing Game V. Actually both are playing Game IV.

The idea behind this variant was to see how the *impression* of asymmetry would affect the performance. Using an actual asymmetric game would not do. We wanted the *objective* situation to be the same for both players, while each *imagined* the situation to be different for the other.

Psychologically the situation invites some interesting questions. For example, is the large temptation *attributed* to the other (and the concomitant large sucker's punishment) sufficient to bring the frequency of cooperation in this game substantially below its value in Game IV, in spite of the fact that the actual payoffs which each player receives are exactly as those of Game IV? On the other hand, we would not expect the amount of cooperation in this game to be as low as in Game V, where the payoffs with large magnitudes, T and S, are actually realized by the players.

Comparison of this game (IV-F) with Games IV and V in the Pure Matrix Condition is shown in Table 26.

TABLE 26

Game	IV	IV–F	V
CC	.56	.50	.21
CD	.10	.10	.06
DC	.10	.12	.06
DD	.24	.28	.67
C	.66	.61	.27

Although IV-F does fall between IV and V, it is much closer to IV than to V.

Comparison of propensities is shown in Table 27.

TABLE 27

	IV	IV–F	V
x	.962	.952	.962
y	.453	.500	.352
z	.377	.391	.229
w	.189	.136	.047

One might interpret these results as an indication that one's own payoffs have a stronger influence on the conduct of the game than the payoffs one attributes to the other. On the other hand, we must keep in mind that because of the deception, the payoffs of the other were not *announced* by the experimenter (as they were in the Pure Matrix Condition). The other's payoffs had to be "looked up" in the matrix. To be sure, the matrix was in front of the subjects all the time, but we have no assurance that subjects looked up both their own payoffs and those of the other player every time. Some might have paid attention only to their own payoffs and so were effectively playing Game IV. It might be interesting to perform the same experiment with an apparatus which displays the payoffs separately to each subject to see whether the absence of announcements might have been responsible for our results.

It should also be kept in mind that the nature of Prisoner's Dilemma is such that an argument can be made for either of two contrary results. In this case, the same features of the game which make it appear "severe" (inducing a strong motivation to defect) can also be interpreted to make the game seem mild. The first line of reasoning which may occur to a player goes something like this:

"He stands to gain 50 if he defects. Also, he stands to lose 50 if he cooperates alone. Therefore he will probably not cooperate. Consequently I will not cooperate either."

However, the reasoning might also go as follows:

"If I defect and he cooperates, I gain 2, but he loses 50. This does not seem fair. Besides, this will make him angry, and he is sure to retaliate. Better to cooperate to show him that I am not taking advantage of his precarious position."

Especially if the other does make a cooperative choice, the interpretation might go this way:

"He risks to lose 50 if he cooperates alone. Nevertheless he did cooperate. He must be a decent fellow. I will go along with him."

As we have said, it is typical of arguments in support of a particular style of play in Prisoner's Dilemma that the features of the game which support the argument can be turned around to support the opposing argument. We had intended to build a strong self-fulfilling assumption into Game IV-F. But in doing so, we may have brought an opposite self-fulfilling assumption into play which all but offsets the first one.

If the arguments we have just developed are valid, they ought to be reflected in the propensities x, y, z, and w. We would expect x in Game IV-F to be greater than in Game IV and w to be smaller. This is because the lock-ins (results of self-fulfilling assumptions) ought to be stronger in IV-F. On the other hand, both y and z ought to be greater in IV-F, especially the latter ("repentance") if the conscience-motivated abstention from continued defection is a fact. Comparing the propensities in IV-F and IV (Table 26), we see that our conjecture is corroborated with respect to y, z, and w, but not with respect to x. The question, therefore, remains open.

The Case of $S \neq -T$ and Asymmetrical Games

One question which has remained entirely unanswered in our investigations is whether the temptation to defect or the fear of being left holding the bag is the stronger motive in inducing defection (or inhibiting cooperation). In all our experiments we had $S = -T$. Consequently any changes in one were always accompanied by the same changes in the other. To assess the effects of each separately, we should keep one of the parameters constant while we vary the other. The following set of games could suggest the answer to our question about the relative importance of T and S.

	C	D
C	1,1	−3,2
D	2,−3	−1,−1

Matrix 18.

	C	D
C	1,1	−2,3
D	3,−2	−1,−1

Matrix 19.

Each of these two games is to be compared with Game IV (Matrix 10). In one of them the game is made more "severe" by increasing the magnitude of S while keeping T constant; in the other by increasing the magnitude of T while keeping S constant.

Games with Third Choice

An interesting modification of Prisoner's Dilemma can be made by adding "third choices." An example is shown in Matrix 20.

	C	S	D
C	5,5	−1,−1	−10,10
S	−1,−1	−1,−1	−1,−1
D	10,−10	−1,−1	−5,−5

Matrix 20.

In this game either player can escape from the Dilemma situation by playing strategy S ("Sanctuary"). For in that case, there is nothing the other can do to change the outcome. Thus each player can on any given play "refuse" to play. The payoff of this "sanctuary" strategy can now be taken as an independent variable. It can, in particular, be decreased to almost P, which each player can guarantee himself in the two-choice Prisoner's Dilemma, and we can see how unattractive, albeit still sought after, the sanctuary can become. On the other hand, the sanctuary payoff can be increased to almost R. Interesting questions arise if the sanctuary payoff becomes less than P or greater than R. Failure to take advantage of the sanctuary in the latter case clearly indicates an "irrational" choice or else points to considerations other than payoffs, e.g., the attraction of the game itself. On the other hand, if the sanctuary payoff is less than P, or even less than S, its use may indicate acts of revenge, where a player punishes the other (and incidentally himself) more severely than he could if he simply chose D, possibly as a demonstration of disapproval of the other's failure to cooperate.

Sanctuary payoffs need not be equal for the row and the column player. A difference offers the opportunity to observe the differential effect in the case of linked subjects, while symmetric sanctuaries but with different payoffs in different games can be compared in the case of independent subjects. Thus the effect of linkage can be assessed. Is there an imitative effect in choosing the sanctuary?

In a comparative study made by E. Travis (unpublished) on fifteen pairs of mental hospital patients diagnosed as schizophrenic and fifteen pairs diagnosed as nonschizophrenic, the results indicate that the frequency of choosing the "sanctuary" or "escape" strategy S was about twice as great among the schizophrenics as among the nonschizophrenics.

As another example of a game with a third choice, consider the game represented by Matrix 21.

We note that this is a modification of the well-known divide-the-dollar game. In the latter game, each of two subjects names the fraction of the dollar which he claims for himself. The payoffs are determined by the amounts named. If these amounts add up to a dollar or less, each gets what he has claimed. If, however, the two amounts add up to more than a dollar, neither gets anything. Matrix 21 would be a representation of this game if all the three entries below the secondary diagonal (the three lower right entries) were zero. (The players are

	25	50	75
25	25,25	25,50	25,75
50	50,25	50,50	−25,75
75	75,25	75,−25	0,0

Matrix 21.

assumed to be confined in their choices to 25¢, 50¢, and 75¢.) Experimental evidence indicates that in the divide-the-dollar game, subjects predominantly choose 50¢, which is the so-called "prominent" solution proposed by T. C. Schelling (1960).

In the present modification, the player who claims 50¢ is penalized if the other claims 75¢. Moreover, the player who claims 75¢ gets his 75¢ if the other claims the equitable share of 50¢. We see from Matrix 21 that if we delete the first row and the first column, a Prisoner's Dilemma game results. Thus the game is a sort of cross between divide-the-dollar and Prisoner's Dilemma.

Consider now the three responses of the column chooser to the row chooser's claim of 75¢. The column player can "give in" to the claim by settling for 25¢. Let us call this the accommodating response. Or the column player can counter with his own claim of 75¢ and so deprive both of any gain. Let us call this the tit-for-tat response. Finally the column chooser can make the equitable claim of 50¢. This results in the greatest loss for him and the greatest gain for the other. One would conjecture that such outcomes would be rare compared with the outcomes (25,75), (50,50), (75,25), and (0,0). Nevertheless they may occur, and it is interesting to look for a psychological explanation if they do. Responses of 25¢ to the other's persistent claims of 75¢ are easily explained. Here the more ruthless player has bullied the more accommodating one into submission, that is, has made him accept the lesser evil. The outcomes (o,o) are also easily explainable: they are the results of "confrontation." The outcome (75, −25) appears as simply the result of misplaced trust. Its *persistence*, however, could indicate something else, namely the insistence of the player who suffers the loss that he is neither giving in nor punishing the other for his greed, that he stands pat on his equitable choice, because that is where the mutually beneficial outcome lies if both should make this choice. This attitude can, of course, also be attributed to the "martyr" in the Prisoner's Dilemma, but it is more pronounced in the three-choice game, because the nonaggressive individual has the additional choice of accommodating to the aggressive player's demand and saving a portion of his share of the reward, which he did not have in the Prisoner's Dilemma game. This game could be subjected to the same variations as the previous games.

Games with Communication of Intent

Some investigators have directed their attention to questions related to the role of communication in nonzero-sum games (Deutsch, 1958). For example, one might ask how the structure of Prisoner's Dilemma is affected if one of the players announces his choice of strategy to the other. If the announcement is binding, it amounts to a move in a game, in which the first player has a choice of two moves, and the second player a choice of two replies to each of the first player's choices. Note that this game is not at all of the sort we have called Prisoner's Dilemma. In order to be compared, the two games both must be in so-called "normal form," i.e., both must be reduced to a form in which each of the players has only one move and their moves must be made *independently of each other*. One of the fundamental results of game theory is that this reduction can always be carried out provided the situation depicted meets the criteria of a game, as games are formally defined. That is to say, regardless of how many moves there may be in a game described as a sequence of moves, where the choices open to one player are contingent on the choices made up to that point (which is the usual situation in games of strategy), the game may be represented in normal form as a matrix, whose rows and columns represent the possible *single* choices of the respective players. Each player needs to choose only once in a play of the game: he chooses a *strategy* (not a move) and this choice (it is shown in game theory) contains all the possible choices, including the contingencies of these choices, which the player might make when the game is played sequentially.

Now Prisoner's Dilemma, as we have been studying it, is already in normal form, because each player must choose only once per play of the game, and the choices must be simultaneous (that is, independent). If one player is asked to choose first, the game is no longer in normal form. However, as we shall now show, it is now a new game which can also be reduced to a normal form.

The first player now has two strategies, which for him are equivalent to the two moves open to him, namely

S_1: Choose C.
S_2: Choose D.

The second player, however, now has *four* strategies at his disposal, namely

S_1':   Choose C regardless of what player 1 chooses.
S_2':   Choose C if he chooses C, otherwise D.
S_3':   Choose D if he chooses C, otherwise C.
S_4':   Choose D regardless of what he chooses.

In normal form, this game is now represented by a matrix with two rows and four columns, as shown in Matrix 22. The payoffs are those corresponding to our Game IV.

	S_1'	S_2'	S_3'	S_4'
S_1	1,1	1,1	$-2,2$	$-2,2$
S_2	2,-2	$-1,-1$	2,-2	$-1,-1$

Matrix 22.

We see that this is not at all a Prisoner's Dilemma game. For one thing, the number of strategies available to one player is not equal to that available to the other. And, what is perhaps more important, the essential feature of Prisoner's Dilemma is missing: Player 1 has no dominating strategy. Note that if the column chooser can announce his choice of strategy (he now has four), he can force the row chooser to take S_1 by announcing S_2' (his tit-for-tat strategy). To the row chooser, on the other hand, no advantage accrues from the privilege of announcing his strategy. If we now assume that the column player has the privilege of announcing his strategy, *this* game, reduced to normal form makes four strategies available to the column chooser and *sixteen* to the row chooser, as shown in Matrix 23.

This is again a different game. Here the best choice for the row chooser is strategy S_{0100} and for the column chooser S_2'. Translated into English, this solution states the following.

If the second player has a choice of announcing one of the four strategies S_1', S_2', S_3', S_4', he cannot do better

	S_1'	S_2'	S_3'	S_4'
S_{0000}	2,−2	−1,−1	2,−2	−1,−1
S_{0001}	2,−2	−1,−1	2,−2	−2,2
S_{0010}	2,−2	−1,−1	−2,2	−1,−1
S_{0011}	2,−2	−1,−1	−2,2	−2,2
S_{0100}	2,−2	1,1	2,−2	−1,−1
S_{0101}	2,−2	1,1	2,−2	−2,2
S_{0110}	2,−2	1,1	−2,2	−1,−1
S_{0111}	2,−2	1,1	−2,−2	−2,2
S_{1000}	1,1	−1,−1	2,−2	−1,−1
S_{1001}	1,1	−1,−1	2,−2	−2,2
S_{1010}	1,1	−1,−1	−2,2	−1,−1
S_{1011}	1,1	−1,−1	−2,2	−2,2
S_{1100}	1,1	1,1	2,−2	−1,−1
S_{1101}	1,1	1,1	2,−2	−2,2
S_{1110}	1,1	1,1	−2,2	−1,−1
S_{1111}	1,1	1,1	−2,2	−2,2

Matrix 23.

The row player has decided in advance what he will do in case the column player announces each of his four strategies. For example, S_{1001} means that the row player has decided to play C if the column player announces either S_1' or S_4', but he will play D if the column player announces either S_2' or S_3'.

than announce S_2'. The first player cannot do better than to decide, "I will play cooperatively if and only if you announce your strategy S_2'" (which is to say, "I will play cooperatively if and only if you will").

If games are to be analyzed strictly formally (as is done in game theory), the reduction to normal form is mandatory. Analysis without such reduction has been undertaken by some investigators. This sort of analysis of necessity remains incomplete. There is no reason, however, why it should not be pursued in the context of *psychological* rather than game-theoretical investigations of games. After all, reduction of a game to normal form is only a formalistic device and needs to have no counterpart in the players' views of the game. Communication, on the other hand, is very definitely a human phenomenon with rich psychological implications. We shall therefore depart from formal game-theoretical analysis and introduce communication, not formally as moves in the game (as must be done in game-theoretical analysis), but as something sui generis imposed upon the game.

Let us suppose Prisoner's Dilemma played in the following way. Before the choice is made, each player reveals to the other (simultaneously) what choice he is going to make, with the understanding that this revelation is not binding. No payoffs are associated with either announcement.

We now have essentially two games played consecutively. The first game is represented by Matrix 24, and the second game is Prisoner's Dilemma. From the purely strategic point of view the choice between C and D in

	C_2	D_2
C_1	0,0	0,0
D_1	0,0	0,0

Matrix 24.

the first game is obviously arbitrary and has no bearing on the choices in Prisoner's Dilemma which follows. Psychologically, however, the situation is very different. The first game gives the players an opportunity to declare their intentions without cost. In repeated plays of Prisoner's Dilemma, the way one plays can also be used to communicate intentions, but in that case there are costs attached, for example, to unreciprocated cooperative choices.

Suppose now both players announce C. Is the choice of C by either player on the next play more or less likely than if either or both had announced D? Or, to put it more generally, in a sequence of plays in which announcements alternate with payoff games, is there likely to be more or less cooperation than in a sequence of payoff games, such as the ones we have been studying?

As with all questions related to Prisoner's Dilemma, one can argue in favor of either answer. On the one hand, it stands to reason that there should be more, rather than less, cooperation when announcements alternate with games, since the declarations of intent serve the purpose of facilitating collusion. On the other hand, the temptation to renege on the declaration of intent is always there. (The rules of the game must specify that the declaration of intent is not binding.) If players renege on their declarations, the resulting mistrust may be even more severe than in the case of a sequence of payoff games, since such a switch is more likely to be interpreted as a doublecross than a straight D response, which can be attributed to "self defense." All the other psychological questions involving the conditional response probabilities, etc., remain in force.

Interpreted Games

So far we have assumed that Prisoner's Dilemma is presented to the subjects as a parlor game played for money. Several variants are possible in which monetary gains and losses are replaced by other kinds of rewards and punishments. Along with these changes, one can introduce different interpretations of Prisoner's Dilemma. The original anecdote involving the two prisoners is one such interpretation (cf. p. 24). Several other interpretations are possible. For example, the two players can be asked to imagine that they are two firms in competition. Each has a choice of selling its product at one of two price levels. If one firm sells at a high level while the other sells at a low level, the second firm reaps the profits (by winning the market). If both sell at a high level, both profit (though not as much as when competition is eliminated). If both sell at a low level, both lose money. Clearly, this situation is isomorphic to Prisoner's Dilemma. Or, the players can imagine that they are rival power blocs who have made a disarmament agreement. The cooperative choice now means keeping the agreement; the defecting choice, breaking it. There is supposedly an advantage accruing to the bloc which breaks the agreement unilaterally, etc.

The central point of interest in these interpretations is the question of whether the pattern of play will change markedly in each variant, and, if so, in what direction. In other words, one can design experiments to tap the relative strength of the subjects' ethical convictions or their cognitive sets on various matters. In the case of the original Prisoner's Dilemma, the question is either whether one should snitch on one's partner in crime or what the subjects think is the likelihood that two prisoners in such a situation will trust each other to hold out. In the case of business competition, the question pertains to the likelihood of tacit price fixing (in the subjects' estimation). In the case of international relations, the question pertains to the role of trust or mistrust (again, of course, in the subjects' estimation, not necessarily in reality).

Note that the experiments provide answers to these questions entirely in behavioral terms, not in terms of verbal responses as in questionnaires. However, there is also an opportunity to compare behavioral data with verbal responses from the same population and to note whether behavioral patterns correlate with verbally expressed convictions.

We have already indicated that attempts to correlate frequency of cooperative responses with independently assessed personality characteristics of *individuals* in repeated plays cannot be expected to yield much information, because of the strong interaction effects. However, we have also suggested that this difficulty may be overcome by "distilling" out other variables, which are more immune to interaction and so may be expected to reflect more faithfully individual personality characteristics. Also it is entirely feasible to correlate behavior patterns in the Prisoner's Dilemma game to personality characteristics of *populations* (as distinct from individuals). The experiments can thus become a source of information about the hierarchy of values in a given population. Our comparison of male and female populations was an example of such an approach.

Prisoner's Dilemma with Group Decisions

As a final example of an intriguing variant, consider Prisoner's Dilemma played by two teams each consisting of three individuals. We shall suppose that there is no communication either between the opposing teams or among the members of each team. The decisions to play C or D are made by a silent vote. The players can see how their own teammates are voting but not how the individual members of the other team are voting. (Of course they know the result of that vote because the outcome is announced after each play, as in the preceding versions.)

In addition to all the other information about this game, we now obtain a great deal more. Previously, we were concerned with the way one's own previous choice and the other's previous choice affected the probability of cooperative (or noncooperative) choice on the next play. Now we have also the effect of one's team's choice, which is not necessarily identical with one's own choice. Here, then, we have an opportunity to observe not only "martyrs" (players who choose unilateral cooperation persistently) but also nonconformists, i.e., players who consistently are in the minority of one in their own group.

Another interesting question is whether introducing communication among teammates makes a difference. Preliminary investigations (Martin, unpublished) suggest that the effect of intra-team communication is quite large and in the direction of greater cooperation between the two teams (in spite of the fact that no inter-team communication is allowed).

One might explain this effect as follows. Suppose the two teams are locked in on *DD*. Suppose one member of one of the teams gets the idea that it might be possible to break out of it. (The probability that this idea will occur to two or more members *simultaneously* is small, since in the absence of communication the events are independent and the corresponding probabilities must be multiplied.) The lone would-be cooperator's vote does not change the team vote, and so his persistence (if he continues to vote for *C*) fails to produce any response from the other team. Thus the lone vote for *C* remains doubly futile and is given up more quickly than in the case of two individuals playing Prisoner's Dilemma. Besides, once given up, the attempt to get one's own team to cooperate may be quite unlikely to be made again, because it has failed on two counts—getting the other team to cooperate and getting one's own team to start cooperating. Thus it may be more difficult to break out of the *DD* trap in the team-vs.-team game.

Suppose now intra-team communication is introduced. The players who see the advantage of cooperation may induce the team to adopt a cooperative strategy on a trial basis. It may be agreed to try a few cooperative plays to be continued or discontinued depending on whether they are or are not reciprocated by the other side. Thus at least attempts to break out of the *DD* trap will be more likely. Because of the inherent instability of the game, these attempts may be all it takes to throw the plays into a *CC* run.

It may be argued at this point that the same reasoning applies to the *CC* run. Suppose an idea occurs to one of the players to defect from *CC* (recall that the temptation is always there). The lone vote in favor of *D* cuts no more ice than the lone vote in favor of *C*, and so the stability at *CC* ought to be greater in teams (without intra-team communication) than in individuals. This may very well be the case and yet the balance may be in favor of more defecting responses in the case of non-communicating teams. The reason for this is that *CC* runs are already quite stable in individuals. Making them still more stable will not make a great difference. On the other hand, the *DD* runs are not as stable in the case of individuals as *CC* runs. Strengthening the lock-in effect on *DD* may be expected to induce greater changes in the overall play patterns than strengthening the already strong lock-in effect on *CC*.

It would be interesting to note whether the results are opposite in the case of populations in which the lock-in effect on *DD* is stronger. This seems to be the case in women subjects. The conjecture, therefore, is that teams of women playing Prisoner's Dilemma without intra-team communication ought to show more cooperation than individuals in contrast to men subjects.

If this turns out to be the case, the sort of explanation we have offered gains credibility.

Other Related Nonzero-Sum Games

Consider the game shown in Matrix 25.

	C_2	D_2
C_1	1,1	−2,2
D_1	2,−2	−5,−5

Matrix 25.

It shares an important feature with Prisoner's Dilemma. Each player is tempted to play D in order to get a bigger payoff, but if both do so, both get punished. However, the basic inequality in terms of which we have defined Prisoner's Dilemma, namely $T > R > P > S$ (cf. p. 34) is violated in Matrix 25, since in that game $T > R > S > P$. We see, also, that a fundamental feature of Prisoner's Dilemma is absent: D no longer dominates C. Strategy D is still best against the other's strategy C, but not against the other's strategy D. The motivations of this game are, therefore, different. According to strategic analysis, C responses on the part of one player should elicit D responses on the part of the other; and vice versa. In Prisoner's Dilemma, strategic analysis indicates that both C and D responses on the part of one player ought to elicit D responses on the part of the other (because of the fact that D is dominant). In practice, this is not at all the case: predominantly C responses elicit C responses, while D responses elicit D responses. Will the game-theoretical prediction be borne out in the case of games represented by Matrix 25? If so, the ρ_i and the $\rho_{C_1 C_2}$ associated with such games (cf. Chapter 3) should be substantially smaller than in the case of Prisoner's Dilemma games, perhaps even negative.

Let us examine more closely the psychology of the game represented by Matrix 25. The interesting feature of this game is in the opportunity it offers for "pre-emption." Suppose one of the players plays D persistently. In the case of Prisoner's Dilemma, the other had no choice but respond with D to D in self-defense (if he were guided entirely by the payoff matrix). In the game now considered, the other player has a choice of either punishing the D response (and, of course, himself as well) by responding with D or of "giving in" in the face of a "determined stand" on the part of the first player. It is clear that the game is psychologically isomorphic to the now famous game of Chicken. Here the C response stands for "chicken" and the D response for "daring." The DD outcome can also be interpreted as "disaster." Matrix 26 presents Chicken in an especially severe form:

	C_2	D_2
C_1	1,1	$-2,2$
D_1	2,-2	$-100,-100$

Matrix 26.

Like Prisoner's Dilemma, Chicken in its symmetric form has four independent parameters, which we may now label R (reward for prudence), T (temptation to bank on the other's giving in), S (surrender), and P (perdition). The inequality to be satisfied must be $T > R > S > P$. The experimental program described here and all the methods of analysis can be directly applied to this interesting class of games.

It appears, then, that the nonzero-sum game offers excellent opportunities to develop programs of laboratory experiments and mathematical theories in which clearly psychological concepts and interpretations are coupled with the generation and analysis of hard, replicable data.

Appendix I

Instructions Given to Subjects Playing Prisoner's Dilemma in the Pure Matrix Condition

YOU WILL BE PLAYING A GAME which has certain payoffs. You cannot by yourself control the specific payoff for a given game. Rather, the outcome will depend on what your partner does, as well as on what you do. Each of you has a payoff sheet in front of you.

The game is played as follows: You are players *A* and *B* respectively. In front of you are 2 cards, labeled R for right and L for left. On any given trial each of you may play, i.e., by pointing to either your left or right card. Any decision is final, i.e., you cannot change your mind once you have pointed to a card. The payoffs resulting from such a move are indicated on your payoff sheets. E.g., if you both move right, each loses _____ points. If *A* moves left and *B* moves right, *A* loses _____ points, and *B* wins _____ points. If *A* moves right and *B* moves left, *A* wins _____ points and *B* loses _____ points. If you both move left, each wins _____ points.

Each point is worth $\frac{1}{10}$ of a penny. During the course of the experiment you will play this type of game a large number of times, i.e., for approximately 1 hour. Each player's total gains and losses will be added together at the end of the experiment and converted into money.

The experimenter will read off after each move the number of points gained and lost by each person. Each of you will then record your particular gain or loss on the record sheet in front of you. After each series of 25 moves you will be asked to total your gains and losses.

It is of the essence that you do not *communicate* with

each other in any form whatsoever. This includes sighing, laughing, or any other form of communication which might indicate how you feel about given outcomes, or how you would like your partner to behave. The reason for this condition of *no communication* is that the experiment becomes useless for our purposes should any communication take place. In view of this, it will be a condition of the experiment that the experimental session be disbanded *without compensation to the subjects for time put in* should communication between group members occur. The same condition holds if a subject leaves the experiment before it is completed.

The gains or losses accumulated by each of you by the end of the experiment will be added to or subtracted from your hourly pay of $1.35 per hour.

Please DO NOT TALK about this experiment to others. They might participate in later experiments and they might be influenced to play differently if they know about it.

Appendix II
Estimates of Significance
(Games Compared)

ONE OF THE FIRST questions we asked at the beginning of our investigation concerned the relation between the payoffs of a Prisoner's Dilemma game and the associated pressures toward cooperation and defection. Such relations were found throughout to be in the expected direction, the most consistent relations being observed in sets of games differing with respect to only one payoff parameter. Thus our weakest hypothesis (Hypothesis 1) was by and large corroborated. Neither of the alternative strong hypotheses (H_3 and H_4) was consistently corroborated, therefore the question about the significance of observed differences in the frequency of cooperative choices observed in the several games must be raised. We wish to know what role the payoff structure plays in determining the value of C (as well as of several other variables), regardless of conditions under which the game is played and regardless of the population. We thus compare the values of these variables between all pairs of games and note the significance of the difference in each case.

Estimates of significance are shown in Table A.

We now rank order the games according to the magnitude of the observed values of the variables, ignoring differences which are not significant. The result is shown in Table B.

Now we apply the rank order correlation coefficient, comparing the observed rank order with those prescribed by our various hypotheses. The results are summarized in Table C.

TABLE A

Kolmogorov-Smirnov Two Sample Tests for thirteen of the variables. Roman numeral entries indicate significance at .01 level, the entry indicating the game in which the variable in question has the greater numerical value.

Games Compared

Variable	I/II	I/III	I/IV	I/V	I/XI	I/XII	II/III	II/IV	II/V	II/XI	II/XII	III/IV	III/V	III/XI	III/XII	IV/V	IV/XI	IV/XII	V/XI	V/XII	XI/XII
CC	I	I	IV	I	o	I	II	IV	II	XI	II	IV	III	XI	o	IV	XI	IV	XI	XII	XI
CD	II	o	IV	I	o	XII	II	o	II	II	o	IV	III	o	XII	IV	IV	o	XI	XII	XI
DC	II	o	IV	I	o	XII	II	o	II	II	o	IV	III	o	XII	IV	IV	o	o	XII	XII
DD	o	III	I	V	I	XII	III	II	V	II	XII	III	V	III	o	V	XI	XII	V	V	XII
C	I	I	I	I	o	I	II	IV	II	XI	II	IV	III	XI	o	IV	o	IV	XI	XII	XII
x	I	I	I	I	o	I	o	o	II	XI	II	IV	III	XI	o	IV	IV	IV	XI	XII	XI
y	I	I	I	I	o	I	II	o	II	II	o	IV	III	o	III	IV	o	o	XI	XII	XI
κ	I	I	I	I	o	I	II	IV	II	o	II	III	III	XI	XII	IV	IV	IV	XI	XII	o
w	o	I	IV	I	I	I	II	II	II	II	II	IV	III	o	o	IV	IV	IV	XI	XII	XII
ξ	II	I	IV	I	o	I	o	IV	II	XI	II	IV	III	XI	III	IV	XI	IV	XI	XII	XI
η	I	I	I	I	o	I	II	IV	II	XI	II	IV	III	XI	III	IV	IV	IV	XI	XII	XII
ζ	I	I	IV	I	o	I	II	o	II	II	II	IV	III	XI	XII	IV	IV	IV	X	XII	XI
ω	II	I	IV	I	o	I	II	o	II	II	II	IV	III	XI	III	IV	IV	IV	XI	XII	XI

TABLE B

Roman numerals indicate rank order of the games prescribed by the corresponding hypothesis except in the case of *DD* where the reverse order is prescribed. The entries indicate the actually observed rank order of the games with respect to each of the variables. Absence of differences significant on the .01 level are indicated by tied ranks.

Variable	H_{1a}			H_{1b}			H_{1c}			H_2		H_3							H_4						
	I	XI	III	IV	III	V	II	XII	III	IV	XI	I	IV	II	XI	XII	III	V	II	IV	I	XII	XI	III	V
CC	1.5	1.5	3	1	2	3	1	2.5	2.5	2	1	1.5	3	4	1.5	5.5	5.5	7	4	3	1.5	5.5	1.5	5.5	7
CD	2	2	2	1	2	3	1.5	1.5	3	1	2	2	2	2	5	2	5	7	2	2	5	2	5	5	7
DC	2	2	2	1	2	3	1.5	1.5	3	1	2	5	2	2	5	2	5	7	2	2	5	2	5	5	7
DD	2	1	1	3	2	1	3	1.5	1.5	2	2	4.5	7	4.5	6	2.5	2.5	1	2	7	4.5	2.5	6	2.5	1
C	1.5	1.5	3	1	2	3	1	2.5	2.5	1.5	1.5	2	4	4	2	5.5	5.5	7	4	2	2	5.5	2	5.5	7
x	1.5	1.5	3	1	2	3	1.5	3	1.5	2	1	1.5	3	4.5	5	6	4.5	7	3	4	1.5	6	1.5	4.5	7
y	1.5	1.5	3	1	2	3	1.5	3	1.5	1.5	1.5	1.5	3.5	4.5	4	1.5	4.5	6	3	2	1.5	4	1.5	4.5	6
z	1	2.5	2.5	1	2	3	1	2.5	2.5	1	2	1.5	4	4	1.5	5	6	7	4	4	1.5	4	1.5	6	7
w	1.5	1.5	3	1	2	3	1	2	3	1.5	1.5	2.5	1	2.5	5	5	5	7	2.5	1	2.5	5	3.5	5	7
ξ	1.5	1.5	3	1	2	3	1.5	3	1.5	2	1	3.5	2	1	3.5	6	6	7	4.5	2	3.5	6	2	4.5	7
η	1.5	1.5	3	1	2	3	1	3	2	1	2	1.5	3	4	1.5	6	5	7	4	3	1.5	6	1.5	5	7
ζ	1.5	1.5	3	1	2	3	1	2	3	1	2	3.5	1.5	1.5	3.5	5	6	7	1.5	1.5	3.5	5	3.5	6	7
ω	1.5	1.5	3	1	2	3	1	2	3	1	2	3.5	1.5	1.5	3.5	5	6	7	1.5	1.5	3.5	5	3.5	6	7

Notes:

H_{1a}: cooperation increases as R increases.
H_{1b}: cooperation decreases as T increases.
H_{1c}: cooperation increases as P decreases (being negative, becomes numerically smaller).

H_2: $(\partial C / \partial r_1) > 0$
H_3: $(\partial C / \partial r_1) > 0$; $(\partial C / \partial r_2) > 0$
H_4: $(\partial C / \partial r_1) > 0$; $(\partial C / \partial r_2) < 0$

TABLE C

Kendall Rank Correlation Coefficient τ and associated a priori probability of observed rank order under the null hypothesis $p(H_0)$, i.e., where each game is assigned each of the relevant rank orders with equal probability.

Variable	H_{1a}	$p(H_0)$	H_{1b}	$p(H_0)$	H_{1c}	$p(H_0)$	H_2	$p(H_0)$	H_3	$p(H_0)$	H_4	$p(H_0)$
CC	.82	.154	1.00	.077	.82	.154	−1.00	.333	.73	.015	.34	.191
CD	0	.231	1.00	.077	.82	.154	1.00	.333	.39	.191	.73	.035
DC	0	.231	1.00	.077	.82	.154	1.00	.333	.39	.191	.73	.035
DD	.33	.154	1.00	.077	.82	.154	1.00	.333	.65	.035	.60	.068
C	.82	.154	1.00	.077	.82	.154	0	.333	.79	.015	.48	.119
x	.82	.154	1.00	.077	0	.231	−1.00	.333	.65	.035	.25	.281
y	.82	.154	1.00	.077	.82	.154	0	.333	.69	.035	.37	.191
z	.82	.154	1.00	.077	.82	.154	1.00	.333	.79	.015	.79	.015
w	.82	.154	1.00	.077	1.00	.077	1.00	.333	.69	.035	.88	.005
ξ	.82	.154	1.00	.077	0	.231	0	.333	.69	.035	.37	.191
η	.82	.154	1.00	.077	.33	.154	−1.00	.333	.69	.035	.29	.281
ζ	.82	.154	1.00	.077	1.00	.077	1.00	.333	.75	.015	.85	.005
ω	.82	.154	1.00	.077	1.00	.077	1.00	.333	.75	.015	.85	.005

From Table C we see that the only hypothesis perfectly corroborated by all variables is H_{1b}, which asserts that cooperation decreases as T increases. It should be kept in mind, however, that the numerical range of T $(2 - 50)$ was greater than that of the other payoff parameters. We conjecture, further, that H_3 has somewhat of an edge over H_4, as has been guessed.

We see also that the variables which agree best with our strong hypotheses H_3 and H_4 are z, w, ζ, and ω, that is, the contingent probabilities of responding cooperatively following *noncooperation* (one's own or the other's). From this we conjecture that the nonpersistence of the defecting response is a more important symptom of the degree of cooperation than the persistence of the cooperative response reflected in CC, x, y, ξ, and η.

Appendix III
Estimates of Significance
(Populations Compared)

EVALUATION OF SIGNIFICANCE of the differences between male and female populations is shown in Table D.

We see from Table D that most significant differences are found between the all-male and the all-female populations. Only in the unilateral responses and in the state-conditioned propensities y and w there are no significant differences observed. In all cases, men have higher indices of cooperation.

Next we see that in the mixed pairs, no significant differences are observed between men and women. The differences between men playing men and men playing women do not reach significance level, with one exception. However, this may be due to the weakness of our test and to the stringency of our significance criterion. In all cases, men playing men have higher cooperative indices.

The rank order of the six comparisons according to the number of significant differences observed is the following:

$MM > WW$ (9); $MW > WW$ (5);

$\left.\begin{array}{l} MM > WM \\ WM > WW \end{array}\right\}$(4); $MM > MW$ (1); $WM = MW$.

We conjecture that it makes more difference to a woman whether she is playing against a man or a woman than it does to a man whether he is playing against a man or a woman. Moreover when men play against women, the performance of the two sexes becomes practically indistinguishable.

TABLE D

Kolmogorov-Smirnov Two Sample Tests for thirteen of the variables comparing all pairs among four populations: MM = men playing opposite men (N = 140); MW = men playing opposite women (N = 70); WM = women playing opposite men (N = 70); WW = women playing opposite women (N = 140). Entries give populations in which the variable in question has the greater numerical value, where the difference is significant at the .01 level. Zero entries indicate failure of the difference to reach that level of significance. Numbers in parentheses indicate the numerical values of the variable in the two populations compared.

Variable	MM, WW	MM, WM	MM, MW	WW, WM	WW, MW	WM, MW
CC	MM(.51, .22)	0(.51, .39)	0(.51, .39)	WM(.22, .39)	MW(.22, .39)	0(.39, .39)
CD	0(.08, .12)	0(.08, .09)	0(.08, .11)	0(.11, .09)	0(.12, .11)	0(.09, .11)
DC	0(.09, .11)	0(.09, .11)	0(.09, .09)	0(.11, .11)	0(.11, .09)	0(.11, .09)
DD	WW(.33, .46)	0(.33, .41)	0(.33, .41)	WW(.55, .41)	WW(.55, .41)	0(.41, .41)
C	MM(.59, .34)	MM(.59, .48)	0(.59, .51)	WW(.34, .48)	MW(.34, .51)	0(.48, .51)
x	MM(.85, .75)	MM(.85, .78)	0(.85, .79)	0(.75, .78)	0(.75, .79)	0(.78, .79)
y	0(.40, .37)	0(.40, .44)	0(.40, .40)	0(.37, .44)	0(.37, .40)	0(.44, .40)
z	MM(.39, .26)	MM(.39, .29)	0(.39, .33)	0(.26, .29)	0(.26, .33)	0(.29, .33)
w	0(.20, .15)	0(.20, .22)	0(.20, .21)	0(.15, .22)	0(.15, .21)	0(.22, .21)
ξ	MM(.74, .55)	MM(.74, .65)	MM(.74, .68)	0(.55, .65)	MW(.55, .68)	0(.65, .68)
η	MM(.76, .60)	0(.76, .69)	0(.76, .71)	WW(.60, .69)	MW(.60, .71)	0(.69, .71)
ζ	MM(.25, .16)	0(.25, .22)	0(.25, .24)	0(.16, .22)	0(.16, .24)	0(.22, .24)
ω	MM(.25, .18)	0(.25, .28)	0(.25, .25)	0(.18, .28)	0(.18, .25)	0(.28, .25)

Appendix IV
Effect of Initial Response

HERE WE EXAMINE the possible effect of the initial response on the final twenty-five responses in all available
data, including data on games VI through X, not discussed elsewhere in this study. This gives us 410 pairs
in all. In Matrix (a) the rows represent the initial
responses *CC*, *DD*, or *N* (*CD* or *DC*); the columns, the
lock-ins, if any, *N* signifying no lock-in. As usual we
call the final twenty-five responses locked in if twenty-
three or more of them are either *CC* or *DD*. In three
instances the final twenty-five responses were all *CD* or
all *DC*. These are included with *N*. The entries of the
matrix are numbers of pairs in each category of lock-in.

		Final		
		CC	*N*	*DD*	
Initial	*CC*	55	46	24	125
	N	85	71	40	196
	DD	29	32	28	89
		169	149	92	410

Matrix (a).

Matrix (b) shows the corresponding expected numbers under the null hypothesis, namely that the category
of the last twenty-five responses is not related to the
initial response.

The differences are in the expected direction. Somewhat more than expected *CC* lock-ins follow initial *CC*
responses and somewhat more than expected *DD* lock-
ins follow initial *DD* responses. However, χ^2 turns out

	CC	N	DD
CC	51	46	28
N	81	71	44
DD	37	32	20

Matrix (b).

to be 6.39, which for four degrees of freedom is only at about .20 level of significance. This result does not speak for the rejection of the null hypothesis.

If we confine ourselves only to the "extremes," i.e., initial CC and DD responses and final lock-ins, we obtain the following matrix.

	CC	DD	
CC	55	24	79
DD	29	28	57
	84	52	136

Matrix (c).

The expected matrix is

	CC	DD
CC	49	30
DD	35	22

Matrix (d).

The value of χ^2 is now 4.61, which for one degree of freedom is at .03 level of significance. Therefore it is reasonable to assume that the initial response, if it is CC or DD, does have some effect on the character of the final lock-in. The relative chi-square, that is $\chi^2/N = 4.61/79$ or .06, is not large; hence the influence of the initial response on the final responses must be considered small. This influence can be attributed to either the common effect of the players' inherent cooperative propensities on both the initial and the final responses or to some impetus given by the initial response to the nature of the subsequent interactions.

Glossary of Symbols

A_1, A_2, B_1, B_2, etc.: Designations of strategies available to players in two-person games. The subscripts refer to players 1 and 2. Player 1 always chooses the rows of the strategy matrix; player 2, the columns.

C, C_1, C_2: The cooperative strategies in Prisoner's Dilemma; also the frequencies of the corresponding choices.

C: If in a sequence of plays of Prisoner's Dilemma a player decides to play C, he is in state C.

$C(1)$: The frequency of cooperative choices on the first play of a sequence of plays in a population of players.

$C(2)$: The frequency of cooperative choices on the second play of a sequence of plays in a population of players.

(C_1C_2) or (CC): The outcome in Prisoner's Dilemma which results when both players choose the cooperative strategy. Also the frequency of such outcomes in a given universe of outcomes.

(C_1D_2) or (CD): The outcome in Prisoner's Dilemma which results when player 1 chooses the cooperative strategy, while player 2 chooses the defecting strategy. Also the frequency of such outcomes in a given universe of outcomes.

D, D_1, D_2: The defecting strategies in Prisoner's Dilemma; also the frequencies of the corresponding choices.

D: If in a sequence of plays of Prisoner's Dilemma a player decides to play D, he is in state D.

$D^{(n)}$: The strategy consisting exclusively of D's in Prisoner's Dilemma played n consecutive times.

(D_1D_2) or (DD): The outcome in Prisoner's Dilemma which results when both players choose the defecting strategy. Also the frequency of such outcomes in a given universe of outcomes.

(D_1C_2) or (DC): The outcome in Prisoner's Dilemma which results when player 1 chooses the defecting strategy while player 2 chooses the co-operative strategy. Also the frequency of such outcomes in a given universe of outcomes.

G_i: Expected payoff to player i ($i = 1, 2$) under steady state conditions.

L_{CC}: Fraction of pairs in a population of paired players of Prisoner's Dilemma who obtained at least twenty-three (CC) outcomes out of the last twenty-five plays of a sequence.

L_{DD}: Fraction of pairs in a population of paired players of Prisoner's Dilemma who obtained at least twenty-three (DD) outcomes out of the last plays of a sequence.

M: The ratio $(1 - y_1)(1 - z_2)/y_1z_2$ or $(1 - y_2)(1 - z_1)/y_2z_1$.

m: The reciprocal of the average life expectancy in a population of processes, each of which may end with equal probability at any moment. It is assumed that m is the same for each process in the population.

MM: The population of players in which both players of a pair are male.

MW: The population of players in which the first player of a pair is male and the second, female.

$N(i)$:   The number of runs (consecutive outcomes of one kind) at least i plays long in a sequence of plays.

P: The payoff to each player in Prisoner's Dilemma when both choose the defecting strategy.

$P(t)$:   The probability that a process, the time of whose termination is a random variable, will not have terminated at time t.

$p_i(t)$:   The probability that a system, passing through a sequence of states, will find itself in state i at time t.

$p_i(\infty)$:   The steady state probability that a system subject to a stochastic process, passing from state to state, is in state i.

R: The payoff to each player in Prisoner's Dilemma when both choose the cooperative strategy.

r_1: The ratio $(R - P)/(T - S)$.

r_2: The ratio $(R - S)/(T - S)$.

$r_{CC}^{(i)}$: The ratio $N(i)/N(i - 1)$, related to runs of (CC) outcomes.

$r_{CD}^{(i)}$ [or $r_{DC}^{(i)}$]: The ratio $N(i)/N(i - 1)$ related to runs of (CD) [or (DC)] outcomes.

$r_{DD}^{(i)}$: The ratio $N(i)/N(i - 1)$ related to runs of (DD) outcomes.

S: The payoff to the cooperating player in Prisoner's Dilemma when the other player chooses the defecting strategy.

s_i: The i-th state of a set of states in which a given system can be.

T: The payoff to the defecting player in Prisoner's Dilemma when the other player chooses the cooperative strategy.

t: Time, measured in terms of the number of plays made in a sequence of plays of Prisoner's Dilemma.

w_i: The probability that player i chooses cooperatively following a (DD) outcome on the preceding play.

$\tilde{w}_i$: $1 - w_i$.

WM: The population of players in which the first player is female and the second male.

WW: The population of players in which both players are female.

x_i: The probability that player i

$\tilde{x}_i$:   chooses cooperatively following a (CC) outcome on the preceding play.

$\tilde{x}_i$: $1 - x_i$.

x^*:   If two players adjust their x_i so as to maximize their expected payoffs, x^* is the value of x_i for which the partial derivative $\partial G_i / \partial x_i$ vanishes.

y_i: The probability that player i chooses cooperatively following a (CD) outcome if $i = 1$ or follow- a (DC) outcome if $i = 2$.

$\tilde{y}_i$: $1 - y_i$.

z_i: The probability that player i chooses cooperatively following a (DC) outcome if $i = 1$ or following a (CD) outcome if $i = 2$.

$\tilde{z}_i$: $1 - z_i$.

α: A learning parameter in a stochastic learning model.

α_{ij}:   The probability that a system, passing through a sequence of states and finding itself in state i, will next pass into state j. Also called a transition probability.

Γ: If in a sequence of plays of Prisoner's Dilemma a player decides (irrevocably) to choose C regardless of outcomes, he is in state Γ.

γ: The probability that a player will pass from state C to state Γ.

δ: The probability that a player will pass from state D to state Δ.

Δ: If in a sequence of plays of Prisoner's Dilemma, a player decides (irrevocably) to choose D, regardless of outcomes, he is in state Δ.

ζ_i: The probability that player i chooses cooperatively following his own defecting choice.

η_i: The probability that player i chooses cooperatively following his own cooperative choice on the preceding play.

λ: The asymptotic frequency of a response in a stochastic learning model.

ξ_i: The probability that player i ($i =$ 1, 2) chooses cooperatively following the other's cooperative choice on the preceding play.

μ: Same as m except that each process may be characterized by a different life expectancy $1/\mu$.

$\rho_{C_1C_2}$ or ρ_C: The product moment correlation between the frequencies of cooperative choices by players 1 and 2 respectively in a population of paired players.

ρ_0: The product moment correlation between two random variables, each referring to one of paired players in a sequence of plays of Prisoner's Dilemma and taking on value 1 or 0 depending on whether the player in question chose strategy C or D.

ρ_1: The same as ρ_0 except that one player's choice is matched with the other player's immediately preceding choice.

$\rho_i \ (i = 2, 3, \ldots 6)$: The same as ρ_1 except that one player's choice is matched with the choice made by the other i plays previously.

$\rho_{w_1 w_2}$ or ρ_w: The product moment correlation between w_1 and w_2 in a population of paired players.

$\rho_{x_1 x_2}$ or ρ_x: The product moment correlation between x_1 and x_2 in a population of paired players.

$\rho_{y_1 y_2}$ or ρ_y: The product moment correlation between y_1 and y_2 in a population of paired players.

$\rho_{z_1 z_2}$ or ρ_z: The product moment correlation between z_1 and z_2 in a population of paired players.

$\rho_{\zeta_1 \zeta_2}$ or ρ_ζ: The product moment correlation between ζ_1 and ζ_2 in a population of paired players.

$\rho_{\eta_1 \eta_2}$ or ρ_η: The product moment correlation between η_1 and η_2 in a population of paired players.

$\rho_{\xi_1 \xi_2}$ or ρ_ξ: The product moment correlation between ξ_1 and ξ_2 in a population of paired players.

$\rho_{\omega_1 \omega_2}$ or ρ_ω: The product moment correlation between ω_1 and ω_2 in a population of paired players.

$\psi(\mu)$: A density distribution function of μ.

ω_i: The probability that player i chooses cooperatively following the other's defecting choice.

$>$: The "greater than" sign, used also to rank order games. Thus $I > II$ means that the frequency of cooperative choices in Game I was observed to be greater than in Game II.

I, II, etc.: Roman numerals designate different variants (with respect to their payoff matrices) of the Prisoner's Dilemma game. Specifically, the seven games discussed are labeled I, II, III, IV, V, XI, and XII.

Notes

1. A zero-sum game is one in which, regardless of the outcome of the game, the winnings of one player are exactly balanced by the losses of the other, or others, i.e., the algebraic sum of the "payoffs" to each player is always zero. If this sum is always constant, not necessarily zero, regardless of the outcome of the game, the game is called "constant sum." From the point of view of game theory, constant-sum games are strategically equivalent to zero-sum games. We shall refer to all constant-sum games as zero-sum games.

2. Nonzero-sum games are all those which are not constant-sum. By definition, then, some outcomes of nonzero-sum games are jointly better for *both* players than other outcomes (assuming that the payoffs can be added). Even if the payoffs cannot be added, it is possible for both (or all) players to prefer some outcomes to others, in contrast to two-person zero-sum games, in which the preferences of the two players must always be opposite.

3. The simplest self-negating proposition is "Every statement within these quotation marks is false." If one assumes the proposition true, it turns out to be false; if one assumes it false, it turns out to be true.

4. This is in consequence of the so-called Law of Large Numbers, which states that if a random variable assumes different values with fixed probabilities, then the average of the values it has assumed over a long sequence of realizations will be very nearly equal the sum of the products of the several values, multiplied by the respective probabilities (the expected value). In the case under consideration, the expected value is $1/2(1) + 1/2(-1) = 0$.

5. Smallest and largest are meant here in the algebraic sense. Of two negative numbers, the numerically larger one is the "smaller."

6. We shall be designating outcomes by pairs of strategy choices which determine them. Thus the outcome (C_1C_2) is the result of player 1's choice of C_1 and player 2's choice of C_2. When

there is no danger of ambiguity, we shall sometimes omit the subscripts. Thus we shall sometimes write (CD) for (C_1D_2), etc.

7. When a game is in normal form, one strategy is said to dominate another for a player, if all the outcomes in the former strategy are at least as good for the player in question and sometimes better as the corresponding outcomes in the latter. That is, no matter what strategy the other player chooses, the dominating strategy yields a larger payoff than the dominated strategy.

8. Note that strategy 2 seems rather reasonable. It starts out by "trying" cooperation. The second move is contingent on the result of the first. If cooperation has worked, it is continued, but not otherwise. These, however, are commonsense arguments. They do not withstand a more thorough strategic analysis according to which it is better to play D in the second move regardless of what happened on the first.

9. Lewis F. Richardson investigated the properties of mathematical models proposed to represent arms races. The most interesting property of these models is their instability when the parameters assume values in a certain range. An arms race represented by a model in the unstable range must either keep going at an accelerated pace (which Richardson interpreted as a drive toward war) or must go into reverse, i.e., toward disarmament. We shall refer to this as the Richardson Effect (cf. Chapter 8).

10. Strictly speaking, when a game is represented in normal form, the payoffs designate the utilities of the associated outcomes to the players. Utilities are so defined that preferences of players with respect to risky outcomes (i.e., preferences among "lottery tickets," each representing an assignment of probabilities to each of the possible outcomes) is determined by maximizing expected utility. Utilities are supposed to be given on an interval scale. That is, if all the utilities u_i of either player are changed from u_i to $Au_i + B$ ($A > 0$), the resulting game is supposed to be identical with the original one. In our experiments the payoffs were in money. We have not, of course, undertaken the very difficult task of determining a utility scale of money for each subject. We have simply assumed that the money payoffs were utilities. In most cases, this is the best one can do. In our situation, the determination of utility scales was not necessary, because we were not testing any game-theoretical result which relates specifically to utilities.

11. When more than two persons are involved, it is sometimes necessary to assume that payoffs are transferable and additive. In that case, it is assumed that payoffs are identified with utilities in the absolute sense.

12. To see this, consider a simpler case, involving only three variables. Let $F(x,y,z) = F(ax + b, ay + b, az + b)$; in other words, let a function of three variables retain its value if all three variables are subjected to a linear transformation. Let $p = (x - y)/(y - z)$, $q = y - z$. Then, given values of p, q, and z, the values of x, y, and z are determined since $y = q + z$, $x = pq + q + z$. But then we can write $F(x,y,z) = G(p,q,z) = G(p,aq,az + b)$ where G is some other function of three variables. Let $a = 1$. Then $G(p,q,z + b) = G(p,q,z)$, which shows that G is independent of z, because b is arbitrary. We can therefore write $G(p,q,z) = H(p,q)$. But then $H(p,q) = H(p,aq)$ and since a is arbitrary, we must have H independent of q. This leaves $p = (x - y)(y - z)$ as a single variable in which $F(x,y,z)$ can be expressed. In other words, if a linear transformation on the variables leaves a function of those variables invariant, the function can be expressed as a function of ratio differences. In the case of three variables, one such ratio suffices. In the case of four variables, two are needed.

13. This is in consequence of the fact that the product moment correlation coefficient is invariant with respect to any linear transformation.

14. The equations of a Markov chain indicate how the probabilities of responses depend on what these probabilities were in the preceding play. Thus our two simpletons will play CC on a given response if either (1) they played CC on the preceding response and neither defected from it, or (2) they played DD on the preceding response. Denoting by $(CC)'$ the probability that CC will occur on the next response, we have the equation

$$(CC)' = x_1x_2(CC) + DD.$$

Similarly,

$$(CD)' = x_1(1 - x_2)CC,$$
$$(DC)' = x_2(1 - x_1)CC,$$
$$(DD)' = (1 - x_1)(1 - x_2)CC + CD + DC.$$

If a steady state is reached, we must have $(CC)' = (CC)$, $(CD)' = (CD)$, $(DC)' = (DC)$, $(DD)' = (DD)$. It is shown in the theory of stochastic processes that in this case a steady state will eventually be approached arbitrarily closely. Setting $(CC)' = (CC)$, etc., we get four equations in four unknowns, namely the asymptotic probabilities of the four states (actually three equations in three unknowns, since the four probabilities must add up to 1). These equations have a unique solution given by Equations (20)–(23) of the text.

15. A partial derivative of a function of several variables with respect to one of these variables is the rate of change of the function as the variable in question varies while the others remain constant. Clearly this rate of change depends in general on the (fixed) values assigned to the others.

16. Cf. Bush and Mosteller, 1955, p. 109.

17. For example, if we are asked to pass a straight line through any two given points, we can always do it: it takes two parameters to determine a straight line given by the equation $y = mx + b$. If we have three points not all on the same straight line, we can always draw a parabola through them, for a parabola is determined by three parameters, etc.

18. A differential equation is one which relates the rates of change of variables to the variables themselves. For example, a population reproducing at a constant rate per individual is described by the differential equation $dp/dt = kp$. The equation says that the rate of growth of the whole population is proportional to the size of the population.

    A solution of a differential equation is obtained when the derivatives (rates of change) have been eliminated and only relations among the variables themselves remain. For example, the solution of the above differential equation is $p = p_0 e^{kt}$, where p_0 is the size of the population at time o ($t = $ o), $e = $ 2.718 approximately, and k depends on the rate of increase per individual. In physical science the most important solutions of differential equations are those which describe how certain variables change with time, i.e., describe processes. In our case, too, we are interested in the way our variables (e.g., C, CC, CD, etc.) change in the course of an experimental session.

19. Recall, for example, that if we assume that the payoffs are given only on an interval scale, i.e., if the zero point and the unit of payoffs must remain arbitrary (as is usually assumed in the theory of the two-person game), we are not free to choose any function of the payoffs as a "cooperative index" of a game. We are confined to functions in which only the ratios of differences of the payoffs appear as independent variables.

20. This is what we did in the case of the two simpletons (cf. Chapter 4 and Note 14).

21. An expression is indeterminate for some value(s) of its variable(s) if substituting the value(s) results in an expression like o/o or ∞/∞. Nevertheless, the limit of such an expression can be often determined as the critical value(s) is (are) approached. For example, the expression $(x^2 - 1)/(x - 1)$ becomes o/o

when $x = 1$. However, as x becomes arbitrarily close to 1, the value of the expression becomes arbitrarily close to 2. Limits of this sort can be evaluated by calculating the ratio of the derivatives (rates of change) of the numerator and the denominator with respect to the variable in question (Hôpital's Rule).

22. $F(1,1)$ designates the value taken by the expression $F(x_1, x_2)$ when $x_1 = 1$, $x_2 = 1$.

23. Recall that the expected payoff is the sum of all possible payoffs multiplied by their respective probabilities of occurrence, which are the outcome probabilities, CC, CD, DC, and DD.

24. Expressions (75) and (76) vanish if and only if their numerators vanish.

25. If the expression is not to exceed 1, the numerator must not be greater than the denominator.

26. Dividing through by R^2, rewrite (81) as $3Q^2 - 8Q - 3$, where $Q = T/R$. There is no upper limit to Q, but 1 is the lower limit, since $T > R$. When Q is large, $3Q^2 - 8Q - 3$ must be positive, and so must expression (81). Q vanishes when $Q = 3$ and remains negative as Q decreases to its lower limit, 1.

27. An "operator" can be viewed as a set of directions which indicate how one quantity is to be transformed into another. In this case the directions are: "To change $p(t)$ into $p(t + 1)$, multiply $p(t)$ by α, then add $(1 - \alpha)\lambda$." In a given context the general form of the directions is the same, but the quantities α and λ may change. They are therefore the parameters of the operator.

28. The order of a differential equation refers to the highest order derivative occurring in it. Thus second order differential equations involve not only rates of change of variables but also rates of change of rates of change. In mechanics these are usually accelerations of masses. In electrodynamics the second derivative of the electric charge is related to the electromotive force.

29. Strictly speaking, we are dealing here not with continuous rates of change dC/dt but with rather finite discrete increments. However, if the increments of time are also considered small compared to the total time elapsed, the ratios of the increments can be considered as derivatives. The advantage of differential equation models is that they can be handled by well-known methods.

30. For that is the pair of values of C_1 and C_2 where their rates of change vanish, hence the values are stationary—a definition of equilibrium.

31. Proof of (1). In this case, as we have seen, $F(C)$ has no real roots. But $F(o) > o$. Therefore $F(C)$ is always positive, and so is dC/dt. Therefore, C will be always increasing.

Proof of (2). In this case $F(C)$ has two real roots, namely

$$r_1 = \frac{(\beta + \gamma + 2\delta) + \sqrt{(\beta + \gamma + 2\delta)^2 - 4(\alpha + \beta + \gamma + \delta)\delta}}{2(\alpha + \beta + \gamma + \delta)},$$

$$r_2 = \frac{(\beta + \gamma + 2\delta) - \sqrt{(\beta + \alpha + 2\delta)^2 - 4(\alpha + \beta + \gamma + \delta)\delta}}{2(\alpha + \beta + \gamma + \delta)}.$$

If $(\alpha + \beta + \gamma + \delta) > o$, it can be easily shown by comparing the numerator with the denominator and the two terms of the numerator that both roots lie between zero and one. Hence this is the same case as is represented by Equations (99) and (100) of the text.

Proof of (3). In this case two real roots of $F(C)$ are guaranteed, because the expression under the radical is positive. We shall show, however, that only the larger root lies between zero and one. Suppose first that $(\alpha + \beta + \gamma + \delta) > o$ so that the denominator of r_1 and r_2 is positive. Then r_1 is the larger root. We shall show that $r_1 \leq 1$ if we show that

$$(\beta + \alpha + 2\delta) + \sqrt{(\beta + \alpha + 2\delta)^2 - 4(\alpha + \beta + \gamma + \delta)\delta}$$
$$\leq 2(\alpha + \beta + \gamma + \delta).$$

This is true if

$$(\beta + \gamma + 2\delta)^2 - 4(\alpha + \beta + \gamma + \delta)\delta \leq (2\alpha + \beta + \gamma)^2,$$

which is true if

$$(\beta + \gamma)^2 - 4\alpha\delta \leq (\beta + \gamma)^2 + 4\alpha(\beta + \gamma) + 4\alpha^2,$$

which is true if

$$o \leq 4\alpha(\alpha + \beta + \gamma + \delta).$$

But this is true, because we have assumed that

$$(\alpha + \beta + \gamma + \delta) > o, \alpha > o.$$

It is clear that $r_1 > o$, because both its numerator and its denominator are positive.

Next suppose that $(\alpha + \beta + \gamma + \delta) < o$ so that the denominator of r_1 and r_2 is negative. Now r_2 is the larger root. By a similar argument we prove that now r_2 lies between zero and one, while r_1 is negative.

In either case, then, the larger root lies between zero and one and is the only such root of $F(C)$. But this is the root associated with the unstable equilibrium. Thus (3) is proved.

32. The situation is analogous to that in classical thermodynamics where a physical or chemical system is assumed to go through a reversible process, i.e., a process so slow that the equilibrium is always reestablished following each minute change. While such a situation is conceivable in the case of certain chemical reactions, for example, where the changes are slow relative to the time it takes for the equilibrium to be reestablished, it is quite unlikely that analogous processes can be found in psychological interactions.

33. Note that the high frequency of *C* observed in Game II (Pure Matrix Condition) is attributed to the large numerical magnitude of $P(= -9)$. But in our model the punishment at *DD* has little effect, because escape from *DD* is immediate $(w = 1)$.

34. To see this, consider a population of runs with a constant mortality. Then the number of runs "dying" at a given moment is proportional to the number surviving. This is expressed by the differential equation

$$-\frac{dP}{dt} = mP,$$

where *P* is the fraction of the population surviving. The solution to this equation is

$$P(t) = P_0 e^{-mt},$$

where P_0 is the fraction surviving at $t = 0$. But this fraction is the entire population at $t = 0$. Hence $P_0 = 1$, and we obtain Equation (120) of the text.

35. Taking negative logarithms of both sides of

$$P(t) = e^{-f(t)},$$

we get

$$-\log_e P(t) = f(t).$$

If $f(t)$ is linear in *t*, the plot of $-\log_e P(t)$ against *t* will be a straight line. If $f''(t) > 0$, the plot will be concave upward. If $f''(T) < 0$, the plot will be concave downward.

36. We were at first intrigued by the good fit given by the formula, because many apparently self-enhancing processes are also well described by it, e.g., distribution of durations of wars and strikes (Horvath and Foster, 1963).

37. The Laplace transform of a function $f(t)$ is by definition $\int_0^\infty f(t)e^{-st}\, dt$. The variable of the integration *t* integrates out, leaving the parameter *s* as the argument of the Laplace trans-

form. In our case, μ plays the part of t while t plays the part of s.

38. Examination of the seven games separately reveals that women cooperate less in every one of the seven games.

39. In mixed pairs, M must be computed as follows: $(1 - y_1)$ $(1 - z_2)/y_1 z_2$ is associated with player 1. Thus if the man is player 1, this M is the ratio of failures to successes of men's martyr runs. If the woman is player 1, it is the corresponding ratio related to women's martyr runs.

40. Pilot studies performed in preparation of the next phases indicate that cooperation in response to the stooge's one hundred percent C in Game III is not minimal but clusters at the extremes. Some subjects cooperate almost completely; others defect almost completely. The latter, however, seem to be in a majority.

41. A tit-for-tat strategy implies $\rho_1 = 1$ (cf. pp. 61–62).

References

This list contains publications referred to in the text or consulted by the authors. For a review of the literature on Prisoner's Dilemma through 1963, see Gallo and McClintock on this list.

Bixenstine, V. E., N. Chambers, and K. V. Wilson. "Asymmetry in Payoff in a Non-zero-sum game." *Journal of Conflict Resolution*, 8 (1964), pp. 151–59.

Bixenstine, V. E., H. M. Potash, and K. V. Wilson. "Effects of Level of Cooperative Choice by the Other Player in Choices in a Prisoner's Dilemma Game: Part I." *Journal of Abnormal and Social Psychology*, 66 (1963), pp. 308–13.

Ibid., Part II. *Journal of Abnormal and Social Psychology*, 67 (1963), pp. 139–47.

Braithwaite, R. B. *Theory of Games as a Tool for the Moral Philosopher*. Cambridge: Cambridge University Press, 1955.

Bush, R. R., and F. Mosteller. *Stochastic Models for Learning*. New York: Wiley, 1955.

Cohen, B. P. *Conflict and Conformity*. Cambridge, Mass.: M.I.T. Press, 1963.

Deutsch, M. "Trust and Suspicion." *Journal of Conflict Resolution*, 2 (1958), pp. 267–79.

Deutsch, M. "The Effect of Motivation Orientation upon Threat and Suspicion." *Human Relations*, 13 (1960), pp. 123–39.

Deutsch, M. "Trust, Trustworthiness and the F Scale." *Journal of Abnormal and Social Psychology*, 61 (1960), pp. 138–40.

Flood, M. M. "Some Experimental Games." The Rand Corporation (1952), RM-789-1.

Flood, M. M. "On Game-Learning Theory." The Rand Corporation (1952), RM-853.

Flood, M. M. "Game-Learning Theory and Some Decision-Making Experiments; Environmental Non-Stationarity in a Sequential Decision-Making Experiment." In *Decision Processes* (R. M. Thrall, C. H. Coombs, and R. L. Davis, eds.), New York: John Wiley and Sons, 1954, pp. 139–58, 287–99.

Flood, M. M. "Some Experimental Games." *Management Science*, 5 (1958), pp. 5–26.

Gallo, P. S., and C. McClintock. "Cooperative and Competitive Behavior in Mixed Motive Games." *Journal of Conflict Resolution* 9 (1965) 68–78.

Horvath, W. J. and C. C. Foster. "Stochastic Models of War Alliances." *Journal of Conflict Resolution*, 7 (1963), pp. 110–16.

Loomis, J. L. "Communication, the Development of Trust and Cooperative Behavior," *Human Relations*, 12 (1959), pp. 305–15.

Luce, R. D. and H. Raiffa. *Games and Decisions*. New York: John Wiley and Sons, 1957.

Lutzker, D. "Internationalism as a Predictor of Cooperative Game Behavior." *Journal of Conflict Resolution*, 4 (1960), pp. 426–35.

Martin, M. W., Jr. "Some Effects of Communication on Group Behavior in Prisoner's Dilemma." Unpublished thesis, Case Institute of Technology.

McClintock, C. G., A. A. Harrison, S. Strand, and P. Gallo. "Internationalism-Isolationism, Strategy of the Other Player, and Two-Person Game Behavior." *Journal of Abnormal and Social Psychology*, 67 (1963), pp. 631–36.

Minas, J. S., A. Scodel, D. Marlowe, and H. Rawson. "Some Descriptive Aspects of Two-Person Non-Zero-Sum Games, II," *Journal of Conflict Resolution*, 4 (1960), pp. 193–97.

Nash, J. F. "Equilibrium Points in N-Person Games." Proceedings of the National Academy of Science, U.S.A., 36 (1950), pp. 48–49.

Pilisuk, M. and A. Rapoport. "Stepwise Disarmament and Sudden Destruction in a Two-Person Game: A Research Tool." *Journal of Conflict Resolution*, 8 (1964), pp. 38–49.

Rapoport, A., and C. Orwant. "Experimental Games: A Review," *Behavioral Science*, 7 (1962), pp. 1–37.

Rapoport, A. "Formal Games as Probing Tools for Investigating Behavior Motivated by Trust and Suspicion." *Journal of Conflict Resolution*, 7 (1963), pp. 570–79.

Rapoport, A. "A Stochastic Model for the Prisoner's Dilemma." In *Stochastic Models in Medicine and Biology* (J. Gurland, ed.). Madison: University of Wisconsin Press, 1964.

Rapoport, A. "Tacit Communication in Experiments in Conflict and Cooperation." In *Communications in Clinical Practice* (R. Waggoner and D. Carek, eds.). New York: Little, Brown and Co., International Psychiatric Clinics, Vol. 1, No. 1, 1964.

Richardson, Lewis F. *Arms and Insecurity* (N. Rashevsky and E. Trucco, eds.). Chicago: Quadrangle Press and Pittsburgh: Boxwood Press, 1960.

Schelling, Thomas C. "Experimental Games and Bargaining Theory." In *The International System* (K. Knorr and S. Verba, eds.). Princeton, N. J.: Princeton University Press, 1961. pp. 47–68.

Schelling, Thomas C. *The Strategy of Conflict*. Cambridge: Harvard
    University Press, 1960.
Scodel, A., J. S. Minas, P. Ratoosh, and M. Lipetz. "Some Descrip-
    tive Aspects of Two-Person Non-Zero-Sum Games," *Journal of
    Conflict Resolution*, 3 (1959), pp. 114–19.
Solomon, L. "The Influence of Some Types of Power Relationships
    and Game Strategies upon the Development of Interpersonal
    Trust." *Journal of Abnormal and Social Psychology*, 61 (1960),
    pp. 223–30.
Shubik, M. "Some Experimental Non-Zero-Sum Games with Lack
    of Information about the Rules. Cowles Foundation Discussion
    Paper No. 105, January, 1961.
Suppes, P., and R. C. Atkinson. *Markov Learning Models for Multi-
    person Interactions*. Stanford: Stanford University Press, 1960.
Wilson, K. V. and V. E. Bixenstine. "Effects of a Third Choice on
    Behavior in a Prisoner's Dilemma Game." Nebraska Psychiatric
    Institute and Kent State University, 1962 (mimeographed).